Developing Library Collections for Today's Young Adults

Amy S. Pattee

THE SCARECROW PRESS, INC.
Lanham • Toronto • Plymouth, UK
2014

Published by Scarecrow Press, Inc.
A wholly owned subsidiary of The Rowman & Littlefield Publishing Group, Inc.
4501 Forbes Boulevard, Suite 200, Lanham, Maryland 20706
http://www.scarecrowpress.com

Estover Road, Plymouth PL6 7PY, United Kingdom

British Library Cataloguing in Publication Information Available

Library of Congress Cataloging-in-Publication Data

Pattee, Amy.
Developing library collections for today's young adults / Amy S. Pattee.
pages cm
Includes bibliographical references and index.
ISBN 978-0-8108-8734-3 (cloth) -- ISBN 978-0-8108-8735-0 (ebook) 1. Young adults' libraries--
Collection development--United States. 2. Libraries--Special collections--Nonbook materials. 3.
Multimedia library services--United States. 4. Libraries and teenagers--United States. I. Title.
Z718.5P38 2013
027.62'6--dc23
2013018596

™
The paper used in this publication meets the minimum requirements of American
National Standard for Information Sciences Permanence of Paper for Printed Library
Materials, ANSI/NISO Z39.48-1992.

Printed in the United States of America

Contents

Preface

Since recognition of the young adult as a legitimate patron of the public library in the early twentieth century, librarians have been piloting and formalizing best practices in teen services. The library's collection of material selected expressly for young people has always been at the center of these efforts. Whereas early library collections for teens included more books for adults than novels we would today consider "young adult literature," as young adult publishing came of age in the last quarter of the twentieth century, library collections for young adults diversified to include expressly teen novels—hardbacks, paperback originals, and series—juvenile and adult titles, as well as graphic and multimedia forms. Since the turn of the twenty-first century, young adult publishing has expanded even further, and young adult literature has become much more popular—and not just among teens. Adults whose heads were turned by the Harry Potter series are now reading young adult series such as Suzanne Collins's Hunger Games trilogy and Stephenie Meyer's Twilight series. That these series have been translated into successful mainstream films has only heightened their status. This diversification—not to mention proliferation—in young adult publishing is both a boon and a challenge to the YA librarian: With so much to choose from, how do librarians ensure that the selections we make and the materials we purchase are the right ones?

Taking on the job of collection development for young adults positions a librarian on the crest of a relatively new wave of library services. Between 1994 (when such statistics were first collected) and 2007 (when the Public Library Data Service annual survey last included questions about young adult services), the number of libraries with dedicated collections of young adult material (housed separately from other materials in the library) had risen from 58 to 83.9 percent in central or main libraries and to 72.2 percent in branch libraries (Mustafoff and Teffeau 2008, 13). These dedicated collections are distinguished by their patron-centric definition: young adult collections are developed primarily for members of the wide demographic we define as "young adult," those between the ages of twelve and eighteen. Teen patrons are not the only readers who consult young adult collections, however. Preteen readers who are interested in "reading up," parents of teen readers and nonreaders, teachers and school librarians, and adults with a penchant for young adult fiction are among the patrons of the public library YA collection. This diversity

among users means that the librarian developing a young adult collection
must consider how the collection supports the scholastic and recreational
information and reading needs and interests of its adolescent patrons, as
well as the needs and interests of its secondary users. Ensuring such
coverage is a challenge that involves thinking about the YA collection as
a single entity, as well as in terms of its relationship to the library's
greater collection of material. Ultimately, librarians developing young
adult collections should strive to meet the collection goal set by the
American Library Association's (ALA) Young Adult Library Services Association (YALSA), as articulated in its white paper "The Importance of a
Whole Library Approach to Public Library Young Adult Services: A
YALSA Issue Paper," and develop collections that include "a full complement of materials such as magazines and books in the adult, teen, and
children's areas of the library are required in order to support the recreational and personal growth needs of teens at all levels of development"
(Braun 2011a, "Collection Development"). To ensure that these goals are
met, young adult librarians engage in a dual process of collection assessment and development.

COLLECTION ASSESSMENT AND COLLECTION DEVELOPMENT

In this book we use "collection assessment" and "collection development" as umbrella terms to describe the two categories of activity that
contribute to the creation and maintenance of a library's collection of
young adult material. Here, "collection assessment" refers to those practices in which librarians engage to ensure that library collections are fresh
and relevant. These include examining circulation records of individual
titles or groups of titles with an eye toward gauging their use by the
population and weeding and discarding outdated and unused material
from the collection. "Collection development" indicates those practices in
which librarians engage to select material for and add material to a library's collection. Although collection assessment and collection development can describe two distinct and discrete processes, this book emphasizes their relationship and encourages librarians to consider them in
tandem.

General guides to collection development note two primary approaches to the assessment and development of library collections: collection centered and user centered. The collection-centered approach focuses on the size and composition of a library's collection: how many
titles it houses, the variety of these titles, and the breadth of coverage. The
user-centered approach focuses on the needs and interests of the user of a
library's collection; the characteristics of patrons who use the collection,
their patterns of past use, and their expectations for the collection are all
factors to consider when taking this approach. Librarians developing col-

lections for young adults must also consider a third perspective, curriculum centered. Because the primary users of young adult collections are typically students, librarians must also consider how the collection meets the curriculum-inspired information needs of the young adults who use it.

Public librarians who develop young adult collections strive to balance all three of these approaches. This means that YA librarians must think about the size of their collections relative to their population of users, the variety of titles in their collections, the composition of these collections, their users' needs and interests, and the demands of the local curriculum, then work to balance these concerns. Assessing and developing collections from this perspective means that librarians have to determine what titles might be considered "core" in a YA collection and work to preserve and include those titles that might be less popular but expected (collection-centric development). For example, most library collections of adult fiction include classic literary novels like *Jane Eyre* and *Crime and Punishment*. These titles are arguably not the most frequently checked out of a library's collection, especially when compared to the works of perennially popular authors like Stephen King and Mary Higgins Clark; however, library patrons expect these classic novels to be among the library's collection, if only because they are "classic." Young adult literature has its own body of classic novels that have a place among the popular titles; the number and extent of a YA collection's classic titles depend on how its developing librarian balances collection-centric approaches against user-centric and curriculum-centric approaches. Sometimes "core" titles are also relevant to the local curriculum, which means that developing from a collection-centric perspective often involves thinking from a curriculum-centric perspective. For example, Robert Cormier's *The Chocolate War* is considered by many to be a classic young adult novel; it is also often included among summer reading list titles or assigned as required reading for English classes. Although Cormier's novel is not necessarily at the top of a teen patron's "must-read" list of recreational reading, its classic status and curriculum connection make it a must-have in the young adult library. Of course librarians developing young adult collections must also be attuned to popularity and add and weed material accordingly. This means that though Stephenie Meyer's Twilight series will probably never be considered a "classic" alongside Cormier's *The Chocolate War* and will probably not make high school and junior high required reading lists, multiple copies of all the novels in the series should be included among the library's collection of YA material to meet young adult library users' demands (user-centric development). The first chapter of this book describes these perspectives in greater detail and offers suggestions for balancing them during collection assessment and development.

ACCESS: A KEY ISSUE IN COLLECTION DEVELOPMENT

Developing library collections—for any population—is a formidable task. When a librarian is acting as a collection developer, he or she is essentially making choices on behalf of users that affect the range and nature of information and material to which current or future users might have access. Although this responsibility is a serious one in any context, librarians developing collections for teenagers face unique challenges. The primary challenge is access: How do libraries ensure that teen patrons can find, borrow, and read material that, in the words of YALSA, "supports the recreational and personal growth needs of teens at all levels of development?" Because the primary users of the library's young adult collection are indeed at "all levels of development" and thus have a variety of personal growth and recreational needs and interests, ensuring that these materials are available to them can be tricky. Members of all large, demographically defined populations have distinct and divergent individual beliefs, interests, and needs, and young adults are no different. However, when it comes to selecting material for minors, librarians sometimes shy away from material that addresses "hot button" issues like sexuality and drug and alcohol use and abuse, worried that material describing or depicting these activities and issues—whether in a fictional or informational context—might somehow harm the developing psyches of young patrons or result in a challenge to library material. Christine M. Allen, writing for *Young Adult Library Services*, has observed that "[s]election can be a very subtle form of censorship, particularly in schools, because it is so often fraught with fear of objection by teachers, principals, parents, or the school board" (2007, 5). Recognizing this potential for selection activities to, ironically, limit access as potential additions to the collection are rejected or censored, this book aims to infuse its discussion of collection development with notes on access and threats to access. The second chapter of this book, devoted to developing collection development policies to guide selection, marks the beginning of this discussion. Chapters in this book that describe the selection of library materials by type revisit these intellectual freedom concerns.

As libraries respond to public interest and developments in technology by installing more public use computers, developing collections of computer and video games, and adding audio books and electronic books to the library's collection, access is again a consideration. When developing collections that include multimedia material, librarians must ask whether and how their patrons can physically access that material. Allocating public use computers for teen patrons gives teens who visit the library access to its subscription databases and online resources; however, how does the library ensure that its patrons—including its young adult patrons—can access and use its other electronic and multimedia material? This issue of access via connectivity is a central one for libraries in general, but teen connectivity is a special case, especially as teen access to and use of electronic devices can be monitored by or circumscribed by parents or guardians. For example, demographic research indicates that nearly four in five teens own an iPod or an mp3 player (Lenhart et al. 2010), and that over half of audiobook users prefer to borrow rather than buy their audiobooks (Pew Internet 2012). Considered together, these data suggest not only that audiobooks are a good investment for libraries, but also that making audio content available in portable file or streaming form for those four in five teens with mp3 players might be the best primary format choice for a young adult audiobook collection. Recognizing that although a majority of teens do own a portable audio device, 20 percent don't, librarians thinking in terms of access and connectivity should consider adding preloaded portable devices, like the Playaway, to the collection as well, so that all users can experience audio versions of titles.

As libraries add video games to their circulating collections, the issues of access multiply: first, libraries have to decide which gaming platform or platforms their collections will support; second, librarians selecting individual games must wrestle with the issue of video game ratings systems and consider how or if a video game's rating will affect their purchase; and third, libraries must address how to make this portion of the collection accessible to users who may not have game consoles at home. Public libraries are recognizing the relevance and appeal of circulating video game collections, especially to teen patrons; as this movement grows, it is likely that the video games will have an increasing place in young adult library collections. Throughout its discussion of materials selection, this book addresses the issues unique to developing multimedia and electronic collections, with an emphasis on best practices for ensuring access.

GETTING STARTED

Chapters 1 through 4 of this book describe the work librarians must do before getting their hands dirty in the library's collection. This predevelopment work involves authoring or editing a collection development policy and conducting a needs assessment of the library's young adult service population. These are key elements of the larger collection development process and should be undertaken on a regular basis. Creating, revisiting, and editing the library's policy for developing collections for teens allows librarians to ensure that their collections remain in line with the library's mission and vision as well as to account for the addition of new media forms. By outlining a library's collection development process—for example, by noting which staff members or librarians participate in weeding and selection and what sources are consulted during the materials selection process—the policy serves as a contract between the library and its patrons. The Arizona State Libraries, Archives and Public Records' collection development training guide asserts the importance of collection development policies, pointing out that the policy becomes a "point of reference for staff to consult when deciding on whether to acquire, discard, or reject an item," and, as a touchstone, this policy ensures consistency in collection development (2012a). Perhaps most important, because collection development policies outline selection criteria—which may include popularity or "popular demand" as a rationale for adding items to the library's collection—these policies are important reference points when or if library material is challenged.

A needs assessment, sometimes considered in broader terms as a "community assessment" or a "community scan," can be an initially large undertaking; however, if updated and revisited on a regular basis, a librarian's needs assessment report is a valuable source of information for collection development. A complete needs assessment results in a description of the service population in terms of demographics as well as local information needs and interests. When considering the local needs of young adult patrons, librarians conduct user surveys, review circulation records to uncover information-seeking patterns, and consult state and local curricula. The information gathered can have a major impact on a library's collection. For example, if a local school system revises its curriculum to require all students enrolled in laboratory science courses to participate in the school science fair, the library would do well to take a closer look at its collection of science fair project manuals and texts and consider bulking up the collection in anticipation of student need. Information about the community itself—particularly any demographic shifts that occur as communities grow and change—informs collection development as well. An influx of residents who speak a language other than English as a primary language might inspire a librarian to add or increase non-English-language material and include easier to read material with teen appeal (hi-lo material) in the collection.

Chapters 5 through 8 detail the work librarians do in and with the collection. Ideally, they apply the policies they have developed for their collections as well as the data they have gathered during the needs assessment to assessing and developing the library's collection of young adult material. With the guidance of policy and armed with information about primary and secondary users, young adult collection developers examine their existing collections; note local classics, favorites, and duds; and weed and add material to construct a balanced collection with relevance and appeal to users. And when they have finished working through a collection, they go back and do it again! Collection development is a continual process: communities and young adults change—their needs and interests wax and wane—and library materials become worn and outdated. This means that a library's collection must be regularly monitored; continuously reviewed; and developed to ensure that the best, most relevant, and most up-to-date material is always available for library patrons.

Acknowledgments

I am grateful to Simmons College for granting me the sabbatical release that allowed me to complete this resource. Special thanks go to my colleague Terry Plum, the assistant dean for technology and GSLIS West at the Simmons College Graduate School of Library and Information Science, for providing advice and guidance regarding the implementation and evaluation of networked resources and e-books in libraries. Thanks are due as well to Linda Braun for her willingness to examine sections of this manuscript. I appreciate the guidance of editor Charles Harmon; his kind words, comments, and suggestions resulted in the creation of an infinitely more readable book. Finally, I wish to thank my husband, Ben Florin, for his love and support, and give a shout out to Cambridge (MA) Public Library youth services librarian Beth McIntyre, who has provided friendship and professional insight throughout this book's march to publication.

ONE

Developing and Managing Young Adult Collections: An Overview

Since public libraries first began recognizing children as library patrons, librarians have argued that special collections for the young housed in space allotted for their service are a necessity. As Christine Jenkins writes in her review of research documenting the history of public library youth services, "youth services librarianship began with specialized collections. Specialized space, personnel, services, and networks began with the establishment of public libraries. Collections, however, greatly predate the other elements of youth services librarianship, and the librarian's knowledge of the collection—the texts—is the bedrock of expertise upon which the profession rests" (2000, "Specialized Library Collections," para. 1). The same is true of young adult librarianship. Following the establishment of compulsory education laws requiring young people to continue schooling into their teens, librarians serving youths began to recognize "young people"—today's "young adults"—as a service constituency distinct from both children and adults. Advocacy for special collections for young adults and the establishment of professional organizations and guidelines for service soon followed. Today, 67 percent of public libraries report hiring staff members dedicated to the service of children and youths, and 69 percent of these libraries have carved out dedicated spaces for teens in their buildings (Miller and Girmscheid 2012).

Whether public libraries delineate physically separate collections of young adult material or interfile young adult material among children's or adult books and media, young adult literature and media represent a small part of most libraries' budgets, but account for up to a quarter of a library's circulation. According to a recent *Library Journal* survey, although young adult fiction averages 24 percent of public library circulation, monies allotted for the purchase of YA materials make up only

1

between 8 and 13 percent of public library budgets, with spending totals between $3,100 and $193,000 (2012a). As reports of looming budget cuts remain in the news, public librarians surveyed in 2012 predicted increases in the circulation and use of material for the coming year (Miller and Girmscheid 2012). These data have significant repercussions for librarians charged with developing youth library collections in general and young adult collections specifically. With budget allocations for material for young adults typically being the smallest piece of the library's budgetary pie (on average, libraries allocate 63 percent of their budgets to adult materials and 28 percent to children's books, compared to an average of 9 percent for YA materials [*Library Journal* 2012a]), the importance of canny materials selection comes to the fore. Young adult librarians are expected to operate from reduced or stagnant budgets to serve greater numbers of patrons, meaning that decisions about the allocation of these limited funds—to fiction, curricular nonfiction, high interest nonfiction, or media, for example—are becoming ever more complicated.

The rapidly expanding world of YA literary publishing and the growing availability of a variety of literary and informational forms—including audiobooks, databases, and e-books—challenge young adult librarians as they strive to squeeze the most from skimpy budgets. In addition, as libraries and librarians are urged to account for spending decisions by assessing their collections in terms of use, developing plans for collection assessment—as well as plans to apply the results of assessment to future collection development practices—become new tasks that collection development YA librarians must address. Librarians serving adults and youth alike are confronting these issues, but the minor status of the library's young adult patrons complicates collection development for this group and requires us to be attentive to issues of access and appropriateness when developing collections that meet both the self-generated informational and reading needs and interests of young people as well as what Melissa Gross (2006) calls their "imposed" information needs—those requests for information motivated by third parties or school assignments. Thus, although as Kay Bishop has written, "the general principles and techniques of collection development are applicable to most library settings" (2007, ix), the unique characteristics of the young adult population and the variety of contexts in which the collections we develop for them exist suggest a need for specialized practice.

This overview provides readers with a broad introduction to the young adult patron and introduces the professional principles that underlie our establishment and development of library collections for this user group. The remainder of this chapter answers two key questions that inform the development and maintenance of library collections for young adults: Who is the young adult? What is the young adult collection? The answers to these questions provide an introduction to the issues; however, collection development—for all library patrons—does not occur in a vacuum, and the importance and influence of local context should not be discounted. This local context can be described following a needs assessment of the service population, the results of which should be reflected in the establishment of policy for young adult collection development and management and in the library's collection itself. Suggestions for assessing the needs of the library's young adult patrons and discussion of collection development policy for this patron group are covered in greater detail in chapters 3 and 4.

WHO IS THE YOUNG ADULT?

The idea of adolescence as a distinct demographic and category of development is a rather new one. G. Stanley Hall's *Adolescence: Its Psychology and Its Relations to Physiology, Anthropology, Sociology, Sex, Crime, Religion and Education* (1904) is considered the first treatise on the population that would come to be known as "youth," "young adults," or "teenagers." Hall's assertion that young people between the ages of twelve and eighteen occupied a separate state of development took hold following the Great Depression in the United States, during which young people and their families looked to secondary education for training in the competitive and increasingly specialized and mechanized job market. The growth of this population in the mid-twentieth century—in 1940, young people aged fifteen to nineteen made up the largest segment of the American population (Hobbs and Stoops 2002, 53)—made adolescents even more visible and spurred interest in (and concern for) their healthy development into productive adults. The institutionalization of the term "adolescent" has enhanced its literal and symbolic meanings; young adults can be considered as such from developmental, institutional, social, and cultural perspectives. That is, the way we (adults) think about and conceive of young adults has a bearing on the assumptions we make about their abilities and capability for understanding and complexity, the rules we enforce on their behalf, and the decisions we make about the material to which they will have access. Each of these perspectives on adolescence has an impact on our work on behalf of young people in libraries, making it important to attend not only to the unique characteristics of our local service populations, but also to the outside factors that shape adolescence in general, particularly as adult librarians operate outside of these constraints to develop collections for a population of which we are no longer members.

Most students of education and human development are familiar with the developmental perspective on adolescence and the influence of the work of psychologists Erik Erikson and Jean Piaget on our understanding of physical, intellectual, and social development. These psychologists' theories of development have contributed to our understanding of adolescence as a life "stage," a period of development distinct from child-hood and adulthood. Following Hall—as well as the work of Sigmund Freud—Erikson posited that all humans develop physically and socially in stages, facing particular psychic challenges, the resolution of which affect behavior and personality. During the period of adolescence, Erikson asserted, young people begin to recognize themselves as individuals and try on, adopt, and discard identities as they work to develop the self. Erikson's theory of development has contributed to our popular under-standing of teenagers as young people in a stage of identity flux, a conception that affects our collection development decisions. If, as Erikson theorizes, young adults are in the process of developing and cementing identity, our concern for the healthy direction of this development might lead us to block access to materials we fear might have a negative effect on it. Although these censorious impulses are understandable and born of genuine concern for young people and their development, they can lead to the infringement of young people's freedom to access information. Unlike Erikson, who places adolescence within a greater continuum of human development from birth to death, Jean Piaget's theory of progressive development places adolescents at the pinnacle of cognitive growth. Piaget argued that our last significant developmental stage occurs during adolescence, when young people develop the capacity to think in more complex, logical, hypothetical, and abstract terms. Piaget's theory has a bearing on our collection development decisions as well, particularly as we consider the complexity of the literature and information resources we collect and recommend.

The belief that adolescents occupy a particular and "developing" place in the world has probably contributed to the establishment of institutions, rules, and regulations meant to guide their healthy progression from childhood to adulthood. Age-based laws regarding school attendance, military conscription, employment, and motor vehicle operation exemplify the institutionalization of adolescence as a particular stage of life during which young people may enjoy progressively greater freedoms (to drive, to vote, to join the military, to purchase alcohol). Although most of us would agree that many of the legal restrictions on young people's behavior are reasonable and reflect best practices in light of our understanding of young people's capacity for reasoning and decision making, other local rules and laws contribute to the institutionalization of adolescence in less productive terms. Larry Grossberg is critical of such rules and identifies some of the inequities:

> In most states in the United States, at 16 today, you cannot get your ears pierced without the permission of your parents. You cannot get a tattoo, and you cannot buy cigarettes. In fact, people under 16 cannot go to the Mall of America in Minnesota . . . after 6 P.M. on Friday or Saturday without a parent. But you can be tried and jailed as an

adult . . . you can be put to death as a penalty. (Grossberg 2001, quoted in Giroux 2003, 107–108)

Rules that restrict the movement of young people by making their presence in public places during certain time periods illegal or that bar their access to information and resources may also be in place in libraries. Library policies that restrict teenagers from using unfiltered computers or restrict teen borrowing privileges based on age are examples of ways in which libraries participate in this restrictive form of institutionalization. The spaces and collections libraries create for teens are ways of counteracting these restrictions on teen life; in library teen rooms and collections, young adults find space they don't have to concede to adults.

From a social and cultural perspective, young adults occupy a symbolic place in our worlds. Henry Giroux writes, "Youth haunts adult society because it represents our need to be attentive to a future that others will inherit" and "[youth] simultaneously serves as a symbol of how a society thinks about itself and as an indicator of changing cultural values, sexuality, the state of the economy and the spiritual life of a nation" (1996, 10). This perspective has influenced the development of library services to young adults in particular. If, as Giroux writes, young people are reminders of our own adult mortality, ensuring that young adults have access to the materials and resources they require to assume our places in the world can be considered the YA librarian's most important responsibility. Unfortunately this also means that young people often bear the burden of our anxieties about the future as we project our own worries about the world onto them and seek to control their movements in an effort to secure our own freedom. These anxieties often emerge when we consider material for the library's young adult collection in terms of "appropriateness," a descriptor Mary K. Chelton calls a code word that means "something kids will like but won't make adults mad" (2006, 11). Our anxiety about potential effects of literary content is often masked in discussions of "appropriateness"; when we worry, for example, that the sensual content in a novel may be a bit too arousing, we argue that it must be inappropriate for young people, whose sensuality and sexuality we—as advocates for youth—are arguably concerned with. Debra Lau Whelan's provocative essay "Dirty Little Secret," published in *School Library Journal*, offers this truism: "[N]o one ever really knows which books might end up changing a kid's life, helping him find comfort, or gaining a better understanding of the subject" (2009, 30). Because we truly can't predict, for better or worse, how any reader will interpret a book, our professional task as developers of young adult library collections is to open those collections as wide as they can go and replace anxiety with idealism as we consider their reception.

The Young Adult Library Services Association defines the "young adult" as anyone between the ages of twelve and eighteen, but this definition ignores the influence of developmental psychology, institutions, and the greater social and cultural world on our understanding of this population. If we consider young adulthood from these conceptual points of view, we can begin to see the influences of adult ways of thinking about young people on our library collections and services for teenagers. For example, recognizing most teenagers' status as students, we develop collections that meet their needs as participants in educational institutions. In addition, as we select material for young adult collections, we wrestle with the slippery ideology of "appropriateness" as we try to collect material that is relevant to young people and meets their needs. From this point, however, we move from concept to context and incorporate what we know, broadly, about young people and their needs with what we observe in our work with local populations. Although we might read broad statements about the general interests and information needs of young adults, we should strive to meet the real needs and interests of our local population of teenagers. Engaging in a detailed needs assessment—discussed in chapter 4—is one of the primary means of ensuring that we develop library collections for our teen patrons and, as such, should be a key factor in young adult collection decisions.

WHAT IS THE YOUNG ADULT COLLECTION?

Although we recognize "young adult literature" as a category of fiction and nonfiction characterized by its attention to the presumed interests and needs of adolescent readers, young adult library collections are not composed solely of this material. The broadest conceptual definition of the "young adult collection" includes all materials—print, audiovisual, and electronic—purchased to address the needs and interests of the library's young adult patrons. To be sure, YA literature is a key component of any library's collection of young adult material; however, these collections often include much more. As Patrick Jones has argued, a library's young adult collection is "a collection for young adults, not a core collection of young adult books in a YA area" (2003, 49). This means that library collections for young adults are unified by the motivation for their selection and consist of that fiction and nonfiction designated by publishers as "young adult," as well as any material that addresses the needs and interests of the local young adult population. Young adult collections may include books written by popular figures with significant adolescent audiences (*Decoded* by Jay-Z is an example of one such title), memoirs popular among adults and adolescents alike (for example, *Into Thin Air* by Jon Krakauer), and works of fiction by adult authors like Stephen King that have young adult readership. In the library, "young adult" is both a literary and a functional designation, describing fiction and nonfiction about and for adolescents as well as any material selected for young adult library users.

Although the library's young adult collection is defined by its function of meeting the needs and interests of adolescent library patrons, where it is located and how it is organized affect its composition as well as how it is used. Many libraries have physical space devoted to housing young adult material, and how a library allocates this space and plans for its use have a significant bearing on the makeup of the young adult collection shelved there. For example, libraries with separate rooms furnished with seating, books, and computers just for teen patrons often house collections that are distinctly different from those young adult collections located on a couple of shelves in a corner of the library or interfiled among adult and children's books and media. The physical space available in the library, as well as the library's intentions for any space designated for the primary use of a particular population, will ultimately impact the organization and selection of any materials purchased for young adults. For example, libraries with teen spaces that function as after-school "hangouts" for young people may consider that space more of a community recreation center than a quiet study space and will collect and display popular fiction and nonfiction, movies, music, and video games in this space, shelving any curricular titles among the adult or children's nonfiction. Those libraries that allocate a corner of the library to the library's young adult collection might shelve only young adult fiction in this area, defining the space in terms of the "young adult" status of the literature rather than the user. In a case like this, other materials selected for young adults—nonfiction to meet recreational and curricular needs, movies, music, video games, and magazines—may be found throughout the rest of the library's collections.

The structure of a library's materials budget and its method of fund allocation will also have an impact on how material is selected for its young adult patrons and where this material is housed. Peggy Johnson writes that most library materials budgets are "line-item budgets . . . which list allocations and expenditures, classified by type, in a detailed line-by-line format" (2009, 89). The nature of the "lines"—the amount of money budgeted and spent for particular categories of materials—may be determined by location (library branch or department), user type (adult, child, young adult), format or genre (books, periodicals, reference materials, fiction, online resources), or publisher type (Johnson 2009, 89). Libraries may organize budgets hierarchically, allocating funds first by user and then by material type, or first by material type and then by user; the organization and breakdown of a library's materials budget are determined by criteria developed by an individual library or library system. Depending on how a library breaks down its budget, the responsibility for various "lines" may belong to more than one person. In libraries that organize their budgets by categories of user, the responsibility for the selection of all material for young adults may lie with the library's youth services librarians. In libraries that organize their budgets by material type and subdivide some or all of these designations by user, the responsibility for the selection of material for young adults may be more widely dispersed.

Because all materials selection is governed by the library's budget, and because budgetary allocations are not equivalent across user or material type, collection development is always a political activity. As noted previously, material for young people often comprises a small portion of the library budget, which reflects a need for advocacy for the young in collection development. This means that those librarians charged with selecting material for young adults should lobby for the purchase of material on their behalf, even if that material is not covered by the young adult "line." As Patrick Jones notes, "Developing a collection is customer focused: it does not matter that much to the teen where the book is shelved as long as the library owns it" (2003, 49). To take this observation further, it doesn't matter at all to the teen which "line" of the library's budget is responsible for the purchase of a desired item, as long as the library owns it.

This book uses the broadest definition of "the young adult collection," describing this entity as the sum total of all material selected with the needs and interests of the library's young adult patrons in mind. This definition allows us to consider a full range of material types and genres: print fiction and nonfiction published for adults and young adults, graphic novels and graphic nonfiction, electronic resources and databases, e-books, and audiobooks. Although much of the selection guidance provided in the following chapters echoes that provided in more general collection development resources, its consistent and particular focus on young adult patrons and how to select material to meet their interests and needs distinguishes this book from others in the genre. This distinction reflects the traditional belief among youth services librarians that young people—children and young adults—have needs and interests that are distinct from those of adults (and distinct from those adults want them to have), and that developing library collections for these populations means putting their interests ahead of our own as we evaluate and select material on their behalf.

TWO

Young Adult Collection Development: Multiple Perspectives

Several philosophies underlie collection development, and librarians' adherence to any or all of these has less to do with our personal perspectives than with the aims and goals of the institutions for which we are selecting material. The library's organizational mission and goals ultimately inform the collection development decisions librarians charged with this task make; as the library's mission statement describes the library's focus and articulates its values, it also suggests the nature of the materials the library will prioritize for selection. The library's collection development policies follow from this mission and, as Peggy Johnson notes, "to the extent that they match collection to mission . . . guarantee that the collection being developed serves the educational, entertainment, and research mission of the parent institution or community" (2009, 74). Most public library mission statements are broad and, as Sandra S. Nelson writes, similar in spirit, if not in content, to this: "The library is dedicated to meeting the educational, recreational, informational, professional, cultural, and social needs of all residents" (2008, 80). This statement describes a library with services and collections that address the "educational, recreational, informational, professional, cultural and social needs" of all the library's patrons. School libraries focus their mission statements more narrowly and describe their purpose in terms of the support the library and its collection offer to the curriculum. Special libraries and athenaeums may describe their services and collections even more narrowly, focusing on conservation or the development of topical collections. The particularity of the library's mission statement will ultimately suggest the perspective(s) the institution relies on to evaluate its collection and select material for its service populations.

Generally speaking, professional guides and handbooks describe two primary approaches to collection development: collection centered and user centered. These map broadly to institutional missions that position the library as curator of material deemed significant by the institution (collection centered) or by the institution's patrons (user centered). These approaches not only inform how and what the library selects for its collection, but also suggest how its collection may be assessed. The collection-centered approach considers the library's collection an entity unto itself. It can be weighed and measured to determine how many titles it contains, what subjects it covers, and to what degree, and can be compared to other collections and to standard catalogs. The user-centered approach considers who is using the collection, what items from the collection they are using, and how they are using these items. Librarians charged with developing user-centered collections select material in anticipation of user need, interest, and demand. From the user-centered perspective, a library's collection is only as good as its ability to meet the needs of the library patron, a metric that takes into account library user opinion and behavior (circulation, reference questions).

When developing collections for young adults, many of whom look to the library to address information needs imposed by the school curriculum, a third perspective must also be considered: the curriculum-centered perspective. Although, as H. Fisher notes, "as part of a much larger collection development issue, a common mantra is that the public library should not be responsible for having curriculum based books in its collection—that this is the responsibility of the school" (2003, 8), surveys of young adult library use and information-seeking behaviors have acknowledged teen patrons' use of public libraries to address school-inspired information needs. Although it is not the place of the public library to replicate the school library's collection, realistically, public librarians serving young adults should consider how and if the local curriculum affects their use of the public library and look to their demands to inform collection development in curricular areas. Patrick Jones and the Young Adult Library Services Association's "Itinerary for Quality Library Services to Young Adults," detailed in *New Directions for Library Service to Young Adults*, advocate for collection development informed by the user- and curriculum-centered perspectives, arguing that libraries should develop collections for young adults that include material "which responds to trends and fads, particularly in the areas of popular culture" as well as material "which supports the formal education needs of students" (2002, 61, 60).

Most general guides to library collection development and assessment consider the collection-centered, user-centered, and curriculum-centered perspectives as they relate to the assessment of the library's collection, not necessarily to the selection of materials. There are, indeed, distinct methods of collection evaluation associated with each of these three perspectives; however, because collection development and assessment are complementary procedures, many of the methods and materials used to guide assessment can also be used to guide selection. For example, although a library's materials might be compared to a standard bibliography, as is done when using a collection-centered perspective for assessment, the same bibliography used as a comparative checklist can also inform materials selection. It is useful to think of the perspectives discussed in this chapter as philosophies underlying the development and assessment of collections in general, as each suggests a distinct way to build a collection or prioritizes a particular collection's function.

THE COLLECTION-CENTERED PERSPECTIVE

The collection-centered perspective associated with collection development and assessment, more so than the user- or curriculum-centered perspectives, is concerned with external standards and measures of collection excellence. Although the use of external measures or established standards lends the collection-centered perspective an air of objectivity, this perspective is not unbiased. From the collection-centered perspective, the size of the collection, the age of the material it contains, the number of items it contains that are featured in standard bibliographies, and its resemblance to other, similar collections determine its value. This means that a library's collection can be evaluated in comparative terms and its effectiveness or strength determined by its adherence to standards for age or the percentage of recommended titles it contains. The methods used to evaluate a collection from this perspective include "list checking," the comparison of the library's collection to a list of recommended titles or a standard bibliography or catalog; "age analysis," an estimation of the average age of the materials in the collection; the compilation of "comparative use statistics," the comparison of one library's collection and its use to that of a peer library; and a comparison to "collection standards" for size, age, and scope suggested by local or national professional organizations.

During or following a collection-centered assessment, librarians relying on these methods of evaluation will make use of a number of resources that can also aid in the development of the collection. For example, many public libraries use the H. W. Wilson standard catalogs *The Senior High Core Collection, The Middle and Junior High Core Collection,* and *The Graphic Novels Core Collection*—recommended fiction and nonfiction titles compiled by librarians and professionals and updated or issued annually—as guides to "optimal" collections against which to compare a local collection, as well as lists of items to recommend for selection. These bibliographies can aid a librarian in the retention and selection of "classic" works in subject areas in which the librarian has little expertise.

Libraries may use lists of award-winning titles or bibliographies compiled by professional associations for the same purpose, comparing the
library's local collection to them to determine the depth of its holdings of
award winners and to suggest titles for purchase.

Collection-centered development and assessment techniques may be
applied in any library setting; however, exclusive use of these techniques
to aid in the assessment and development of the library's collection suggests a particular type of library and collection. The Boston Athenaeum, a
subscription library that includes children's and young adult material of
historical and contemporary interest, relies on a selection policy that suggests an underlying collection-centric philosophy of development and
assessment. According to its website, the mission of the Boston Athenaeum is to "serve its members, the broader community, and scholars
throughout the world by preserving and augmenting its collections of
books and art, by providing library services and cultural programs, and
by preserving and enhancing the unique atmosphere of its landmark
building" (2012b). This mission is exemplified in the children's and
young adult collection, which "contains a wide variety of both old and
new books, and aims to have the most distinguished books of children's
literature from all periods" (Boston Athenaeum 2012a, IV.D.). According
to the selection policy, the books selected for this collection "are primarily
by American authors, with a sizeable secondary selection by British authors. The emphasis is on literary quality and artistic expression in works
of classic and current interest" (Boston Athenaeum 2012a, IV.D.). The
Athenaeum's definitions of "literary quality" and "artistic expression"
are implied in the description of material it does not collect. Among the
policy's "guidelines for materials the library does not generally acquire"
is a list of the types of books the athenaeum avoids, including "how-to
books, and self-help books, science fiction, horror fiction, evangelical inspirational fiction, and romance novels" and "paperbacks when hard
covers exist" (Boston Athenaeum 2012a, III.B.). In this library, each collection is described in terms of its level of coverage; the children's and
young adult collection is a "Level 2" collection, which includes "general
reference works, standard works, selected current materials, and a few
major serials" (Boston Athenaeum 2012a, II.). The note regarding the library's intention to acquire and retain "standard works" implies a collection-centric development philosophy, though the sources the library uses
to determine the standard nature of these works are not indicated in its
collection policy. Furthermore, its mission to collect works of "literary
quality" suggests its adherence to a collection-centric standard of "quality" that its collection development policy implies.

Special collections of children's and young adult material housed in
college and university libraries or in larger public libraries are often developed from a collection-centric perspective. The Children's Literature
Research Collection at the Philadelphia Free Library is an example of one

such library, with collection-centric emphases in particular areas of children's and young adult literature. According to the library's website, the Children's Literature Research Collection "emphasize[s] juvenile books associated with the Pennsylvania region; books about human sexuality; serial fiction; folk literature; toy and moveable books; and books written or illustrated outside the field of children's literature" (Philadelphia Free Library 2012). This description of the collection's scope suggests the depth of its development in certain topical areas (e.g., human sexuality) and media forms (e.g., serial fiction). Here, the focus seems to be on the collection-centric task of developing a deep and complete collection of certain types of material and media. The Kerlan Collection of children's material at the University of Minnesota is another example of a collection-centric collection. Although the larger collection of over 100,000 books contains a variety of material in various forms, the collection's emphasis on the acquisition of award-winning manuscripts (the library seeks to acquire manuscripts of books that have been honored with the Newbery Award, the Newbery Honor, and the Minnesota Book Award, as well as manuscripts and original illustrations for books that have been honored with the Caldecott Award and Honor) suggests its collection-centric focus. The Kerlan Collection also publishes a list of its holdings that peer libraries may use as a basis for comparison, making this research collection a collection-centric development and assessment tool.

Most public library collections are not collection-centric in their entirety; however, public librarians may rely on collection-centric techniques to evaluate and develop their young adult collections. Many public libraries collect and house award-winning YA titles, selecting annual Printz and National Book Award winners for inclusion in the library's collection or maintaining collections of work by authors who have received the Margaret A. Edwards award. Although the popularity of these award-winning titles among patrons may vary, these selections are often made with the expectations of patrons in mind. That is, although award-winning titles may not be the most read of the library's collection, patrons tend to expect the library to house collections of these "classic" works of young adult literature. How deep the library's collection of award-winning titles is (whether the library collects award as well as honor books and the length of time it maintains these collections) depends on the library's mission, its historical patterns of service, and the amount of shelf and storage space available. In this way, decisions about the use of collection-centric techniques of development can be seen as related to a library's understanding of its users, itself an indicator of a particular collection philosophy: the user-centered collection development stance.

THE USER-CENTERED PERSPECTIVE

Unlike collection-centered practices, user- or use-centered collection development and assessment depends on local context and focuses on how the material collected by the library is used by library patrons. One of the primary ways libraries determine how and if a collection is being used is by studying its circulation. G. Edward Evans and Margaret Zarnosky Saponaro assert that two "basic assumptions" inform library reliance on the circulation study method: "(1) the adequacy of the book collection is directly related to its usage and (2) circulation records provide a reasonably representative picture of collection use" (2005, 326). By examining circulation records, Kay Bishop has argued, libraries can easily identify "(1) low-usage materials, which may be ready to be removed from the collection; (2) high-usage materials, which may be titles to duplicate; (3) patterns of use in selected subject areas or by format; and (4) materials favored by certain user groups" (2007, 140). Bishop's description of the utility of circulation statistics in evaluating library collections also highlights the relationship between this form of evaluation and materials selection. Identification of areas of high use in the collection suggests a need to purchase more or duplicate materials in that area, whereas notations of particular patterns of material use—by subject or format—suggest a need for further or deeper development.

Not all of a library's material may be circulated, however; thus librarians should also examine how noncirculating material is used in-house to determine the strength of, for example, its reference and database collections. Jennifer Burek Pierce's intriguing 2003 study of noncirculating and missing young adult library materials indicates the relevance of studies of in-house library use and exposes the limitations of circulation studies. Following the researcher's identification of noncirculating material (i.e., items listed among the library's holdings that had not been checked out for a significant period of time), Pierce noted that many of these items were no longer on the library's shelves and had likely been removed by library users. That these missing items dealt with sensitive topics like sexuality, romantic relationships, and controlled substance use and abuse suggested the popularity of these topics among readers who may have been reluctant to check out these items at the circulation desk. In this case, whereas Bishop suggests that material identified in circulation records as "low use" may represent topics no longer of interest to teen patrons, Pierce discovered that "low use" in circulation terms may represent "a particular kind of use" by young adult patrons (2003, 71).

Because most public libraries consider "community need . . . the dominant factor in selection" (Evans and Saponaro 2005, 75), evaluation of the collection in terms of its use by the communities and patrons for whom library material is selected aligns with the library's service mission. "Community need" encompasses not only the information needs of the library community, but also its interests, and because, as Evans and Saponaro note, "anticipating public interest is a challenge for the public library selector" (2005, 76), determining how and if library material selected in anticipation of public interest is being used informs collection evaluation as well as development. User surveys and interlibrary loan statistics provide two measures of use- and user-centered data that can help libraries determine if the current collection is meeting its patrons' needs and suggest areas for future collection development. Sarah Ludwig recommends the use of focus groups, surveys, and circulation data to "discover trends and patterns in the books [teens] borrow and ask about" (2011, 58). Focus groups and surveys can measure patrons' current library use or solicit patron feedback and suggestions for collection development. Circulation data—especially interlibrary loan data—can help librarians "identify subject or format weaknesses in the collection [and] identify specific titles needed" (Bishop 2007, 153). Determining what material is checked out most often, what material is "held" most often, and what material is requested from other libraries can help librarians identify the patterns of use about which Ludwig writes as well as specific titles to add to the collection.

Some resources for collection development make anticipated popularity and use the primary criteria for the recommendation of materials. YALSA's Popular Paperbacks for Young Adults list, a collection of recommended adult and young adult titles widely available in paperback and chosen for how they represent a variety of what the organization calls "accessible themes and genres" (YALSA 1997–2012), is one example of a selection list created with user interest in mind. Similarly, the McNaughton plan, created by the library materials vendor Brodart, makes popularity a criterion for selection and offers libraries popular titles for lease to fulfill patron demand. Librarians may select titles from a list of high-demand items compiled by McNaughton and Brodart and arrange to lease these titles for an established period of time to meet inflated demand following a book's release. Of the benefits of such a program, Evans and Saponaro write: "There are no processing costs, because the books come ready for the shelf, and the leasing fee is considerably lower than the item's purchase price. Users will be happier about shorter waiting times for the high interest books" (2005, 255). Lists and services like these are useful, because they draw attention to and make available nationally popular titles of interest to young adult librarians; however, these lists alone cannot address all of a library's local patron needs and interests. In fact, one of the benefits of user-centered collection assessment and evaluation lies in its tendency to uncover and recognize unique titles of high interest to the local user population.

THE CURRICULUM-CENTERED PERSPECTIVE

Increasing interest in school accountability and the development of state-wide or national curricular standards has an impact on school as well as public library collections for young people. School library media collections are built to support the educational work of the school library media specialist, the school's educational staff, and the information seeking of children and are responsive to local, state, and national curricula; their function to provide informational support to the school community indicates these collections' close relationship to the school curriculum. Public libraries also often make the education of the public a component of their mission, and as their collections function to support young people's every day information needs as well as those imposed by the school curriculum, curriculum-centered collection assessment and development techniques become relevant to the public library selector as well. Although historically there has been a "turf war" between school and public libraries with regard to each institution's responsibility to local curricula, the recommendations of Shirley Fitzgibbons, in a study commissioned by the U.S. Department of Education on the role of public and school libraries in education reform, remain as true today as they were when the study was published at the turn of the twenty-first century. Arguing that the roles of the school and public library are "unique and complementary," Fitzgibbons asserts, "there is a need to make cooperative decisions on nonfiction titles to provide a diversity of titles while still duplicating titles in high demand" (2000, "Cooperation," para. 3).

The curriculum-centered model of collection development typically guides the development of school library collections. As Bishop notes, "A major purpose of the [school library] collection is to support the school curriculum" (2007, 179). To develop collections to support the curriculum, Bishop continues, school library media specialists "must understand the school's approaches to education, be knowledgeable about the curriculum, and be aware of any educational trends that might affect the curriculum" (2007, 179). Sandra Hughes-Hassell and Jacqueline Mancall argue that to "have a clear picture of the enacted curriculum," school library media specialists must familiarize themselves with the curriculum's "major subjects and topics, state and local standards or benchmarks, essential questions that focus instruction and assessment, skills and processes, teaching methods, assessment strategies and end products, [and] classroom organization" (2005, 37). Hughes-Hassell and Mancall encourage media specialists to gather data about the school's curriculum by "observing in classrooms, participating on curriculum and technology committees, analyzing local curriculum documentation, reviewing state and local academic standards, analyzing student work, [and] conducting teacher and student surveys" (2005, 37). This data collection allows media specialists to identify "the types and number of resources needed to support learning, when, how and where learners need access, utility software and other technology needed to complete assessment products [and] budget needs for resources to support the curriculum" (Hughes-Hassell and Mancall 2005, 36). Because school library budgets are typically limited, Evans and Saponaro observe, "library media specialists often build a core collection that provides some breadth and then concentrate on building emphasis collections that target curricular goals" (2005, 78).

When assessing library collections from a curriculum-centered perspective, school library media specialists often create curriculum-keyed collection maps to aid in the discovery of strong and weak areas. At their most basic, collection maps are tables of data listing the number of titles the library holds in a given subject area or Dewey class, the average age of the material in each subject area, and the percentage of total circulation represented by that area of the collection. More detailed collection maps may describe the level of curricular support offered by each area of the collection in broad or narrow terms, labeling areas of the collection that house a few, general resources as providing "weak" support for in-depth research and considering those areas of the collection that feature general topical overviews addressed to multiple audiences as well as more narrowly focused topical monographs as providing more "in-depth" support in a subject area. Pat Franklin and Claire Gatrell Stephens describe collection mapping as a three-step process involving data collection; physical inspection; and consultation with faculty, students, and school support staff and encourage librarians to gather general collection and circulation data, focusing on the "number of volumes in a particular subject area or the age of the books in that same collection" (2009, 44). These data can be used to compare the local collection to others in the district or can be compared to collection standards for age, because "if the resources are outdated, they might give false or inaccurate information to users" (Franklin and Stephens 2009, 44). The authors then recommend a physical examination of the collection to determine the condition of the materials, with an eye toward gauging their appeal to student users. Finally, Franklin and Stephens recommend consulting with teachers and students to determine how and if a topical area of a collection meets their teaching and research needs. In these ways, the collection-mapping process combines elements of collection-centered and user-centered approaches, but maintains a focus on curriculum support and relevance. While school library media specialists may develop collection maps that adhere to the understood local demands of the curriculum, public librarians may also create maps to identify broadly understood curricular areas of strength and weakness in the collection.

School library media specialists consider a number of formal and informal documents and information sources when assessing and developing the school library's collection, and public librarians may not have access to the same sources to use in structuring their own curriculum-centered evaluation or development activities. They can and do, however, have access to key documents and data that can be used to inform collection assessment and development, including state and local curriculum standards. The Common Core state standards, which to date have been adopted by forty-five states, serve as the primary informative document for many public librarians. Christopher Harris has noted how the Common Core standards, with their focus on literacy and reading in subject areas, will affect library collections, advising librarians to "buy more world-class nonfiction texts" to meet content area reading requirements, while making an effort to include primary source material that young people can "consider more deeply" than the "predigested tertiary writing found in many of today's textbooks" (2012, 28). The text of the standards—available for download from the Common Core State Standards Initiative website—describes in detail the reading and comprehension benchmarks for students through grade 12 and offers excerpts and short lists of exemplary texts that represent leveled requirements. It is important to note that although widespread adoption of the Common Core State Standards suggests the development of a national curriculum, states remain free to structure and implement these standards as they see fit. In Massachusetts, for example, the state Department of Education incorporated Common Core requirements within its existing Curriculum Frameworks, a process that resulted in the development of a number of state curricular guides. These guides describe topical parameters of education associated with each grade level and include bibliographies of recommended resources for teachers and students.

Although public library mission statements typically position the library as a purveyor of educational as well as recreational reading and information sources, few public libraries collaborate with school libraries to develop public library collections to meet student academic needs. A recent study undertaken by *School Library Journal* revealed what the authors called a "disturbing trend": "only 30% of respondents say their library collaborates with local schools to coordinate book purchases to support the curriculum" (Miller and Girmscheid 2012, 26). Arguing that "there's no better time than now" for librarians serving youths in school and public libraries to "join forces to deliver the best services we can," Rebecca Miller and Laura Girmscheid, interpreters of the *School Library Journal* survey results, urge public and school librarians to collaborate and share resources and to consider the relevance of the school curriculum to public library collections. Noting that "teens approach the reference desk with two main types of questions: the imposed query (usually a school assignment) and the personal query (often a popular culture interest)," Sarah Flowers justifies guideline 4.0 of YALSA's "Guidelines for Library Services to Teens": "Provide and promote information and resources appropriate to both curriculum and leisure needs of teens"

(2008, 6). With these professional standards guiding our collection development activities, it is clear that public libraries would do well to pay attention to the curricular needs of young patrons and develop collections that complement—rather than merely reproduce—the school library's collection.

CONSIDERING MULTIPLE PERSPECTIVES

Few public library collections reflect allegiance to a single collection assessment and development perspective; these institutions typically rely on a mixture of collection-centric and user-centric techniques to assess and develop the library's collection of print and media. Fewer public libraries (see Miller and Girmscheid's observation, above) recognize the local curriculum as a potential source of information for collection development; however, as young people turn to the library to meet personal and educationally inspired information needs, this perspective remains important. Blanche Woolls's guidance and recommendation for collection development that is responsive to curricula is especially relevant here. In a paper presented at the 2009 annual conference of the International Association of School Librarianship, Woolls argued:

> No single library collection can or should attempt to meet all the needs of students in schools. Library services to students is the joint responsibility of school and public libraries with school library media center activities concentrating upon curriculum-oriented programs and the public library offering its wide range of reading and other varied program possibilities. (8)

This realistic perspective—"no single library collection can or should attempt to meet all the needs of students in schools"—encourages collaborative collection development across two youth-serving institutions.

Young adult librarians responsible for collection development should recognize their position as purveyors of recreational, informational, and educational material for young people and should strive to balance these concerns—and the collection development and assessment perspectives each implies—as they develop and maintain the YA collection. The nature of this balance is ultimately influenced by context: the space—if any—allotted to the young adult collection; the demographic makeup of the primary and secondary users of the young adult collection; and the extent and type of young adult services offered will affect the emphasis the young adult librarian will place on any of the collection development perspectives described in this chapter. This means that the development of the young adult library collection should ultimately be informed by the service mission of the library and the mission of the collection itself and should be responsive to primary and secondary users and their expectations for the collection. Thus, a library with a strong after-school homework help program might look to the local curriculum to inform much of its collection development, whereas the library with a small collection of young adult fiction used primarily for recreational reading purposes might look to the user- and collection-centered perspectives to inform the majority of its collecting and assessment activities. As Vicky L. Gregory notes:

> Knowledge of the service community . . . is the keystone of effective collection development. The more the collection development staff knows about the work roles, general interests, education, information and communication behavior, values, and related characteristics of potential library users, the more likely it is that the collection will be able to provide the necessary information when it is needed. (2011, 15)

Young adults and, to a lesser extent, the general public comprise the YA collection's "service community," and effective collection development will hinge on how well that collection meets the needs of the patrons who use the library for personal or school-inspired information seeking or for recreation and entertainment. Libraries engage in needs assessment activities to determine the information and recreational needs and expectations of their patrons, and the results of the needs assessment of the young adult collection will be a key factor in the library's collection development perspective.

THREE

Collection Development Policies

Developing collections of material for young adults can be a formidable process. Adding to and subtracting from the library's collection changes its face, and although these changes can make the collection more relevant, useful, and appealing, they can also be perceived as challenging and even threatening. Young adult library collections are created primarily for teen users of the library, but the number of stakeholders invested in this collection exceeds this population; library administrators, parents, teachers, and adult patrons use, comment on, and sometimes criticize this collection of material curated for minors. Because the real tastes and interests of young adults do not always coincide with the tastes and interests of adults, grown-up stakeholders may dispute the selection and addition of popular and controversial titles on the grounds that these materials are inappropriate for teen library users. By providing guidelines for collection development that outline the intent and mission of the library's young adult collection and describe and explain how the collection is built and maintained—essentially outlining the library's criteria for "appropriateness"—collection development policies can guard against such disputes while ensuring consistency in the selection and maintenance processes.

When developing library collections for young adults, librarians act as teen advocates by selecting material to meet their adolescent patrons' expressed and anticipated interests and needs. This process of collection development is informed not only by the YA librarian's knowledge and appreciation of young adult literature and the teen service community, but also by the mission and goals of the institution in which the librarian works. The relationship between the library's mission and goals and its collections of material is spelled out in the library's collection development policy, a formal document that describes the library's collections of

material and documents its goals for collection development. Unfortunately, many libraries' collection development policies fail to mention or
describe young adult collections or characterize them with a broad brush
under the heading "children's services." Ensuring that the library's
young adult collection is represented in the collection development policy is one way of formalizing the library's plan of service to the young
adults in its community. Because library policies serve not just to document practice, but also to communicate and defend library practices to
library staff members and the public, library collection development policies help justify many of the library's major purchasing decisions by defending the right of patrons to access materials of their choice and information that addresses and answers their needs.

WHAT IS A COLLECTION DEVELOPMENT POLICY?

A library's collection development policy is a component of its greater set
of policies and procedures and exists as a detailed description of a library's plans for developing and maintaining its collections of materials.
Vicki Gregory calls these policies "blueprints for the operations of a library," arguing that "it is through these policies that the library carries
out its central tasks of acquiring, organizing, and managing library materials. These policies also typically set up the general framework for establishing the library's collection goals, in terms of both new acquisitions
and the maintenance of existing items" (2011, 31). Although collection
development policies vary in detail and depth, they contribute to and
structure the heart of library services: the selection and maintenance of
collections of material and information for library users. Peggy Johnson
(2009) argues that a library's collection development policy serves a pro-
tective function as well as the informative function that Gregory identifies. To this end, collection development policies draw clear lines of
cause and effect between the library's mission and its collection of materials, explaining and defending the selection and evaluation practices of
the institution and outlining the rights of patrons to access and even
challenge the library's collections. Collection development policies connect the library's collection practices to its service mission and describe
how and by whom material is selected, how and by whom the collection
is evaluated, and procedures for weeding and maintaining the collection,
as well as offering recourse for patrons with complaints about or concerns with items in that collection.

A library's collection development policy serves a number of internal
and external functions: it provides information and guidance to library
staff with regard to selection, acquisition, and deselection procedures,
thus ensuring procedural consistency and emphasizing the importance of
balance, and provides information about the library's selection practices

to library patrons, allowing for transparency in the process and offering opportunity for patron comment or complaint. G. Edward Evans and Margaret Zarnosky Saponaro note that the library's collection development policy "provides a framework within which individuals can exercise judgment" (2005, 52). By establishing guidelines that can be referred to by current and future library staff members and by outlining criteria for collection-based decision making, the library's collection development policy ensures that its collection of materials is consistently developed in a way that reflects the institution's mission and values. Furthermore, by detailing the responsibilities of the library and its collections to the community it serves, the policy protects the intellectual freedom of its patrons and defends its collection against challenges.

Because library policies make the library's mission and goals explicit and provide a formal road map for collection development, it is important that these policy statements be inclusive and describe any collection building efforts on behalf of the library's service population of young adults. Unfortunately, as noted previously, many collection development polices do not include explicit statements describing the library's services to and collections for young adult patrons. In these policies, young adult services and collections are subsumed under adult and children's services or not mentioned at all. Any library with a YA collection should include a detailed description of the collection and explicate its development and evaluation processes within the library's greater collection development policy. This inclusion formally authorizes young adult collections and services in the library; implies a plan for the continuing development and maintenance of a young adult collection; and, as Linda Braun, Hillias Martin, and Connie Urquhart explain, "create[s] a safety net for all the risks taken via collections" (2010, 28) by asserting its young adult patrons' "freedom to read" and the library's "intellectually free" development of the YA collection.

CREATING COLLECTION DEVELOPMENT POLICIES

Creating and formalizing public library policy is akin to a legislative process and requires the involvement of library administration, the library's board of trustees, and in some cases guidance by the state library or state library agency. Involvement of the library's community stakeholders may also be necessary to this process, especially when entire policy statements are being created from scratch or rewritten; if new statements are being added to existing policy or policies are being revised, the same stakeholders should be alerted or consulted, but may not be involved in the formal drafting process. Because in the United States state law dictates how and by whom public libraries are governed and authorizes public libraries' parameters of services, any library policies—

including those related to collection development—must be approved by
the necessary governing boards and must conform to state law. This
means that when policy statements are drafted, they must be passed by
the library's governing board—in most cases, the board of trustees—
before they are enacted.

When designing policies from scratch, Karen Muller (2011), writing
for *American Libraries*, suggests first contacting the library development
office of the state library to ensure that any planned policy reflects the
laws of the state. To aid in such legal policy development, state library
offices may offer policy guidelines or templates for policy writers that
highlight, explain, or list state laws affecting library policy. For example,
the Maine State Library makes a "Complete Library Template" available
for libraries to use when creating policy. This template is a complete
policy document with "blanks" left for the library to fill in its name and
particular details of local rules and procedures (e.g., amounts charged for
overdue materials). Similarly, the Indiana State Library has created a
guiding document for library directors that details the state laws applicable to library services and policy creation. Muller also encourages new
policy writers to consult the "Positions and Public Policy Statements"
that have been approved by the Council of the American Library Association. These address topics such as serving underserved populations,
intellectual freedom, and personnel policy development.

Young adult librarians interested in adding statements about services
and collection development for young adults to existing library policies
should first consult library administration. Depending on the size and
hierarchal structure of the library, the administrators to consult will include the library's branch head, head of youth services (for the library
branch or the entire library), head of collection development, and library
director. The administration may then assemble a committee of librarians
and staff to draft the new policy statements and communicate this intention to the library board of trustees, members of which might also serve
on the policy drafting committee. After a draft of the proposed policy has
been written, the library administration will likely ask for the advice of
the library's legal counsel, to ensure that the policy adheres to state laws
governing libraries and their use. Following approval by the legal counsel, the policy additions may be presented at an open meeting of the
library board of trustees and the community so that members may provide feedback. When a final revision is prepared, it must be voted on by
the library's board of trustees; the board's approval allows the policies to
be added and implemented.

COMPONENTS OF THE COLLECTION DEVELOPMENT POLICY

Although their purposes are identical—to describe the library's materials selection, evaluation, and collection maintenance programs—individual libraries' collection development policy statements are seldom alike. Frank Hoffmann and Richard Wood advise that a library's collection development policy should ideally "reflect all activities concerning the collection management process—including the evaluation, selection, acquisition, and weeding of information resources" (2005, xiv). Although, as Hoffmann and Wood note, the diversity—in content, tone, and structure—of collection development policies created by public libraries reveals that there is little professional "consensus" on their content, comparison of published guidelines and handbooks reveals a number of common recommended policy elements. These include general and more specific categories and subcategories of information related to the library's mission, its service population, the content of its collections of material, and its goals for development and maintenance. A number of professional resources (e.g., Arizona State Libraries, Archives and Public Records' Collection Development Training Manual [2012a, 2012b, 2012c], Evans and Saponaro's *Developing Library and Information Center Collections* [2005], Hoffmann and Wood's *Library Collection Development Policies* [2005], and Kay Bishop's *The Collection Program in Schools* [2007]) recommend optimal elements to include in the public library's collection development statement. Although each resource's list of components is distinct, the following elements appear consistently among the descriptions:

1. Statement of purpose (a brief statement describing the purpose of the library's collection development policy)
2. Library mission, goals, and objectives (documentation of the library's mission statement and any formal goals or objectives established for collections and services)
3. Description of the library's service communities (a description of the population served by the library, including articulations of who is eligible to use library services)
4. Description of budgeting or funding for collections (details of the library's sources of funding and how this funding is allocated)
5. Details of who is responsible for collection development and management (statement of responsibility for collection decisions)
6. Description of subject areas or formats included in the library's collections (description of the scope of the library's collection, including subject areas, material format [e.g., DVD, mp3], and any special collections of material)
7. Material selection and evaluation criteria or procedures (criteria for evaluating and selecting library material)

8. Collection maintenance and weeding statements and procedures (criteria for weeding, replacing, preserving, or updating library material)
9. Collection evaluation statements and procedures (criteria for evaluating the library's collections)
10. Gift policies (details of how or if the library accepts donated material)
11. Intellectual freedom statements and concerns (affirmation of the intellectual freedom of library patrons)
12. Complaint procedures (details of how the library handles any complaints by patrons)
13. Revision statements (including the date and extent of any revisions to the library's policy)

Many existing library policy documents might not be divided in just this way or include each of these components, but most do attempt to link the library's mission and purpose with its collection and services and demonstrate this with formal policy.

Explicit descriptions of a library's young adult collection and its collection development practices may be found in a number of places in a library's greater policy; these descriptions may be "embedded" within the policy or may comprise a supplemental or adjunct policy attached to the general collection development policy. "Embedded" descriptions of YA collections and services may be found throughout library collection development policies: young adults may be named as members of the library's service community and be described in the policy's introduction; responsibility for development of the young adult collection may be assigned to a specific librarian, office employee, or staff member in a detailed statement of responsibility for collection development; the YA collection might be described as a special collection within the library and be detailed within a description of the formats and subjects of material collected by the library; and sources specific to young adult literature may be listed among the sources consulted from which to select material for young adults in libraries. Arguably, any library that includes a dedicated space for the collection and display of material selected for young adults should also feature policy statements that detail how that material is chosen and how the collection is maintained. Depending on the size of the library and the scope of its collection of material for young adults, these policy statements may be embedded within general policy or may take the form of what Johnson (2009) calls a "supplemental policy" and exist as a separate document featuring a narrative or "classed" description of the YA collection that articulates goals for the 'collection; connects these goals to the library's mission; and describes the procedures for selecting, weeding, and evaluating library material in detail specific to the YA collection.

WRITING SUPPLEMENTAL POLICIES FOR YOUNG ADULT LIBRARY COLLECTIONS

As Johnson (2009) observes, many general library policies may be supplemented by statements describing the processes for selecting material within particular subject areas or for specific communities of users. Libraries with newly developed collections of material in a variety of formats for young adults may find that creating a set of supplemental policies to describe the collection's user community, as well as the processes associated with selecting, evaluating, and deselecting material for this group, is easier than editing the institution's entire collection development policy document. As YA library collections grow to include a greater variety of media types and forms, the procedures for developing collections for this user group become more complex and harder to protect or defend with general or multipurpose policy statements, making greater specificity in "embedded" policies a necessity or suggesting the need for supplemental policy. A set of supplemental policies specific to the library's YA collection serves an advocacy purpose as well as a practical one: when formalized, the library's YA materials policy affirms the primary motivation for the development of young adult collections in general. If, as YA librarians argue, the needs and interests of young people are distinct from those of adults and children, libraries serving populations that include young people must also develop specialized procedures to create collections to meet their unique needs.

Johnson also notes that a supplemental policy may take one of three forms: it may be presented as a narrative document describing the collection, its purpose, and procedures for materials selection, collection evaluation, and maintenance; it may take the form of a "classed" document that "describes the collection and current collecting levels in abbreviated language and numerical codes, typically according to the Library of Congress or Dewey Decimal Classification scheme" (2009, 80); or it may combine both the narrative and classed formats. Whichever format a supplemental policy takes, Braun, Martin, and Urquhart recommend that the policy include at least the following information:

1. The age(s) of the primary population for which the young adult collection is created
2. A description of the genres and formats of material collected for young adults
3. A list of the criteria and resources used to make material selection decisions
4. Weeding guidelines
5. The outline of a procedure to follow when responding to challenges of library material (2010, 27–28)

When creating a supplemental policy for the library's young adult collection, policy writers should look to the library's general collection development policy as a model of organization and terminology. Supplemental YA collection policies mirror the general collection development policies of their institutions in content and tone and describe the young adult collection's service population, scope, and procedures for its development and maintenance in detail not typically found in descriptions of young adult collections that are "embedded" in general collection development policy statements.

Describing the Young Adult Population and the Young Adult Collection's Service Intent

Supplemental policy statements for YA collections should begin with a description of the primary population they serve and should be as broad as possible while reflecting the service mission of the library. When crafting statements to be included in this part of the policy, YA librarians should strive to use language that is broadly encompassing and suggests the collection's primary purpose to meet the needs of the library's young adult users. The "priority needs" for young adults that libraries identify vary among libraries and reflect each library's mission for its young adult collection. Sarah Ludwig (2011) argues that the size of the space allocated for young adult material; the scope of the library's existing adult collection and its accessibility to young adults; the size of the young adult materials budget; and the availability, accessibility, and relevance of the library's databases will inform how and for what purposes the library envisions this collection will be used. In general, public library collections for young adults may be designed to meet both the popular and school-inspired (or required) reading and information needs of the library's teen population or their popular and educational needs individually and exclusively. The scope of the population the library considers "young adult" will also vary across communities. In some libraries the young adult population is defined as exclusively high school students (grades 9–12 or ages fourteen to eighteen), whereas other libraries define the population more broadly to include middle school (grades 6–8 or ages eleven to fourteen) or junior high school (grades 7–8 or ages twelve to fourteen) students as well as high school students. The age and grade level configurations of the local school system will probably affect the library's definition of "young adult," as will the definition of "children" employed by the library's children's services staff. The age at which the library's children's services "end"—the upper range of ages and grades of the students for whom the library selects children's material—is a useful lower age boundary of the library's young adult services population.

The supplemental policy description of the library's YA collection and the population it serves should reflect local and community definitions of "young adult" and the library's institutional definition of the "young adult collection." However the library chooses to define its service population and its service mission, its description of its service population and intent will define its population in terms of an age range and, because very few libraries serve monocultural communities, should also describe the population's cultural, economic, and linguistic diversity, specifying the presence of linguistic, ethnic, or cultural groups the library may have a goal of serving. This section of the policy should also specify the goal of the young adult collection itself and characterize its mission to meet the particular reading and information needs it has defined as "priority" for the collection.

The following examples describe a fictional public library's collection for young adults meant to serve the popular and educational reading and information needs of a diverse population of adolescents, a young adult collection of popular materials to address the recreational reading needs of a diverse population of young people, and a collection built to meet the educational research and assignment needs of a diverse young adult population.

Popular and Educational Materials Collection:
The Anytown Public Library's young adult collection has been created with the popular and curricular reading interests and needs of the town's racially, socioeconomically, ethnically, culturally, and linguistically diverse population of young people between the ages of twelve and eighteen in mind and to that end includes a variety of popular, high interest, and educationally supportive material and media that reflect the interests and needs of this group.

Popular Materials Collection:
The Anytown Public Library's young adult collection has been created to serve the popular and high interest recreational reading needs and interests of the town's racially, socioeconomically, ethnically, culturally, and linguistically diverse population of young people between the ages of twelve and eighteen and includes popular material and media created for and enjoyed by this diverse young adult audience.

Educational Materials Collection:
The Anytown Public Library's young adult collection has been created to meet the educational and curricular needs and interests of the town's racially, socioeconomically, ethnically, culturally, and linguistically diverse population of young people in grades six to twelve enrolled in local schools or involved in other educational endeavors. This collection reflects state and local curricular guidelines and includes classic fiction, summer reading titles, nonfiction, and other media selected to support the educational and research needs of the young adult population.

These sample policy statements identify the primary audience for whom material included in the Anytown Public Library's young adult collection has been selected, using, in the first two examples, YALSA's age-based definition of young adulthood (ages twelve to eighteen) and, in the last example, a more institutional definition of young adults (grades 6–12), which suggests the more curricular focus of that collection. All of the policies define the primary user population in broad terms, noting the diversity of the population in terms of race, socioeconomic factors, ethnicity, language, and culture; as the policies suggest that the collections are created to meet the needs of such a diverse audience, they support the development of a diverse collection. Each policy statement includes language that emphasizes the development of a collection reflecting specific population needs and interests and begins to define the parameters of those "needs and interests."

Describing the Genres and Formats of Material Collected for Young Adults

Just as general collection development policies include descriptions of the subjects, genres, and formats of material collected on behalf of the library's service population and housed throughout the library, supplemental policies for young adult collections should indicate the formats and subjects of the material collected for young adults and make note of the general criteria used for their selection. Because young adult collections are not composed solely of young adult literature and may include, for example, adult and children's fiction and nonfiction, it is important that any supplemental policy describing the material selected and collected for the young adult audience, like the description of the collection's primary user population, be as broad as possible. Braun, Martin, and Urquhart recommend that the language used to describe young adult collections in policy statements be "encompassing, flexible, and allow for taking risks" (2010, 27); the library should develop statements that encourage what Lester Asheim might call a "positive" rather than a "negative" orientation to the collection and support the selection of material based on criteria that allow for breadth rather than limiting scope.

Although the descriptions of the genres and formats of material collected by the library for its young adult patrons would seem somewhat neutral, a policy's description of this material collected for any population operates as an effective description of the collection's scope and can thus be cited to defend the addition of nontraditional material or condemn the selection of material that does not fit within the scope of the collection as described in library policy. Statements like the fictional one that follows describe the library's collection of young adult material broadly, allowing for the inclusion of a variety of forms of print material published for multiple audiences:

The Anytown Public Library's collection of print material for young adults is selected to reflect the diverse recreational and educational reading interests, needs, and abilities of the Anytown Public Library's teen population. This collection includes popular and literary young adult fiction as well as works of popular and literary fiction published for adults and children that are of interest or relevance to the library's teen population. To meet the varied informational needs and reading abilities of this population, the library collects nonfiction of recreational or daily life interest and relevance to its young adult patrons as well as material that addresses their educational and curriculum-related information needs. In addition to collecting material in traditional book form, the library embraces new formats of interest to its teen patrons, including fictional or informational graphic novels, comic books, magazines, zines, and newspapers.

This description suggests a rich young adult collection of print material in multiple formats of potential interest to a diverse population of young people. It reflects the intention for the library's young adult collection to include material that meets the recreational and school-inspired reading needs of the young adult population, including material published for adults and children as well as young adults. Space and budgetary demands typically disallow the development of a collection with a scope as broad as the dream collection described here; however, more narrowly defined young adult collections can be described in policy statements to allow for flexibility as well. The following is a description of a more narrowly focused fictional collection of material selected to reflect the recreational reading interests of young adults:

The Anytown Public Library's young adult materials collection was created to meet the recreational and high interest fiction and informational reading needs and interests of young adults. This collection includes popular and literary young adult literature and nonfiction addressing topics of recreational, popular, or high interest to the library's diverse population of teen readers. Duplicate copies of material published for and shelved in the library's collections for adults and children that have been requested by young adults and works by adult and children's authors that have proven popular among young adults are also included within this recreational reading collection. In addition to material in book form, this collection also includes fictional and information works in formats of interest to young adults, including graphic novels, comics, magazines, and zines.

This description connects the library's collection of recreational reading material to the needs and interests of the young adult population, characterizing it as "diverse" and implying a variety of material by subject and type. It allows for the inclusion of children's and adult material in this collection. As does the previous description, this one uses the word "includes" to suggest the parameters of the library's collection of nonbook material without narrowing its scope in absolute terms.

As material for young people emerges in multiple nonprint formats, it is important for the library to describe any multimedia or electronic formats the library collects for its teen patrons. Although the library's young adult collection may not include material in every available nonprint format, those that are collected should be described. Because many collections of material for young adults that include multimedia and electronic formats may be in constant flux, as old technologies are superseded and new technologies emerge, it may be wise, as Gregory advises, to indicate in the library's description of multimedia formats that "the library will collect in new formats where feasible" (2011, 48). Gregory continues: "A statement such as this will suffice when a new technology first comes along, but the new format should be incorporated into the policy as soon as possible" (2011, 48). Although libraries may collect multimedia material for a variety of audiences, lack of space may not allow these materials to be housed within audience-specific physical collections. This means that although the library may collect multimedia material for its teen patrons, it may not be housed in the library's physically delineated young adult collection, but rather within a general collection of material by format. Whether the library's multimedia material is housed in the physical space created to hold the library's young adult material or interfiled with the library's general collection of material by format, any multimedia material selected for teens should be described in the supplemental collection development policy.

The supplemental policy's descriptions of multimedia collections of material selected for teens should be, as is the description of the library's print collection, as broad and encompassing as possible. This description may note where the library houses the multimedia material collected for young adults as well and should, as do the preceding descriptions of print material, connect this collection activity to the needs and interests of the library's young adult patrons. The following sample describes a fictional collection of multimedia material selected for teens but housed in format-specific collections throughout the library:

> The Anytown Public Library collects nonprint material to meet the varied recreational, informational, and educational needs of its diverse clientele of young adults. Audiobooks in various formats, musical and spoken word recordings, and films on DVD are among the formats collected with the library's adolescent patronage in mind; as new technologies and formats emerge and are adopted by the public, the library will consider collecting material in these formats where feasible. The library's multimedia materials for young adults are interfiled with material in the same format collected for adults and children and are available to all library patrons.

This description suggests the library's mission to meet the "recreational, informational and educational needs" of its service population and provides examples of the types of multimedia material collected by the library, noting, as Gregory suggests, the potential for the addition of material in new formats. This fictional library organizes its multimedia material by format in collections of audiobooks, musical and spoken word recordings, and films that include selections for children, young adults, and adults. The descriptive policy statement notes that material selected for young adults is included among these format-based collections and affirms the right of all patrons to select material from them.

In keeping with the American Library Association's "Diversity in Collection Development" statement (2008a), in supplemental policies descriptions of the library's materials selected for young adults should affirm and advocate diverse resources and perspectives in library collections. In this interpretation of the "Library Bill of Rights," the ALA asserts that "librarians have an obligation to select and support access to materials and resources on all subjects that meet, as closely as possible, the needs, interests, and abilities of all persons in the community the library serves" (2008a, para. 1). Furthermore, the statement argues:

> Access to all materials and resources legally obtainable should be assured to the user, and policies should not unjustly exclude materials and resources even if they are offensive to the librarian or the user. This includes materials and resources that reflect a diversity of political, economic, religious, social, minority, and sexual issues (2008a, para. 2).

By emphasizing the "needs, interests and abilities" of the young adult community served by the library's young adult collection and by noting that these "needs, interests and abilities" reflect "a diversity of political, economic, religious, social, minority, and sexual issues," a library's policy becomes a statement of advocacy for the needs and interests of the library's or collection's service population.

The ALA's "Diversity in Collection Development"—as well as "Labeling and Rating Systems" (2009)—has particular relevance for developers of young adult collections where graphic novel and media formats are concerned. Because many graphic novels, comics, movies, and video games have audience labels or "ratings" attached to their packaging, it is important to develop policy that describes how the library will handle "rated" material. In its "Labeling and Rating Systems" statement, the ALA notes that "[m]any organizations use rating systems as a means of advising either their members or the general public regarding the organizations' opinions of the contents and suitability or appropriate age for use of certain books, films, recordings, Web sites, games, or other materials" (2009, para. 6). These ratings systems include the system of movie ratings developed by the Motion Picture Association of America (see "What Each Rating Means," http://www.mpaa.org/ratings/what-each-rating-means), the video game rating system developed by the Entertainment Software Rating Board (see figure 3.1), and the rating systems developed by comics and manga publishers like Marvel and Tokyopop. Some libraries use the ratings systems to guide collection development and indicate in their collection development policies that only material that falls within a particular ratings continuum may be purchased for a specific age group. The ALA's "Labeling and Ratings Systems" statement allows that when used as "viewpoint-neutral directional aids [that] facilitate access by making it easier for users to locate materials" (2009, para. 4), ratings or labels may be employed in a way that does not infringe upon a library user's intellectual freedom. If, for example, the library as a whole collects video games that have been assigned ESRB ratings across the ratings spectrum and shelves those with EC, E, and E 10+ in the library's children's room; those with T ratings among the young adult material; and those labeled M with the adult material, these ratings labels can become "directional aids" that indicate both rating and physical location of the item. If, however, the library uses a rating system to delimit collecting—if, for example, it refuses to carry or shelve material in any part of the library that bears a rating higher than T, despite its popularity—or if the library uses a system to restrict access by not allowing checkout of material bearing certain ratings by teen or child users of the library, these ratings are being employed in a way that has the potential to infringe upon library users' rights. The ALA's advice here—that "the library should seek legal advice" regarding the labeling issue—should be heeded by YA librarians developing media collections for young people, to ensure that both legal mandates and intellectual freedom are maintained.

Describing Selection Criteria for Young Adult Materials

One of the primary functions of the library's collection development policy is to explain to the public exactly how the library selects materials on their behalf. In general, as well as in supplemental young adult collection development policy statements, this content, Hoffmann and Wood note, "represents the core of the collection development policy" as it "provides a blueprint as to why certain information resources are chosen over others for library holdings" (2005, 41). Selection criteria may be outlined in general or specific terms and may include descriptions of criteria unique or specific to particular formats or genres. Most policies include statements similar to the following, describing general criteria for the selection of materials:

1. As the library seeks to offer a diversity of viewpoints on current and historical issues, materials collected by the library represent multiple points of view.

Rating Designation	Description
EC	*Early Childhood:* Games for ages 3 and older that "[c]ontain[] no material that parents would find inappropriate"
E	*Everyone:* Games for ages 6 and older that "contain minimal cartoon, fantasy or mild violence and/or infrequent use of mild language"
E 10+	*Everyone Ages 10 and Above:* Games for ages 10 and older that "may contain more cartoon, fantasy or mild violence, mild language and/or minimal suggestive themes"
T	*Teen:* Games for ages 13 and above that "may contain violence, suggestive themes, crude humor, minimal blood, simulated gambling, and/or infrequent use of strong language"
M	*Mature:* Games for audiences aged 17 and above that "may contain intense violence, blood and gore, sexual content and/or strong language"
A	*Adults:* Games for adults aged 18 and above that "may include prolonged scenes of intense violence and/or graphic sexual content and nudity"
RP	*Rating Pending:* Games that have not been assigned a final rating

2. The library seeks to provide material to meet the entertainment, recreational, and informational needs of all of its constituents; thus, the library will not exclude material from its collection based on the racial, social, ethnic, religious, political, or gender identity or point of view of its creator.
3. The library seeks to collect and provide library users with access to information in a cross-section of media formats and types.

These broad selection guidelines draw from the ALA's "Library Bill of Rights" (1996) and reflect most public libraries' mission to provide access to information from multiple points of view and in multiple formats. Libraries that do not adhere to the '"Library Bill of Rights" or that have partisan missions (e.g., a church or synagogue library may have a mission to collect only material that supports and proclaims its particular religious and ideological stances) may not include such liberal guidelines for selection. Further selection guidelines may address issues specific to the selection of materials for particular populations or in particular media formats and may include lists of resources consulted by the collection development librarian during selection as well as information regarding any standing orders of popular material or media maintained by the library.

Supplemental policies for young adult collections should include, at the very least, general criteria for selection that emphasize and assert the library's mission to develop a collection that meets the diverse needs and interests of the young adult population. Just as general criteria for selection often reflect the '"Library Bill of Rights," criteria for the selection of material for young adults may draw from the ALA's "Access for Children and Young Adults to Nonprint Materials" (2004) and "Free Access to Libraries for Minors" (2008b). It is important to note that in many communities, and in many libraries, ALA's perspective is considered liberal, especially where minors are concerned. Guidance from and approval by the library's legal counsel should be sought when developing both general and specific selection criteria for young adult collections. General criteria for the selection of material for young adults might read as follows:

1. Material for young adults is selected to meet the diverse entertainment, information, educational, and recreational reading needs and interests of the library's young adult patrons and reflects a diversity of points of view and perspectives.
2. The library's collection of young adult material includes media in a variety of formats, including audiobooks, music, electronic databases, and video games. These multimedia items are selected to reflect the informational, recreational, entertainment, and educational needs of the library's young adult population and, like the library's print resources, reflect a diversity of points of view and perspectives.
3. The library cannot assume the role of parent or guardian of the young adult patrons who use the library's collection of materials selected for them. To aid parents and guardians in guiding their reading and viewing choices, the library will provide published reviews or reference works that contain information about the content, subject matter, and recommended audiences for the material selected for the young adult collection.

The first two statements reiterate selection criteria for library material in general, but speak to the young adult collection specifically. The third statement uses language from "Access for Children and Young Adults to Nonprint Materials" and "Free Access to Libraries for Minors" to reaffirm the intellectual freedom rights of the library's young adult patrons as well as to support the broadest possible selection of material for young adults.

More specific criteria for the selection of material for young adults should reflect the library's mission statement and its mission to serve young adults, as well as address any format-specific collection goals for the library's YA collection. For example, although many libraries make curricular support a partial goal for the library's young adult collection, most public libraries do not collect school textbooks. This should be noted in the library's specific criteria for selection. Similarly, many libraries seek to develop collections that reflect not only the expressed and observed needs and interests of the young adult population, but also literature created for young adults that has been recognized for its quality. To that end, many libraries' specific selection criteria address their efforts to collect award-winning titles for the young adult collection. A library may also include statements describing its policy for acquiring material recommended or suggested for the young adult collection by library patrons. This section of the library's policy may also include criteria specific to particular media formats and lists of or references to professional and popular resources used to guide selection activity.

In this section of the library's policy a "classed" description of the library's collection and selection criteria might be useful. "Classed" descriptions of library materials break down the library's collections by subject and format, describing their scope and noting any subject- or format-specific criteria used to select material. A classed description of the library's young adult collection should describe all formats of material currently selected for the library's young adult patrons. These "classes" might represent broad categories of fiction, nonfiction, and multimedia material, or they might be more specific and describe the library's collection of fiction selected for young adults, nonfiction in subject areas delineated by Dewey Decimal or Library of Congress class, graphic print forms (comics and graphic novels), and multimedia material by type. Following are examples of classed descriptions of material collected for the fictional Anytown Public Library:

> Young Adult Fiction: The Anytown Public Library's young adult fiction collection includes literary and popular fiction published for young adults as well as fictional material published for children and adults that is of interest or relevance to its teen patrons. Fiction for young adults may be selected based on its adherence to the general selection criteria for fiction used by the library at large, as well these more specific criteria: recommendation in professional review journals or bibliographies; critical review in popular media; current or anticipated popularity of the author, publisher, or series among the local young adult population; and recommendation or request by library patrons. The library seeks to include those fictional titles that have received publishing or literary awards in the field of youth literature among its collected titles, including books that have won the Michael L. Printz Award and the National Book Award. In the interest of diversifying the perspective and authority of the fiction collection, the library makes an effort to collect works that represent multicultural and diverse perspectives. In addition, the library works with local schools to ensure that any fiction titles recommended on summer reading lists are represented in the young adult fiction collection.

> Young Adult Nonfiction: 600–699: This section of the library's nonfiction collection includes material related to physical health and medicine, including sexuality; nutrition; vocations and trades, including vo-

cational guidance; home economics, including cooking and sewing; and building, including construction and carpentry. Materials selected to be included in this section of the library's young adult nonfiction collection meet the general criteria for nonfiction selection established by the library, with special attention given to those titles that address the teen or adolescent reader. Materials are selected to represent multiple perspectives, especially those related to teen sexuality, and the library makes an effort to select material that may be used for student research as well as personal information. Because this section of the collection includes material describing trends and discoveries in health and medicine, the library seeks to purchase only the newest material in these topical areas, replacing titles that are more than five years old.

These descriptions characterize the "classed" model: materials are described as they fall within certain classes of format or information, and format- or subject-specific criteria related to the selection of material in these areas are explained. As with all descriptions of the library's selection criteria, it is important to ensure that these criteria are broad enough to allow for flexibility and diversity in selection without foreclosing possibilities.

Describing Evaluation and Weeding Guidelines

A detailed description of the library's criteria for the selection of materials should be followed by an explanation of its procedures for evaluating and weeding the collection. Evaluation and weeding often go hand in hand, as guidelines for the evaluation of a library's collection often include standards for age in terms of subject and publication date and suggest a timetable for the deselection of material. An evaluation of the library's young adult collection helps librarians make decisions about where and how to allocate monetary resources, especially in collections that include material in multiple formats. For example, a YA librarian might collect circulation data to determine whether games playable on a particular gaming platform are used more or less often to help make decisions about which platform's games to emphasize during selection. However the results of collection evaluation are used, librarians developing statements to describe the evaluation of a collection should consider ALA's "Evaluating Library Collections: An Interpretation of the Library Bill of Rights" (1981), which indicates that

> The continuous review of library materials is necessary as a means of maintaining an active library collection of current interest to users. In the process, materials may be added and physically deteriorated or obsolete materials may be replaced or removed in accordance with the collection maintenance policy of a given library and the needs of the community it serves. Continued evaluation is closely related to the goals and responsibilities of all libraries and is a valuable tool of collec-

tion development. This procedure is not to be used as a convenient means to remove materials presumed to be controversial or disapproved of by segments of the community.

This statement affirms the library's mission to create and maintain a collection "of current interest to users" and ensures that the collection remains diverse in form, format, and point of view.

Ideally the young adult collection development policy will include separate sections describing its evaluation procedures and its weeding criteria. Gregory reminds us that because "collection evaluation and assessment are usually studied together with weeding . . [many] think the terms are synonymous, but they should not be so viewed" (2011, 113). As Evans and Saponaro (2005) note, the results of a library's evaluation of its collection can be used in arguments for increasing budgetary allocations in specific directions or in promotional material distributed by the library. A policy statement describing plans for evaluating the young adult collection does not have to be lengthy; however, like all other components of the collection development policy, it should reflect the library's mission, as this fictitious statement from the Anytown Public Library does:

> The young adult collection at the Anytown Public Library is under continuous review to ensure its timeliness and relevance to the population of young people who are its primary patrons. Periodic evaluation of the young adult collection will ensure that the collection is meeting its service goals. The collection will be evaluated annually to ensure that it is up to date, and that its holdings reflect minimal criteria for timeliness as recommended by professional standards. Circulation figures, usage statistics collected by library vendors to measure the use of subscription databases and electronic resources, interlibrary loan requests, and patron requests to purchase or add material to the collection will be examined on a regular basis as the library seeks to maintain an effective collection.

This description is brief, but it refers to a number of collection evaluation techniques employed by libraries to aid in collection decision making that can be used to determine when items may need to be added, weeded, or replaced (these techniques are discussed in greater detail in chapter 7). This statement, and the following weeding statement, both draw from ALA's "Evaluating Library Collections" (1981), which emphasizes continuous review and judicious weeding of library collections. A statement describing the library's procedures for weeding may read like the following fictional description:

> To ensure the timeliness and relevance of the library's collection of young adult material, the library updates the collection with new material on a regular basis; replaces worn but still relevant material; and removes or discards physically deteriorated, superseded, obsolete, and

outdated material. Decisions regarding the retention, preservation, or removal of material are made following professional guidelines for young adult collection development, which provide maximum age guidelines for informational texts, and include consideration of the physical condition of the material, its historical significance or relevance, the availability of duplicates, the currency of the information, the material's appropriateness to the collection, and its contemporary and historical use by patrons.

Weeding library materials can be somewhat fraught with difficulty, because it involves actually removing and discarding or recycling material in the library, a practice that connotes censorship and book burning. As Donna J. Baumbach and Linda L. Miller point out, however, weeding "is something all librarians and library media specialists must do regularly if they want to maintain the best possible collections. . . . It is a professional responsibility that cannot be taken lightly" (2006, 3). Developing a policy that defends weeding as an important professional practice that benefits the library and its users helps to communicate to the public—and to library staff—the importance of this activity.

Describing How the Library Responds to Challenges to Material

All library policies should include a description of the library's policies and procedures regarding challenges to library material. The ALA's "Challenged Materials: An Interpretation of the Library Bill of Rights" states that "it is the responsibility of every library to have a clearly defined materials selection policy in written form that reflects the Library Bill of Rights, and that is approved by the appropriate governing authority" (1990). If, as Johnson (2009) notes, the library's collection development policy statements are created in part to inform the library's service community of its mission and communicate the steps the library takes to fulfill this mission with its collection, the policy offers library patrons the opportunity both to view documentation of the library's practices, and, in the case of challenges to library material, to comment on the results of these practices. This section of the library's policy also provides an opportunity for the library to reaffirm its commitment to intellectual freedom, an important professional ethic that underlies many libraries' mission statements. As Johnson notes, "the presence of a carefully prepared and board-approved policy will not decrease the likelihood of a challenge to a specific controversial title, but it does increase the likelihood that challenged materials will be fairly reviewed and retained" (2009, 75). By outlining the steps required for a patron to lodge a formal complaint against a specific item, as well as the steps the library will take to respond, the policy ensures that any patron with a concern about the library's collection has an opportunity to voice it and have it heard in a fair and consistent forum.

A supplemental policy may reiterate the formal process for dealing with challenged materials as documented in the library's general collection development policy. It should not describe an alternate procedure specific to the young adult collection. To this end, this section of the supplemental policy for the YA collection may summarize the library's formal process and refer to the procedures outlined in the general collection development policy. It is here that the library may wish to affirm the principles of intellectual freedom specific to minors and cite, reprint, or affirm the principles outlined in ALA's "Library Bill of Rights" (1996), "Access for Children and Young Adults to Nonprint Materials" (2004) and "Free Access to Libraries for Minors" (2008b) as these reflect the library's mission statement.

ADDING "EMBEDDED" POLICY STATEMENTS DESCRIBING THE YOUNG ADULT COLLECTION

Libraries with young adult collections comprising only one or two formats (e.g., print material and audiobooks), defined by genre and format, and consisting solely of literature published for young adults, or with collections of young adult material that is interfiled with the library's children's and adult material, may not require such detailed supplemental collection development policy statements. If the library's service community consists of few adolescents or young adult readers, or if the size of the library precludes the development of a stand-alone young adult collection or the purchase of a significant amount of material for young adults, an "embedded" collection development policy statement may be the best way to advocate for young adult collections and services. "Embedded" collection development statements are specific to distinct populations or collections and are included within the body of the library's general collection development policy. As the Arizona State Libraries, Archives and Public Records, Hoffmann and Wood (2005), Evans and Saponaro (2005), Gregory (2011), and Bishop (2007) have noted, although collection development policies are diverse documents, they tend to share core content. It is at this "core content" level that librarians seeking to add young adult collection concerns to the library's collection development policy should operate.

Young adult services and collections may be referred to throughout the library's general collection development policy (see figure 3.2). If a library's general policy is detailed but flexible, and its mission is clear but broad, as most library mission statements are, any concerns about the development of the young adult collection may already be broadly addressed in the general policy. It is important, however, to ensure that the library's young adult collection and the population for whom it is created are mentioned and described within the greater collection development policy, as this inclusion is an act of advocacy on behalf of the young adult population. Most library mission statements include young adults by default, subsuming their needs under descriptions of a service community that consists of "all residents" or "all community members." Some libraries choose to expand the boilerplate mission statement description of "all residents" to reflect the more specifically inclusive language of ALA's "Library Bill of Rights," which extends the right to use the library to all persons regardless of "origin, age, background, or views" (1996). This inclusion of "age" is politically important, as it asserts the rights of minors in general and young adults more specifically to use the library. A collection development policy statement of purpose typically follows the library's mission statement and, as the rest of the policy will continue to do, reflects the library's mission as it describes what Hoffmann and Wood (2005) consider to be the policy's "communication function." This statement of purpose describes the greater policy's intention to outline its collection development processes and operations.

Description of the Library and Its Service Community

The collection development policy's description of the library and its service community is an important first place to consider the inclusion of explicit statements about the library's young adult collection and its teen service community. The Arizona State Libraries, Archives and Public Records' "Collection Development Policy" argues that the description of the library and its service community places the collection development policy in context. A description of the service community, the library, and its services provides information regarding "specific needs or situations that are influencing the library's collection decisions and priorities" and "should aid the user of the policy and the community to understand the relative size of the library's resources and the character of its collections and programs" (2012b, "Description of the Community," para. 1; "Description of the Library," para. 1). Hoffmann and Wood observe that most general descriptions of libraries and their service communities presented in policy statements include

1. geographical data;
2. a demographic breakdown of the constituency as a whole;
3. a listing of notable business, political, educational, and cultural entities in the immediate (or surrounding) area;
4. the social services required by citizens;
5. the location of library facilities and general statement of purpose; and
6. a description of networking agreements. (2005, 9)

Within this description of the library and its service population, it is important to include young people as part of the "demographic break-

Table 3.1. Opportunities for Including Embedded Young Adult Collection Development Policy Content

General Collection Development Policy Component	Young Adult Services and Collection-related Additions
Library Mission Statement	(none)
Library Statement of Purpose	(none)
Description of the Library and Its Service Community	Should include mention of the young adult demographic (ages 12 to 18) within the greater service population
Explanation of the Collection Development Process	Should describe procedures for selecting young adult material, including • responsibility for selection of young adult material, • the application of broad criteria for selection material in general to the library's collection of young adult material, and • the application of broad evaluative criteria used when comparing the library's collection in general to the young adult collection.
Descriptions of the Library's Collections of Material by Format and Subject or Clientele	Should include the library's young adult collection as a category of material and should describe • the target audience of the young adult collection, • formats and subjects of material collected for the young adult collection, • specific criteria used for the selection of young adult material, and • sources and resources used to aid young adult collection development.
Descriptions of the Library's Goals for Collection Development	Should include statements of any goals related to the continuous development and maintenance of the library's young adult collection.
Descriptions of Procedures for Evaluating and Weeding Library Collections	Should include the library's young adult collection as a category of material to be evaluated and should specify the application of the library's general weeding guidelines to the young adult collection and articulate any specific criteria used to weed or evaluate the young adult collection.

Procedural Policy Statements (Gifts, Donations, Requests for Reconsideration)	Should mention the "chain of command" when and if young adult materials are challenged or reconsidered.
Appendixes	Should include copies of or reference to ALA's "Access for Children and Young Adults to Nonprint Material" (2004) and "Free Access to Libraries for Minors" (2008b).

down of the constituency" and consider local schools serving adolescents in the "listing of notable business, political, educational and cultural entities." A description of the library's facilities and services should note any physical space set aside for young adult collections or teen users and should mention any YA-directed programming or services provided by the library. The policy might mention here any relationship the public library has with school libraries, particularly with regard to the selection of certain types of material and the understood responsibility of each for supporting the local curriculum.

Public library collection development policy statements describing the library and its service community vary in detail and length. Some may use recent census statistics to describe the library's service population, while others rely on narrative description. The size of the library and its service community—whether the policy describes a library system serving a county or geographically large or populous region or one consisting of a single branch—will affect the nature of this description. For example, the description of the Queens Borough (NY) Public Library's service community is necessarily broad:

> The Queens Library consists of sixty-two (62) Community Libraries and a Central Library which serve the culturally and ethnically and linguistically diverse population of the Borough of Queens. Additionally, the Central Library's special subject collections support the academic, professional and technical research needs of the Borough. The sixty-three (63) locations house general and special interest circulating and reference collections for all age groups: children, young adults, college students, adult and senior adult, in languages which represent the ethno-linguistic character of the local community. It is the Library's intention that the collection in each agency or library location addresses the individual needs and interests of its immediate community and to the degree possible, reflect the diversity of the entire borough. (2012, "Collection Development," para. 6)

This description is notable for its inclusion of "young adults" as a specific demographic within the library's service community. It reflects the Queens Borough Library's mission statement ("to provide quality services, resources and lifelong learning opportunities through books and a variety of other formats to meet the informational, educational, cultural and recreational needs and interests of its diverse and changing population" [2012, "Collection Development," para. 1]) as it describes its service population in terms of its cultural, ethnic, and linguistic diversity and asserts its goals of, first, addressing the "individual needs and interests of its immediate community" and second, reflecting the diversity of the greater borough. The Gleason Public Library of Carlisle, Massachusetts, is more specific in its description of its comparatively smaller service community and, in the general text of its description of the community and the library's services, provides a brief description of the area public schools and the responsibility of the public library to the town's student community. Following a note that the town's population of persons between the ages of five and seventeen is the largest, at 1,165, with people aged forty-five to fifty-four comprising the second largest population segment at 1,150, the description of the library's service population concludes with this observation:

> The Carlisle public school is a K-8 school; high school students attend Concord-Carlisle High School. Many K-8 students use the library for assignments and reports. Other users include professionals, consultants, the unemployed, retired people, parents and their children. (Gleason Public Library 2011, "Community Analysis," para. 4)

A description of the library's services indicates the relationship between Gleason Public Library and the Carlisle public schools: "The Library maintains close links with the Carlisle public school in order to provide support services for their educational programs, but serves only as a supplementary resource" (2011, "Library Programs," para. 5). This statement distinguishes the public library's function to provide educational resources from that of the local schools and begins to suggest the scope of the library's collections for young people.

Explanation of the Collection Development Process

Many general collection development policies outline the steps of the collection development process broadly, detailing particular concerns related to audience, subject, and format in sections devoted to the description of particular materials. This section of the general policy document may name the parties responsible for developing the library's collections of material by audience or format and may list the general criteria the library uses for selecting and evaluating material. In many libraries the ultimate responsibility for collection development lies with the library director, who delegates responsibility for specific collections to departments or library staff members. The following statement of responsibility from the Pomona (CA) Public Library is typical: "The authority and responsibility for library materials selection rests ultimately with the Library Director. Under his/her direction, selection and development of the library's collections is delegated to the professional library staff" (2004, 3). This broad statement allows for any changes to the library's larger collection, including the addition or expansion of the library's young adult materials collection. The statement of responsibility for the development of collections at the Johnson City (TN) Public Library is more specific and names the library director as well as the library's adult and youth services managers as responsible parties:

> The ultimate responsibility for selection, whether by purchase, donation, or any other means, rests with the Library Director who operates within the framework of policies determined by the Board of Directors. The Director assigns to the Adult Services Manager and the Youth Services Manager the responsibility of overseeing collection management for their respective departments. All professional staff members have collection development responsibilities. All staff members and library patrons may recommend material for consideration and are encouraged to do so. (2012, 1)

This policy sketches a hierarchy of collection development responsibility, naming the "managers" of the adult and youth services collection and noting that all members of the library's professional staff contribute to collection development.

Following a broad statement of responsibility for collection development, general policies often outline the criteria the library employs to select material. The public library of the city of Pasadena, California, includes a list of criteria used to select material, noting that "[a]ll materials, whether purchased or donated, are considered in terms of [these] criteria" (2012, "Selection Criteria"). The statement continues, "[a]n item need not meet all of these standards in order to be added to the collection" and concludes with the following list (Pasadena Public Library 2012, "Selection Criteria"):

1. popular interest
2. contemporary significance or permanent value
3. currency of information
4. accuracy
5. local emphasis
6. readability or ability to sustain interest
7. treatment of subject for age of intended audience
8. reputation of author, publisher, producer, or illustrator
9. creative, literary, or technical quality
10. critical assessments in a variety of journals
11. format and ease of use
12. circulation as monitored through the automated system
13. cost and availability
14. relationship to existing materials in collection
15. relationship to materials in other area libraries

This broad and encompassing list of criteria allows for flexibility in selection and indicates both user-centered criteria (e.g., the service community's "popular interest" in the material to be selected) and professional criteria (e.g., the "critical assessment" of potential selections in "a variety of journals") used to consider material for addition to the collection. The policy's descriptions of its collection by format and subject outlines further criteria for selection unique to the format or subject of material collected by the library. Deliberately broad selection criteria, Hoffmann and Wood write, "serve as a corrective mechanism to ensure that collections remain focused on overriding institutional goals and objectives" (2005, 41). In the case of the Pasadena Public Library, the selection criterion "local emphasis" supports the library's continued development of its Pasadena collection. A description of this collection notes the "high priority" the library places "on acquiring comprehensive information and resources about Pasadena, past and present" (Pasadena Public Library 2012, "Pasadena Collection").

Some library policies include lists of selection aids and bibliographic resources used by the collection development staff to make selection decisions. Hoffmann and Wood identify three arguments for the inclusion of a list of professional selection resources in a library's collection development policy:

1. The section establishes a benchmark for consistency in the use of these tools;
2. it assists new staff in adapting to a library's established selection practices, and;
3. it communicates the level of professionalism involved in the evaluation process to the community at large. (2005, 137)

Although these are strong arguments for including a list of resources employed by the library to aid in selection, Gregory advises: "Never box yourself into having to use only the sources listed in that section, but rather use it to list the more common sources for selection in your type and size of library" (2011, 48). The Brookline (MA) Public Library's collection development policy includes a list of potential selection aids, introducing this information with language that allows for flexibility in collection development. A section of this library's collection development document entitled "Collection Development Sources" begins with the following broad description: "In determining which materials will be purchased, the assistance of the staff is solicited and requests by borrowers are welcomed. General and specific bibliographic aids, and many leading book reviewing periodicals as well as general magazines, newspapers and publisher's catalogs are consulted" (Brookline Public Library 2007, 4). This description concludes with a list of periodicals, introduced with the flexible statement, "Book reviewing periodicals consulted include but are not limited to" (Brookline Public Library 2007, 4). A list of bibliographic resources employed by the library to aid collection development and of assessment sources is also included, introduced with similarly flexible language. "We also rely on published bibliographies to aid us in collection development and analysis," the policy reads. "The most-often consulted volumes are" (Brookline Public Library 2007, 5). Using the phrases "include but are not limited to" and "most-often consulted volumes" allows the library to include a list of selection and assessment resources for informational purposes, but does not limit the library to just these resources. If the list of resources in a library's collection development policy is meant to be exemplary and represent the type of resources used to select materials and assess the collection, it is a good idea to include at least one or two publications that review and recommend young adult material as a way of, in Hoffmann and Wood's terms, communicating the "professionalism" involved in the development of the library's young adult collection.

Descriptions of the Library's Collections by Format and Subject or Clientele

A library's general collection development policy typically includes a description of its collections broken down by audience group or clientele, format, and subject, or described in terms of general and more specific audience-, format-, or subject-focused criteria for selection. For example, although many libraries include descriptions of criteria used to select all material for the library's collections, the library may have developed more specific criteria to aid in selecting material that addresses particular subjects collected by the library, collections comprising material published for particular audiences, or collections of material that exist in particular formats. Following a general description of selection criteria, many library policies describe the scope of more narrowly defined collections and the criteria associated with the selection of material for these collections. As Kay Ann Cassell and Elizabeth Futas have observed, "Many library policies discuss selection by age, which is useful since it can define some of the special needs and interests of a particular age group" (1991, 95). If there are significant numbers of easily defined groups, Cassell and Futas advise, "policies should be formulated for them" (1991, 95). Thus, if a library serves a significant population of teen patrons and has developed a collection expressly for this population or has begun to select material with these patrons in mind, it should describe its process and criteria for selecting materials for this population in its collection development policy. Although the library's collection of material for young adults may not comprise material in a unique format, young adult collections are often described within greater "format statements" in collection development policies. In many policies "format statements" are actually descriptions of material in particular formats (e.g., DVDs, periodicals) as well as descriptions of material for particular audiences (e.g., adult fiction, adult nonfiction).

If a library has not created a supplemental policy describing its collection of young adult materials, its young adult collection will probably be described and addressed in the greatest detail in this section. As Hoffmann and Wood have observed, library format statements in collection development policies "generally refer to the types of information resources collected—or *not* collected—within" the library's holdings (2005, 52). Thus, a format statement can serve as a description of a collection's scope as well as its limitations and may include justifications for or explanations of any limitations in the collection by subject or format. For example, the Monroe County (IN) Public Library's brief format description of its young adult collection does not detail what formats of material are collected for adolescents; however, it does specify that its collection for young adults does not include textbooks: "Young Adult materials are purchased to support a wide variety of interests from adolescence (age twelve) through adulthood. . . . While local curricula are generally supported, school textbooks and workbooks are specifically excluded from purchase in this collection" (2012, "Young Adult Collection"). The Sharon (MA) Public Library's description of its young adult collection does refer to format, and in its description of its young adult fiction collection in a section entitled "Collection Development for Young Adults," notes: "Paperback format is selected where possible since this is the preferred format for this age group" (2004). The library's description of its collection of young adult nonfiction specifies the format-specific parameters of its collection for young adults and also notes the space limitations that dictate shelving of young adult nonfiction, periodicals, reference, and audiovisual material in the library's general (adult) collections of material by type:

> Young adult non-fiction is selected in all subject areas represented in the adult non-fiction collection. As there are many potential users for this material, young adult non-fiction is chosen with all library users in mind and, in part due to space constraints, shelved along side adult non-fiction titles rather than separated out. . . . The general reference, audio-visual, and periodical collections include materials for young adults (Sharon Public Library 2004, "Young Adult Non-fiction").

Both of these statements were found in sections of the libraries' policies that served as descriptions of both the formats of material the library collects and the audiences for whom the library collects material. Such "multipurpose" descriptions of a library's collections may fall under a general heading like "The Library's Collections" and may describe library collections in terms of both format and audience.

Whether the library's young adult collection is considered a particular "format" of material or described in terms of its intention for it to serve the library's population of young adults, its description in a general collection development policy should include various information, including

1. the ages or grades served by the collection;
2. the scope of the collection in terms of subject or format; and
3. any specific or unique criteria for selection, weeding, and assessing the library's young adult collection.

Cassell and Futas note that this information can be conveyed "in general terms, i.e. how selection for [young adults] differs from that of other groups" or "it can replicate the adult selection policy outlining criteria for fiction and nonfiction and areas of emphasis" (1991, 95). The Pomona Public Library's description of its young adult collection falls within the "general" category of description that Cassell and Futas identify and distinguishes material collected for young adults from that collected for children:

> A limited young adult collection has been established to satisfy the library needs of patrons from the approximate age of 13 to 18 years. It is a transitional collection for the reader moving from the children's collection to the adult collection. The type of materials selected differs significantly from the elementary school level because of the social, emotional, and intellectual maturity required to read them. As this is primarily a browsing collection, fiction and paperbacks are emphasized. Non-fiction paperbacks are purchased in contemporary areas of interest to teens and are shelved in the Young Adult area. Non-fiction hardback titles, intended for research use are integrated in the Adult non-fiction collection. (2004, 15–16)

This general description of the library's young adult collection characterizes the collection's primary users as "approximately" thirteen to eighteen years old and establishes, as Hoffman and Wood suggest, the limitations of this collection by specifying that the library's young adult collection is "primarily a browsing collection" that emphasizes fiction, paperbacks, and high interest nonfiction titles. The Jervis (Rome, NY) Public Library's description of its young adult nonfiction collection uses comparative language to distinguish the nonfiction materials purchased for young adults from those purchased for adult library users, noting that "'YA' non-fiction is not always distinguishable from adult non-fiction" and pointing out that both adult and YA nonfiction are "shelved together in the adult section by Dewey subject number":

> The library chooses "YA" non-fiction which deals with adult-level material, but which is not too difficult for readers grades 8 and up. As with adult non-fiction, clarity, accuracy, and authoritativeness are important selection criteria. Because many "YA" non-fiction books are used for school reports, information in these books should be present-

ed in clearly accessible formats suited to easy extraction. (2000, "Young Adult (YA) Non-fiction and Fiction")

In this description of its young adult nonfiction collection, the library suggests an audience for the material (grades eight and up) and points out that it relies on the same criteria regarding "clarity, accuracy, and authoritativeness" in its selection of young adult nonfiction as it does in its selection of adult nonfiction. Furthermore, the description notes the need for material that presents information in "formats suited to easy extraction" for the benefit of those library users completing school assignments or reports.

The Mentor (OH) Public Library's description of its young adult collections is perhaps one of the most complete ones that is available online. It delineates the age of the service population, describes the formats of material collected for this age group, and refers to both general and specific selection criteria for material in this collection. The policy delineates its collection first in terms of the age of the library's service population and then in terms of format, assuming a "classed" format. Its young adult resources, which include fiction, nonfiction, and graphic novels, are described as follows:

3.1.1 The Young Adult Non-Fiction Collection will provide current general interest and informational materials. This collection will include many points of view to present a balanced selection of material. This collection will meet needs of young adults (12 to 18 years).

3.1.1.1 Specific Criteria for Young Adult Non-fiction:

3.1.1.1.1 Meets criteria for adult non-fiction.

3.1.1.1.2 Can be used for research and school reading.

3.1.1.1.3 Caters to the interests of young adults.

3.1.1.1.4 Is thematically and linguistically age appropriate.

3.1.1.1.5 Presented at a level and in a format that appeals to young adults.

3.1.2 The Young Adult Fiction Collection will provide popular browsing materials that include standard authors and titles as well as special interest titles.

3.1.2.1 Specific Criteria for Young Adult Fiction:

3.1.2.1.1 Meets criteria for adult fiction.

3.1.2.1.2 Appeals to young adult tastes in genre, format, and writing style.

3.1.3 The Graphic Novel Collection will provide fiction and non-fiction titles of interest.

3.1.3.1 Specific Criteria for Graphic Novels:

3.1.3.1.1 Contains quality art work.

3.1.3.1.2 Is durable. (Mentor Public Library 2012)

This section of the policy describes the young adult collection in terms of format, specifying "graphic novels" as a format alongside "young adult fiction" and "young adult non-fiction"; indicates the age range of the audience for whom the collection is developed (twelve to eighteen); and outlines selection criteria specific to material chosen for the young adult nonfiction, fiction, and graphic novel collection. Although this library's collection development policy as a whole includes only one mention of graphic novels (in its description of the graphic novel collection selected for young adults), it appears that graphic novels are a format specific to the library's young adult collection. The policy's later descriptions of multimedia material specify "adults, young adults, and children" as the inclusive audience for whom these collections are developed.

Description of the Library's Goals for Collection Development

Many general collection development policies have a list of goals for collection development that may include general goals for establishing, continuing, and developing library services and collections. These goal statements may be as broad and encompassing as the library's mission statement and may be found in the introductory section of the policy, or they may be more specific and focused on particular collections or formats. The Monroe County (IN) Public Library's statement of goals, found in the introductory section of its collection development policy, exemplifies the broad type of such statements:

1. Provide responsive service that meets the community's needs and interests.
2. Provide high quality and relevant collections with active collection management.
3. Utilize centralized collection management to increase efficiency in the library's acquisition and de-selection cycles.
4. Provide services and collections to address emerging demographic trends. (2012)

These statements are applicable to the library's collections as a whole and operationalize the library's mission statement to "enrich individual lives and strengthen our community by offering equitable access to information and opportunities for literacy, learning and enjoyment" (Monroe Public Library 2012). In contrast, the Mentor (OH) Public Library's goals for collection development are linked to its strategic plan, and though broad, identify particular service initiatives to be supported by the library's collections. For example, two of its goals speak to the library's intention to "create young readers" and collect material that "stimulates the imagination":

> We will Create Young Readers. Our outstanding staff will provide quality materials and engaging programs to support early literacy, and community partnerships to encourage a love of reading. . . .

We will provide a collection to Stimulate the Imagination: Reading, Viewing, and Listening Materials for Pleasure. Our collection will be balanced, in a variety of formats, and will be supported by relevant programming opportunities and a responsive staff. Our programs will promote the joy of reading and meet the leisure interests of our patrons. (2012)

These goals support the development of two particular types of collections: early literacy collections for young readers and pleasure or leisure collections of material—including multimedia material—for all patrons.

Descriptions of Procedures for Evaluating and Weeding Library Collections

As public libraries are experiencing increasing pressure to account for their services and demonstrate their relevance to the community, more institutions are developing protocols to evaluate library collections and services. Evaluation of library collections does not, as Johnson writes, provide an objective measure of "how 'good' a collection is"; instead, evaluation demonstrates how and if the library's collection "matches the goals of the library and its parent institution" (2009, 228). The results of such evaluations can suggest or support a need for continued development of library collections in particular subjects or formats and also can be cited to support decisions about weeding or deselection. Although there are numerous techniques for the evaluation of library collections, general policy statements describe evaluation in broad terms and typically link the process to the library's selection and deselection practices. For example, the Jervis (Rome, NY) Public Library's statement describing its evaluation endeavors reads: "Continual evaluation of the collection is performed by librarians, usually when some limitation in coverage, timeliness, or space is indicated" (2000). The Pasadena Public Library's description of its evaluation process is found under the heading "Collection Maintenance" in its library policy and expresses similar sentiments:

> Maintenance of the library's collection through constant re-evaluation by the library staff ensures its usefulness and relevancy to the community. This evaluation depends heavily on the staff's professional expertise in assessing the needs of the community and the content of the collection. Those materials determined to no longer be of value are withdrawn from the collection (2012).

Though brief, both libraries' evaluation statements assign responsibility for evaluation to professional staff and suggest that evaluation is undertaken to determine the relevance of the library's collection to its changing service community. In comparison, the Campbell County (WY) Public Library System's description of its evaluation practices is exemplary in terms of detail. The policy connects evaluation to the library's mission and describes some of the measures the library uses to evaluate its collection:

> The library collection needs continuous evaluation in order to keep on target with the Library's mission to provide diverse cultural opportunities for reading, learning, and entertainment to all citizens of our community. Collection evaluation and maintenance is a high priority job duty for library managers. Statistical tools such as circulation reports, collection turnover rates, and State Library reports should be used to determine how the collection is being used and how it should change to answer patron needs. The materials themselves should be assessed for their physical condition and their use. (2012)

Like the Jervis and Pasadena statements, the Campbell County statement connects evaluation to the library's mission and names the parties responsible for it. But Campbell County's evaluation statement is notable for articulating its methods of evaluation; the paragraph cited notes the tools the library may use to assess the collection, while the rest of the policy outlines qualitative tools for evaluation, including standard bibliographies to be used for "list checking" and the solicitation of patron feedback.

Because evaluation is often described in terms of its relationship to weeding practices, many library policies refer to evaluation practices in their descriptions of institutional weeding procedures. In general collection development policies, these statements "lay down the general guidelines for weeding based on the needs and collection purpose of the particular library" (Gregory 2011, 50), effectively linking the practice of weeding to the library's collection evaluation process by connecting this practice to the library's institutional goals. In fact, although Gregory has argued that "evaluation or analysis of a collection does not necessarily imply weeding at all," she does recognize that collection evaluation is typically undertaken "with an eye toward determining when and how to weed out or deselect items and materials" (2011, 113). In library policy statements that do not feature explicit discussion of collection evaluation procedures, weeding is described as a practice associated with evaluation.

The Gleason (Carlisle, MA) Public Library's description of its weeding procedures is typical:

> The term weeding is used to describe the activity of seeking out items that are no longer useful or appropriate for the collection. These items are then discarded and may or may not be replaced.
>
> Weeding the library collection is as much a routine as the acquisition of new books. The purpose of discarding materials from the collection is to maintain an accurate and up to date collection for library patrons. Materials which are inaccurate, outdated, unused, or in poor condition detract from the usefulness and aesthetic appeal of the collection. These materials take up shelf space that could be occupied by needed and

requested materials. Weeding the collection is an ongoing process and is the responsibility of the librarians. (2011)

This library's policy statement defines weeding as a process that resembles evaluation (i.e., "seeking out items that are no longer useful or appropriate for the collection") and provides a broad outline of the criteria the library employs to determine which items to weed from the collection. The policy also assigns responsibility for weeding to the library's professional staff, further indicating the professionalism required to complete the activity.

A library's policies about weeding may be as broad or specific as its policies regarding selection. At a minimum, a library's weeding policy should, as Evans and Saponaro assert, describe the "criteria, scope, frequency, and purpose of a deselection program" (2005, 62). Because, as Hoffmann and Wood note, weeding criteria often "mirror" the criteria used to select library material, librarians creating weeding guidelines should endeavor to make these statements, like those used to guide selection, "general enough to provide librarians some degree of latitude in the decision-making process" (2005, 186). Library collection development policies may describe weeding in general terms that suggest the application of general guidelines to the entire collection or, as in policies that outline general and format- or subject-specific criteria for selection, may include specific guidelines for the evaluation and weeding of particular collections within the descriptions of those collections. In library policies that feature general evaluation and weeding guidelines, it is important that the language of these guidelines reflect the entire collection, so that patrons understand the library will be applying the same evaluative criteria to all library material. Just as many library policies refer to bibliographies or aids to selection in their selection policies, library policies related to weeding may refer to guides like *CREW: A Weeding Manual for Modern Libraries* (Larson and Texas State Library and Archives Commission 2008), which outlines general and subject-specific criteria for weeding library materials.

COLLECTION DEVELOPMENT POLICIES: MAKING DECISIONS

One of the best strategies for getting to know the library is reading its collection development policies. New and veteran YA librarians should make examining the institution's collection development policies a priority and, following a thorough reading of these, should determine if and how these existing policies are applied on a regular basis. The gaps and differences between written policy and day-to-day practice demonstrate where policy revision is needed and offer opportunities for the documentation and implementation of new policies and procedures. Undertaking a full-scale revision of the library's collection development policy is not for the faint of heart; however, YA librarians can and should contribute to policy development and revision and act as advocates for the young adults they serve through collection development.

There are a number of ways for the young adult librarian to "ease into" the library's policy conversation. If the library revisits and revises its policies on a regular basis, the YA librarian may wish to begin participating at the next scheduled opportunity. Of course the librarian should attend the meeting prepared to advocate for the explicit inclusion of young adults and young adult collections within written policy if this content is missing from the library's formal documentation. By presenting the library administration and board of trustees with statistics that document the size of the library's young adult service population and the number of young adult library cardholders (if this information is available) and referencing statistics, program attendance numbers, and circulation records that indicate use of the library's young adult collection, the YA librarian should be able to craft a compelling argument for, at a minimum, the inclusion of YA-specific language in revised library policy. When confronting an outdated collection development policy that includes YA-specific language but is incomplete in its descriptions of collections and services to young adults or that contains erroneous information, the young adult librarian should document the differences between policy and practice and present these to the library administration as evidence supporting a need for policy revision.

Proposing the development of a supplemental policy document is a more challenging task. Because young adult collections and services are still considered "new" in public libraries, there are few examples of existing supplemental policies to consult or use as models. Two notable supplemental policies have been published on library websites: the San Francisco Public Library and the Haverhill (MA) Public Library have developed supplemental policies describing their libraries' young adult services population and procedures for developing YA collections. These two libraries are located in distinctly different communities, yet each institution features a collection of young adult material that is diverse in both subject and format. The San Francisco Public Library collects high interest and popular fiction and nonfiction for young adults, material in Chinese and Spanish (two of the most dominant non-English languages spoken in the service community), magazines, graphic novels, CDs, and DVDs. The Haverhill Public Library's collection for young adults includes fiction and nonfiction, graphic novels and comic books, magazines, audiobooks, and video games. Because both of these libraries collect material for young adults in such a diversity of forms, supplemental policy to describe general criteria for selection of material for the young adult audience, as well as more specific criteria for the selection of material in particular formats for the young adult audience, appear to be a necessity to ensure consistency in the collection development process.

Libraries that feature collections for young adults as diverse as those developed by the San Francisco and Haverhill libraries may be best positioned to develop supplemental collection development policies, whereas libraries with smaller and less format-diverse collections may find that general policy inclusion is sufficient documentation.

FOUR

Needs Assessment

Public library collections for young adults are ideally developed with the needs and interests of young adult patrons—the primary users of these collections—in mind. As Peggy Johnson notes, "All selection decisions begin with consideration of the user community and the long-term mission, goals, and priorities of the library and its parent body" (2009, 108). Although the library's policy statements may provide new librarians with details about the library's mission, goals, and priorities in relation to the library's collections and services, and even general information about the library's service population, professionals must look elsewhere to learn about the particular information wants and needs of the patrons in the library's service community. Librarians' broad understanding and conceptualization of the young adult population, as discussed in chapter 1, is informed by society, culture, and the institutions created to educate and enrich young people. Recent research in the field of library and information science provides more data about the information needs and wants of narrower classes of young people—preteens and teens, urban and rural adolescents—and how they use the library, and this work particularizes our broad understanding of this population. Although this research certainly informs professional literature and drives professional decision making, it doesn't completely answer the questions that librarians developing collections for young adults should continually try to answer: What are the information needs and interests of the local population of young adults, and how can I address these with my local library's YA collection? To find these answers, YA librarians should engage in regular needs assessment of their patrons.

"Needs assessment" describes the formal processes libraries and librarians undertake to learn more about the community the library serves. Libraries often engage in community needs assessment as a part of their strategic planning processes and may conduct formal needs assessments every four to six years. Librarians considering new initiatives or planning more discrete services to targeted and well-defined populations may engage in needs assessment activities outside of this time frame. In fact, many libraries regularly solicit informal needs assessment data in the form of feedback from patrons via surveys or suggestion boxes to determine how and if the library's collections and services are meeting existing patron needs. Data from a library's formal needs assessment activities, as well as informal data collected by libraries or librarians on a regular basis that document and illuminate patterns of information needs among library patrons, are key sources of information for collection development. As G. Edward Evans and Margaret Zarnosky Saponaro note, "the more the collection development officers know about user's work roles, general interest, education, information or communication behavior, values, and related characteristics, the more likely it is that the collection will provide the desired information at the time desired" (2005, 20). To that end, the more young adult librarians know about the teen patrons they serve—as well as those they don't serve—the more equipped they will be to develop collections that meet these patrons' needs.

YOUNG ADULTS' INFORMATION NEEDS: WHAT RESEARCH TELLS US

Young adults turn to the library to address a number of information needs: to find information for homework assignments and school projects; to find material to read, watch, or listen to for fun; and to locate information applicable to personal concerns and questions. Whether they are searching in response to an assignment or to address a personal concern, as Ross Todd has observed, young people seek information with a variety of intentions and may look for information to allow them to "get a complete picture [of a situation or concern], get a verified picture, get a changed picture, get a clearer picture, and get a position in a picture" (2003, 39–40). In short, young people are motivated by a diversity of circumstances to visit the library and seek information, and as they search, they may be interested in data that answer their questions as well as information that challenges their assumptions. Because young adults comprise a population defined by what Eric Meyers, Karen Fisher, and Elizabeth Marcoux call common "physical, affective, and social contexts that shape [their] information worlds" (2009, 303), their information needs tend to be fairly consistent and persistent. Research investigating the information needs of young people has sought to identify these topics of consistent and persistent interest and demand and, as it illuminates universal information needs and interests of young people, such research is important for collection development activity.

Researchers argue that young people's information seeking is motivated by their desire to know more about the world and their place in it and is informed by their developmental status as adolescents. According to Denise Agosto and Sandra Hughes-Hassell, teen information seeking ultimately "facilitate[s] the multifaceted teen-to-adulthood maturation process" and emerges from a desire to find information that relates to and supports the development of the social self, emotional self, reflective self, physical self, creative self, cognitive self, and sexual self (2006a, 1399). They assert that information seeking is "self-exploration and world exploration that helps teens understand the world and their positions in it, as well as helping them to understand themselves now and to contemplate who they aspire to be in the future" (2006a, 1399). In other words, young people seek information that, as suggested by Pat Shenton and Andrew Dixon, addresses their "life aims," alleviates their anxieties, helps them make decisions, and bolsters their understanding of a problem or a subject (2003, 10). During this process of exploration, young people search out information that aids in their development of skills; fulfills the requirements of school assignments; addresses immediate and everyday life concerns about purchasing decisions, job and school opportunities and requirements, and transportation; and provides advice and support as well as the opportunity for what Shenton and Dixon call "empathetic understanding" (2003, 10). Whether young people look for information to support their own development or consider resources that may support the attainment of specific goals, it is important to remember, as Todd has observed, that these young adult information seekers are not "passive, robot-like processors of information" (2003, 40), but are driven by various needs to seek information that they may apply or reject in various ways.

In studies of young people's information needs and wants, popular culture information and resources appear at the top of lists of most common information requests. As Shenton (2007), Agosto and Hughes-Hassell (2006b), and Agosto, Kimberly Paone, and Gretchen Ipock (2007) have observed, popular culture and the media are among the central interests of teen information seekers. Young people are interested in finding out and reading about popular music and musicians, sports teams and stars, television shows and movies, and celebrities. They also request information about their hobbies and interests that intersect with popular culture, including electronic games and gaming and anime and manga. Although young people express interest in learning more about these topics of popular cultural, they are also interested in experiencing this popular culture firsthand, and they request movies, television shows, and popular music CDs from the library. To respond to these interests, library collections for young people should include up-to-date biographies and autobiographies of popular figures, behind-the-scenes accounts of popular movie and television productions, books of gaming codes and "cheats," and how-to-do-it books instructing young artists in the techniques used in manga and comic books. Library collections should also contain the "primary sources" of popular culture, such as movies and television shows compiled on DVD, popular music recordings, and copies of popular novels and series.

School-related information is a second commonly expressed information need among young people. Research describing young people's motivations for visiting the library places schoolwork and homework near the top, and libraries respond to requests for this information by developing collections that reflect the demands of the local curriculum. These demands can be understood within the context of the growing standards movement in education, which Hughes-Hassell and Jacqueline Mancall (2005) have observed has clarified and particularized curricular expectations. Although this public clarification is useful, Hughes-Hassell and Mancall remind us that the "translation of these standards to actual teaching and learning still rests with individual teachers and thus varies from school to school and often from classroom to classroom" (2005, 37). This caveat is important to keep in mind and supports the necessity of a local needs assessment for collection development, but professional journals have suggested general guidelines for librarians developing collections to meet new and developing standards. The Common Core State Standards, which so far have been adopted by forty-five states and three territories (Common Core State Standards 2012), are the most common guidelines to curriculum-related collection development. Rebecca Hill's introduction to Common Core standards and their impact on collections notes the increased importance of informational texts to the learning standards; high school curricula guided by a Common Core that emphasizes literacy across the curriculum will require students to engage heavily with informational texts (2012). Specifically, the Common Core "calls for primary sources and short pieces on social studies and scientific topics," a requirement that challenges collections of books of facts and traditional reference sources (Harris 2012, 16). As schools begin to enact this new standards-based curriculum, libraries serving the school-imposed needs of teens will have to attend not only to topical coverage, but also format and develop collections that are rich in narrative nonfiction and primary source material.

Although young adult library users may feel comfortable requesting information related to popular culture or the curriculum, researchers have noted a number of information needs common among young people that teen patrons may be reluctant to express. Questions about personal health, including drug and alcohol use and abuse, sexual behavior, and sexually transmitted diseases, as well as on coming out and GLBTQ identity, represent "hidden" information needs of young people. Because these information needs—particularly those related to sexual activity and the use and effects of controlled substances—deal with topics that can be controversial among adults and young people, they may not be expressed by teens directly; because young people may not feel comfortable requesting information related to these topics, many librarians may ignore these needs. As Elizabeth Rauch has observed, "Teens, reluctant to ask for [GLBTQ] information, make it easy for some librarians to believe that there is no demand or need for these materials, but research shows otherwise" (2010, 216). In fact, Linda B. Alexander and Sarah D. Miselis report, "there is an abundance of evidence in the literature indicating that the GLBTQ population, though not always visible, makes up a significant portion of library users in all areas of the United States" (2007, p. 46). To address the needs of this "invisible" population of information seekers and ensure that young people have access to information about topics they hesitate to broach with librarians, YA collections should include informational material and self-help and support guides on sexual health, pregnancy, and alcohol and drug use, as well as fiction featuring "positive and realistic portrayals of GLBTQ characters" and nonfiction detailing GLBTQ history and culture (Alexander and Miselis 2007, 45).

Research describing young people's common interests and information needs provides us with a basis from which to begin a local needs assessment. Although this research points out often overlooked areas of general interest and concern among young people and encourages us to attend to our library's collections in these areas, we rely on needs assessment to help us clarify and particularize local needs and interests. Using the results of this research as a starting point, we can begin to locate avenues for further exploration. For example, research indicates that sports information is consistently popular among and requested by young adults, so we might identify the sports, teams, and stars that are of particular interest to our local population and develop our collections to include material of local as well as general interest. In addition, as we recognize young people's interest in popular cultural materials, we might find out what music, celebrities, television shows, and movies are particularly popular among our local population and develop collections that include material on these interests. Finally, by pointing out information needs that are often unexpressed by young people but nonetheless exist, research encourages us to modify our collections to include materials discussing health and sexuality so that these resources can easily be found by young information seekers reluctant to ask for our guidance.

YOUNG ADULTS' ACCESS TO LIBRARY COLLECTIONS AND INFORMATION: WHAT RESEARCH TELLS US

As we develop our collections to meet the information needs and interests of young adults, we must also consider the important issue of access and recognize the unique challenges young people face in the search for information. Restricted mobility, variations in literacy, and lack of access to technological tools are real obstacles to young people's information seeking and library use. These challenges impact not only how and if young people use the library, but what materials they use. Research describing barriers to young people's information access has much to tell us about collection development. By considering the factors that affect young people's access to information in general, as well as to specific types of information, we can develop collections that are literally accessible to the young people we serve.

A user's distance from the library, combined with his or her inability to traverse that distance easily, forms a geographic barrier young adults in particular may find difficult to conquer. As Meyers, Fisher, and Marcoux have observed, young people "often rely on adults for transportation, which limits their physical information venues—how often and when they may use them" (2009, 319). Thus, the availability of adult drivers and for older teens, state restrictions on teen driving, including the age at which young people may be granted drivers' licenses and be permitted to drive alone, influence how and if young people visit the library independently, particularly in suburban and rural communities. In both types of communities, the proximity of the library to residential neighborhoods, local schools, and public transportation affects independent teen library use. In rural or suburban communities with no public transportation, the library may be considered inaccessible by young adults except during those brief windows of time during which their schedules coincide with those of the adults who drive them to use this resource. These visits may be limited to greatest need only—when students are required by school to read a particular book or need research support—and may occur primarily in the evenings or on weekends. Although libraries that serve these intermittent teen visitors may feature collections that address their recreational reading needs, if teen visits are primarily motivated by required reading and research project demands, the YA collection should reflect this fact and feature a variety of information resources that support these scholastic pursuits. In addition, libraries serving teen patrons unable to visit on a regular basis may find that remotely accessible collections—e-books and databases, for example—are a strong investment.

Young people's literacy and language challenges may also impede their use of library resources. Struggling adolescent readers who require information and texts to complete school projects and assignments find a barrier to access when faced with a collection created for proficient or advanced readers that they are unable to decode or comprehend with ease. Professional and research literature touts the utility of "high-low"—high interest and easy to read—material to meet the needs of library users challenged by reading. These "high-low" books address the interest-related, school-inspired, and recreational reading needs and wants of those young people who struggle with decoding and comprehension by conveying information and stories in language that is easier for them to read. High-low titles published for young adults are generally more attractive to teen readers because, although they are written in easy-to-read language, they are packaged as adolescent texts and speak to the interests and needs of young people. Audiobooks—available as mp3 files, in CD format, or as self-contained "playaway" devices—can be useful to these young people as well. When required to read a particular title, students may be better able to use an audio version of the text, which presents the text with fluency and expression. Although arguments dissecting the quality of high-low material and challenging the legitimacy of audiobooks as texts that are "read" by listeners abound, these materials are necessary components of a library serving struggling readers, making information accessible by removing some common barriers to comprehension.

The digital divide remains an access issue among adults and young adults alike and is one librarians should consider when developing collections of electronic material and media. Research undertaken by the Pew Research Center has indicated that although the adoption and use of technology among young adults is generally high, discrepancies in access to technological tools and electronic information still exist. According to a report by Amanda Lenhart, Latino teens use the Internet less than Caucasian teens (88 percent versus 97 percent), and households headed by parents with a high school diploma or less are "substantially less likely to have youth who say they 'own' a computer (65 percent versus 80 percent)" (2012b, slide 1). Lenhart reports that although "mobile [technology] is a more universal access point" among young people, cell phone ownership is correlated with age (more older teens ages fourteen to seventeen than younger teens ages twelve to thirteen report owning cell phones) as well as ethnicity (more Caucasian teens [81 percent] report owning cell phones than black teens [72 percent] and Latino teens [63 percent]) (2012b, slide 14, slide 4). Lenhart's report indicates the necessity of considering the local population and its ability to access technology when developing electronic collections for young people, particularly when considering the forms these technology collections might take. Communities in which cell phone, smartphone, and computer ownership is less prevalent may be better served by electronic collections that include content and container (e.g., "playaway" audio material, handheld gaming consoles, preloaded e-books). Furthermore, young people's access to technology—and their use of technology at the library—will impact the selection of and subscription to library databases created for teens. Communities in which computer ownership is lower may be better served by print resources that students may bring home than by databases that the library assumes young people will access from home.

Research describing trends in young people's information needs and interests and common barriers faced by young people in search of information resources provides us with a base from which to begin a local needs assessment and aids us in the interpretation of our needs assessment data. As researchers have noted, young people have a number of broad information needs and interests in common: they are interested in popular cultural information and artifacts, information and data to support school assignments, and information and texts that address their personal needs and recreational interests. The particulars of these needs—for example, which sports stars and teams, musicians, and celebrities are of especial interest—tend to be more localized. For example, public library collections in the Boston area carry a number of resources related to the Red Sox; these libraries collect biographies of contemporary and historically notable players, histories of winning years, and detailed conspiracy theories describing the "Curse of the Bambino" and its supposed "reversal," which reflect young Boston and Massachusetts residents' baseball interests and fandom. Libraries in other parts of the country are unlikely to feature such Red Sox–centric sports collections, because Red Sox fandom, though widespread, is probably not as rabid outside of the Boston area; as such, demands for material related to the Red Sox are probably less frequent. Whereas research describing the tendency of young people to seek information related to sports supports our development of library collections in this area in general, needs assessment informs us of the direction (Red Sox or otherwise) this development should take. Similarly, research describing barriers to information common among young people encourages us to investigate these barriers locally via needs assessment and to develop collections that are accessible to library users and meet their needs.

LEARNING ABOUT THE LIBRARY'S SERVICE POPULATION: CONDUCTING A NEEDS ASSESSMENT

Many guides to collection development link needs assessment to marketing activities, noting the overlapping intentions of the two processes. Marketing, Johnson writes, "is the process of determining the user communities' wants and needs, developing the products and services in response, and encouraging users (i.e., consumers) and potential users to make use of the products and services" (2009, 192). In contrast, a needs assessment involves determining the 'user communities' wants and needs with an eye toward developing and assessing collections, services, and projects in response. As Kay Ann Cassell and Elizabeth Futas assert, a needs assessment provides libraries with a "benchmark position" from which to consider collection development (1991, 63). Generally, Evans and Saponaro note, needs assessment describes the process of learning more about small segments of the population, whereas "market analysis" involves studying people or communities to "assess interest in, or reactions to, a service or product" (2005, 21). Here, *needs assessment* comprises those activities undertaken to learn about a segment of the library's service community—young adults—and we consider how the application of the information uncovered during the needs assessment may affect the development and assessment of young adult collections.

Part 1: Collecting Demographic and Community Data

A number of factors influence young people's tendency to use the public library and its collection, many of which are related to their socioeconomic, racial and ethnic, and social and cultural identities. The existence and use of community, cultural, and recreational services other than the library affect and inform young people's library use, just as the status of the local school library influences their tendency to make use of the public library. Data describing the secondary and postsecondary educational attainment and goals of the young adult population can also inform the development of library collections to suit this group's needs. The geographical location of the library in the community, coupled with its accessibility to young people, is an additional influence on how and if the library is used by its teen constituents. Recognizing the influence of these local factors on library use, the first step in conducting a needs assessment involves gathering data about the community. This section describes the types of demographic and community data that are relatively easily accessible to librarians, as well as their potential to inform collection development. The information resources described in the following discussions are listed at the end of the chapter.

Demographic Information

Handbooks describing needs assessment and collection development procedures for librarians note the essential relationship of demographic information to collection development. Evans and Saponaro (2005) list the following demographic variables as particularly useful areas of potential investigation for those conducting needs assessments: level of education, level of income, cultural background, group membership, and economic considerations. Although some of these variables may seem irrelevant to young adults specifically, we should remember that though our needs assessment may focus on the adolescent members of the population, we must also recognize the income and educational level of the heads of households in which they reside, as well as the economic circumstances of their families, because these factors affect young people's use of public libraries. When collecting these data, librarians should remember to limit their data collection to the library's service community, which may be a county, a town or city, a neighborhood, or a region.

Basic demographic information that describes the population in terms of age-defined segments, as well as household income and educational attainment, may be culled from U.S. Census Bureau data, as well as from data and reports issued through the Census Bureau's American Fact Finder service, which includes data collected by the American Community Survey and the American Housing Survey. KIDS COUNT, a data collection project of the Annie E. Casey Foundation, is an additional source of information, as its data center (accessible online) provides information on the educational attainment and demographics of children and families at the national, state, and local levels. The following demographic information may be collected from these sources:

1. number of young adults (ages twelve to seventeen) in the library's service area
2. number of young adults registered for school
3. racial and ethnic identities of individuals in the library's service area
4. number of households in which a language other than English is spoken at home
5. languages other than English spoken among members of the community
6. educational attainment of the adult population
7. income level of families and individuals

This information can reveal a number of useful facts about the population that have a bearing on collection development. The number of young adults in the current population is the total number of the collection's potential primary patrons and can suggest an appropriate size for the collection. Although no official standards exist that suggest the optimal number of books per public library user, holdings data from comparatively sized libraries can suggest goals for collection size. Furthermore, data describing not only the number of young adults but also the number of children in the community can impact the size of the library's collection. Examining historical population data may reveal a tendency for the local population to remain stable, suggesting the value of the data to predict the potential for growth among the young adult population. This data also provide a general picture of the racial and ethnic makeup of the library's service community, revealing the size of minority populations, the comparative presence of dominant minority groups, and the languages other than English that are spoken in the community, descriptive information that should affect the cultural and linguistic diversity of the library's collection. Annual income figures not only provide a mean and median income for the community, but also reveal diversity and disparities in income distribution.

We cannot say that these data are predictive, but research has noted the tendency for certain types of demographic factors to correlate with library use and information behavior:

1. Race and ethnicity correlate with high school students' library use; whereas Caucasian students tend to use their school libraries with greater frequency, ethnic minority students tend to use the public library in greater numbers (Sin 2012).

2. Race and ethnicity correlate with household library use; larger percentages of black and Asian households report using the library to facilitate the school-inspired information seeking of students than white or Hispanic households (Glander and Dam 2007).

3. Household income tends to correlate with library use; members of households in the top 20 percent income brackets use libraries more often than members of households in the lowest 20 percent (Glander and Dam 2007).

4. Educational attainment of household members tends to correlate with library use; members of households where the highest attained education level is a high school diploma or lower tend to use the library less often than members of households where the highest education level is an advanced degree (Glander and Dam 2007).

5. Teen cell phone ownership correlates with age and family income; younger teens are less likely to own a cell phone than are older teens, and a little over half (59 percent) of teens from households earning less than $30,000 per year own a cell phone, whereas between 73 and 87 percent of teens from higher earning households own cell phones (Lenhart et. al. 2010).

6. Teen computer ownership correlates with age and family income; although 69 percent of all teens report computer ownership, younger teens are less likely to own a computer than older teens, and teens from households reporting annual incomes of $75,000 and above (74 percent) are slightly more likely to own computers than teens from households reporting lower annual incomes (Lenhart et. al. 2010).

7. Although demographic factors do correlate with teen computer ownership, computer ownership and at-home Internet connectivity are not considered factors that negatively impact young people's tendency to visit the public library (D'Elia, Abbas, and Bishop 2007).

8. Over three-quarters of teens (79 percent) own an iPod or mp3 player, a statistic that is unrelated to most demographic characteristics, with the exception of household income and parental educational attainment; teens from families with higher household incomes or from families headed by adults with higher educational

attainment tend to own personal music players in greater numbers (Lenhart et. al. 2010).
9. Although teens enjoy access to the Internet from a variety of locales (including school, home, friends' homes, and the public library), higher percentages of minority youths and young people from homes in which English is not the primary language are more likely to visit the library to access the Internet (D'Elia, Abbas, and Bishop 2007).

These correlations have the potential to affect our development of library collections, especially where the selection of multimedia material is concerned. Recognizing that the majority of all young adults own either an iPod or and mp3 player, libraries may find few barriers affecting teen access to collections of audio files. As teen cell phone and computer ownership tends to correlate with age and family income, libraries should consider the prevalence of youthful and lower income populations when developing collections of digital material to be accessed off-site. Libraries serving populations with limited access to cell phones or computers might consider technology tools—laptop or tablet computers that can be loaned to library users—to be more important additions to the library's collection than overly specialized databases that require patron ownership or technological tools for access. As libraries develop collections of e-books, it is important to consider the multiple means of reading and accessing these texts. Contemporary statistics report a low but rapidly growing incidence of e-reader ownership among young adults, but electronic book readers may access and read these texts via cell phones or desktop, laptop, or tablet computers. Thus, libraries considering the development of e-book collections should assess local teen access to and use of not just e-readers, but also other forms of technology that allow for electronic reading.

Geographic Information

Reports of teen library use note that distance from the library is a significant barrier for teens and underscores the importance of geography for library use. The principle of least effort suggests that people are reluctant to expend effort to access information, which has led to researchers' conclusions that distance from the library is a significant factor in patron library use. The location of the library in a rural, suburban, or urban area, as well as its position within walking or driving distance from residential neighborhoods, youth centers, or schools, affects its use by young adults. Library locations convenient to schools and youth centers may serve as after school "hangouts" for young people who walk to the library after school, whereas libraries at a distance from schools and youth centers may only be accessible to young drivers or those with parents or caregivers willing to drive them there. Thus, the difficulty young people face in getting to the library may be a factor in their library use and influence when and how they use it.

Although distance affects library patrons' tendency to use the library, not all library users make use of the libraries closest to their homes. Sung Jae Park's research examining the geographic accessibility of public libraries found that some library users "use a more distant library instead of the nearest library, suggesting that their library use might be affected by factors other than simple distance" (2012, "Travel Distance," para. 2). A library system featuring a large main or "headquarters" branch as well as several smaller branches with comparatively smaller collections may find that the "headquarters" branch is used by patrons who live closer to smaller branches for specific reasons related to collection size or program availability. Thus the status of a library as a "main" or "branch" library may affect patrons' use of it for recreational or research purposes.

The following factors may be useful when considering the geographic profile of the library:

1. location of the library in relation to branch and main libraries within the same library system
2. location of the library in relation to libraries in other library systems
3. population of young adults residing in the library's immediate neighborhood as well as its larger service community
4. racial and ethnic identities of households residing in the library's immediate neighborhood as well as its larger service community
5. languages spoken within households residing in the library's immediate neighborhood as well as its larger service community
6. location of public and private schools serving young adults in relation to the library
7. existence and schedules of public transportation options that discharge riders near the library

The Public Library Geographic Database, created and maintained by Florida State University's School of Library and Information Studies, is an invaluable resource for much of the data described above. This database allows users to manipulate an online map and view census and some library use data superimposed on the map. The geographically localized demographic information provided by this service allows for the particularization of the general demographic data and may further aid in the characterization of the truly local library user. For example, database users can identify the number of young adults residing in the neighborhood in which the library is situated and can also view a map describing the linguistic and socioeconomic diversity of this neighborhood.

Student Demographic, Curricular, and Educational Attainment
Information

Information about the local curriculum as well as the educational attainment and efforts of the local young adult population has tremendous bearing on the public library's YA collection. The public library exists to complement the school library, but it remains a source of material and information for traditional students as well as one of the primary sources of educational material for homeschoolers and unschoolers. Therefore the public library's YA collection often includes material to address traditional and homeschooling students' information needs. Descriptive data provided by the state department of education, the local school district and local schools, and any local or regional homeschooling organizations help paint a clearer picture of the library's young adult patrons with an eye toward developing collections that are accessible to them, whereas information describing local curricular initiatives can inform our topical development of collections that include material selected to support students' school-inspired information seeking.

State departments of education are rich sources of demographic and statistical information describing students involved in public and special educational initiatives that can be used to particularize and supplement general community demographic information. These data are often provided in the form of school and district assessments as well as student assessments describing the results of student mastery and achievement tests. The KIDS COUNT data service can provide librarians with descriptive data about a number of indicators of child well-being, including teen unemployment, high school dropout rates, and the percentage of young adults in the community who attend college. KIDS COUNT draws its data from a number of sources, including state departments of education and national census data.

The following information may be drawn from these sources and aid in the development of a more detailed profile of the local young adult population:

1. number of students registered in public schools, including the number of students registered in individual grades and individual schools
2. racial and ethnic characteristics of students registered in public schools
3. number of students enrolled in English Language Learning programs
4. number of students enrolled in special education programs
5. student achievement in assessment tests
6. graduation and dropout rates
7. postsecondary plans of high school graduates

When combined with more general demographic data, this information may influence our library collections' topics and nature. For example, information about the number of students enrolled in English Language Learning programs may give us a clearer picture of the number of students in the library's service area who struggle with English. This information, combined with demographic data describing the predominant languages other than English spoken by the community, can inform the development of non-English-language collections, as well as of easier-to-read collections of material. Student achievement on assessment tests may be a controversial metric, because this information provides us with data describing, for example, the number of students who struggle with reading and are at risk of failing as well as the number of students considered proficient and advanced readers, but it can suggest the utility of high interest, low reading material for the population as well as the value of more traditional texts for young adults. Graduation and dropout rates and data describing the postsecondary plans of high school graduates can aid in the development of collections for young adults transitioning to adulthood. For example, communities that feature a high proportion of students who plan to attend college may benefit from a well-developed postsecondary education collection that includes guides to colleges and information about the college application process and scholarship competitions. Communities with fewer students who plan to attend college may benefit from a more diverse selection of material describing careers that do not require a traditional college education.

School and Curricular Information

Information about local schools, including details of their curricula and the condition of their school libraries and school library collections, can also inform the development of our library collections. Joanna Sei-Ching Sin (2012) has noted the relationship between the "school information environment" — that is, whether the school has computers for students to use, and whether the library features an automated book circulation system and makes online information resources available to students — and students' frequency of school library use and their tendency to use the public library for informational or recreational information seeking. Sin's conclusions suggest the particular relevance of data describing local school libraries and their collections to public library collections and services. She argues the following:

1. School information environments that are considered poor — that have few or no computers available for student use, that lack automated circulation, and that make little or no online information available to students — breed students more likely to use the public library for informational as well as recreational purposes.

2. A high level of school library use by students tends to correlate with a lower level of public library use.
3. A high level of public library use tends to correlate with a high level of school library use.

Sin hypothesizes that the convenience of the school library influences students' tendency to use it rather than the public library; however, if the school library's information environment is considered poor, students will turn to the public library for their recreational and informational needs. Sin's observations suggest the utility of information about local secondary school libraries for public librarians developing YA collections.

Information about the state curriculum and its application at the local level can influence the development of collections of informational material for young people. In addition, information on the availability of advanced placement courses and tests suggests the need for informational material that supports these courses as well as test preparation guides for students to study before taking AP tests. The Common Core State Standards inform many states' local curricula and are described in detail on the Common Core State Standards website. The appendixes provide information on gauges of text complexity that may be applied to library collections of material (English Language Arts Appendix A) and exemplary texts assigned to students at each grade level (English Language Arts Appendix B). The adoption of the Common Core State Standards is decided at the state level; however, individual school districts and schools are in charge of implementing these standards and may do so directly or through the lens of a particular secondary curriculum such as "Facing History and Ourselves." Information about what Hughes-Hassell and Mancall (2005) call the "enacted curriculum," the local application of state curricular directives, may be available from the local school districts and accessible via district or individual school websites.

The growth of charter, nontraditional, and specialized public schools may also influence the direction of the public library's YA collection. Charter schools are publicly funded schools that may not be required to adhere to some of the rules and regulations that apply to traditional public schools. In exchange for this reduction of regulatory requirements, charter schools pledge in their "charters" to achieve particular educational results and demonstrate this achievement in the form of specialized assessments. As Barbara Wales has observed, "In the absence of a requirement for a library, many charters have inadequate or nonexistent libraries" (2002, para. 3). If there are no local charter school libraries or they can be characterized, in Sin's terms, as poor informational environments, the public library may emerge as the primary source of school-related information and support for their students. Thus, the prevalence of charter schools within the library's service community and the status of these schools' libraries may affect charter school student use of the library for school support. Charter, nontraditional, and specialized public schools that focus on particular academic and artistic development may require support from the public library as well. For example, schools of science and technology may require student participation in school-wide science fairs, a scholastic event that can tax libraries' collections of books guiding student development of science projects.

Although the degree to which public library collections support students during the school year may vary by locality, most public libraries support school-assigned summer reading initiatives and develop collections of required reading material for students. Therefore an investigation of how and if summer reading programs are implemented by local schools is a necessary component of needs assessment. Broadly speaking, schools may develop short lists of material that all students are required to read in the break between school years, or they may develop longer lists of material from which students choose a specific number of titles to read. To support this initiative, public librarians must understand the "rules" of any school-instituted summer reading program and develop collections that feature multiple copies of required books.

The following information about local schools serving young adults can aid in collection development:

1. number of traditional public and charter schools in the library's service community
2. number of students registered for traditional and charter schools
3. educational or ideological thrust of nontraditional, specialized, or charter schools located in the library's service area
4. status of school libraries in local traditional and charter schools, including hours of operation and information environment
5. existence of special programs and course offerings for students, including the existence of advanced placement programs of study
6. number of students registered for advanced placement courses and AP examinations
7. application of Common Core State Standards (if adopted) to state and local curricula
8. details of local curricula, especially with regard to large or long-term research projects assigned to students
9. details of summer reading initiatives, including lists of required reading

It is important to reiterate the role of the public library in complementing the school library, and there is much the public library can do to develop collections that support student learning and achievement:

- In communities with strong advanced placement programs in which a large proportion of students register for AP courses and complete AP exams, public libraries may consider developing collections of AP course and exam study guides and acquiring multiple copies of literary and informational texts required for these courses.

- In communities that offer students and families the opportunity to choose among a number of specialized public school offerings, public libraries may develop topical or thematic collections of material to address specialized educational initiatives.
- In school districts characterized by school libraries with modest information environments, the public library may develop collections of databases for student use, as well as fiction and nonfiction to support school assignments.
- Public libraries may develop collections that support long-term assignments or major research projects, thus supplementing and complementing the school library's resources.
- Public librarians may apply the Common Core State Standards guidelines for determining text complexity to the evaluation of their collections to determine how and if these collections are meeting curricular guidelines.
- Public libraries may develop special collections of summer reading texts and purchase multiple copies of these titles to support local summer reading initiatives.

Considering Demographic and Community Data

Demographic and community data are key sources of information for libraries' needs assessment and marketing initiatives. These data describe the library's entire service population and, from a marketing perspective, can inform the development of targeted programs and collections. From a needs assessment perspective, these data help determine how and if a library's collection reflects and meets the needs of its user population. Evans and Saponaro point out that "[t]he most important question to ask following a needs assessment is: Do the present objectives of the library coincide with its new knowledge of the community? Are the objectives in line with the current needs of the community, do they reflect a past need, or are they merely self-serving?" (2005, 42). The demographic and community data can help us begin to answer these questions. To reframe Evans and Saponaro's questions in the more specific terms of YA collection development, we might ask if the library's present collection of material for young adults coincides with its new knowledge of the local teen community and its needs. To do this, we must compare the descriptive data we collected to data collected in the library that describes how the library is used in "real life." This allows us to consider who among the library's potential users are using the library and how, when considering the multiple motivations that might compel young people to use the library, these patrons are actually using the facility.

Part 2: Collecting Library Use Data

Information about how the library is used can impact collection development even more significantly than the information that describes the library's service population. Data collected through observation, the assessment of circulation and transaction logs describing database and networked resource use, tabulation and analysis of reference statistics, or the use of surveys reveals which members of the library's population are using the library's collection and helps develop a picture of the library in the lives of its current users. Library use data is often collected as part of collection evaluation programs; however, it is also important to needs assessment. When considered in tandem with the information describing the library's service population as a whole, it helps us answer two key questions that inform current collection development and future collection initiatives:

1. Who is using the library's collection, and why?
2. Who is not using the library's collection, and why?

The answer to the first question can be determined by considering current library use. The answer to the second can be determined by considering current library use against the data we have collected about the library's service population. Ultimately, we want to develop collections that meet current user needs and that attract new users and satisfy their needs and interests as well. To do this, we need to discover what we are doing to satisfy current patrons and then consider what we could be doing to attract new patrons.

Observational Data: How the Library and Its Young Adult Collection Are Used

One of the easiest ways to determine how the library and its YA collection are used is by observing its use. This is easier to accomplish in libraries that have space dedicated to housing a collection of material for young adults; however, it can be done in libraries that interfile young adult and adult or children's material as well. The location of the young adult collection will affect the primary observational approach and the tendency to observe library patrons or the library collection. Depending on the size and layout of the library, it may be possible to observe both forms of activity. Although numerous scholarly resources suggest the optimal conditions and procedures for undertaking a scientific observation, for less formal baseline data collection for internal use, it is not necessary to follow these to the letter. The procedures for conducting an observational study are as follows:

1. Identify the observational parameters: Will you be observing the library's discretely situated young adult collection to determine how this distinct collection of material is used, or will you be observing the entire library to determine how the library is used by young adults?

2. Create an observational schedule: To determine when the collection is used or when young adults visit the library, consider the library's hours of operation and divide this into segments. You may wish to observe the collection or library every hour, half hour, or fifteen minutes. In addition, you will want to observe the library over the course of a number of days, weeks, or even months to ensure that you capture use during the library's evening and weekend hours.

3. Create a data-collecting instrument: When observing use of the library's collection or the use of the library by young adults, you should create an "instrument" to record your observations (see figure 4.1). Your observational record should be divided into sections reflecting when you plan to conduct the observation and may include columns for a "head count" (the number of people occupying the area in which the library's young adult collection is housed or the number of young adults occupying the library), "perceived activity" (what you observe the patrons doing, e.g., browsing the shelves, reading books or print material, using the library's computers), and notes on any special programs or circumstances (e.g., whether school has been dismissed early, whether the library is hosting a teen program) that might affect library use.

4. Conduct the observation: Conduct a visual survey of the library in accordance with your observational schedule, noting the behavior of your target library users.

Information gathered through observational methods will confirm known patterns of use and perhaps illuminate previously unrecognized use. For example, many libraries situated near schools will notice an influx of young adults following class dismissal, a tendency the observation record will capture formally. This record may also reveal the use of the library in less traditionally frequented times and expose its use by homeschooling families that include young adults.

As this observation reveals how young people use the library, it has the potential to affect collection development. Noting, for example, that young people tend to use the library as a hangout after school could suggest the utility of having a browseable collection of magazines and high interest and visual titles. An observation that the library is used during the evening and on weekends as a study and research space could

Table 4.1.   Sample Observation Data Collecting Instrument

Date:
Location:

Time	Head Count	Perceived Activity	Notes
9:00am			
9:30am			
10:00am			
10:30am			
11:00am			
11:30am			
12:00pm			
12:30pm			
1:00pm			
1:30pm			
2:00pm			

suggest the utility of having a curricular reference collection as well as scholastic support material.

Reference Statistics: Patterns of Information Seeking Among Young Adults

Many libraries compile reference statistics that describe the nature of questions asked at the reference desk as well as the results of the reference transaction. Although some libraries may collect this information by hand, many make use of library data software programs such as those provided by Springshare (LibAnalytics), Altarama (Refstats, Deskstats), and Compendium (Desk Tracker). These programs allow libraries to record reference transactions in terms of, for example, type of question, type of patron, and the outcome of the transaction. This information can be useful for identifying information request trends that may suggest an information need associated with a specific subpopulation and can aid in identifying popular titles and sources. For example, consistent requests for information on a specific topic may be motivated by a common school assignment. When considering these patterns of consistent requests over time, a calendar of the school curriculum may begin to emerge. Information related to how and if these transactions were successful can suggest areas of the collection in need of further development or the need for multiple copies of particularly relevant or requested sources.

ILS Statistics: Circulation of the Library's Young Adult Material

Data collected by the library's integrated library system (ILS) provide collection developers with information about the circulation of the library's current collection. This information may be organized by variables such as user group (if the library identifies its users in terms of demographic categories or "youth" and "adult" categories or if the library collects patrons' dates of birth to record in its user database when patrons register for library cards), collection, date of publication, and subject classification. These data can be used to identify high use materials that may be titles the library wishes to duplicate, low use materials that may be titles the library wishes to weed, patterns of use in topical or subject areas, and materials circulated by particular user groups. Reports generated from the library's ILS can identify popular authors and titles as well as topics of informational or personal interest or need.

Circulation reports represent some of the most easily collected information, but Evans and Saponaro and Kay Bishop express caveats about the usefulness of these data. Evans and Saponaro point out: "Two basic assumptions underlie user/use studies: (1) the adequacy of the book collection is directly related to its usage, and (2) circulation records provide a reasonably representative picture of collection use" (2005, 326). Though these assumptions would seem true, Bishop points out the following challenges:

1. In-house use is excluded, thus underrepresenting actual use.
2. It reflects only materials found by users and does not record whether a user did not locate a desired item or the collection did not have that item.
3. Bias may be present because of inaccessibility of heavily used materials.
4. The method is not suitable for noncirculating collections, such as periodicals. (2007, 150–151)

Furthermore, the following factors may affect the representative potential of ILS circulation data for young adult collections:

1. If the ILS does classify users in terms of binary designations of "youth" and "adult," reports of circulation attributed to "youth" may include children as well as young adults.
2. If the ILS issues reports that describe the circulation of materials by collection (e.g., materials designated in the catalog as belonging to the "young adult" versus the "juvenile" or "adult" collection), the use of this material may not be attributed to young adults in its entirety but may include the use of this material by interested adults and children.
3. In libraries that interfile young adult and adult material or young adult and children's material and that process this material in gen-

eral terms (e.g., "adult nonfiction" or "juvenile nonfiction") and rely on spine labels to identify young adult titles, tracking the circulation of young adult material may be close to impossible.

With these caveats in mind, circulation reports provide easily generated data that can be complemented, enhanced, and verified by reference statistics and aid in the identification of high- and low-interest areas of the library's collection.

E-Metrics: Use of the Library's Electronic Resources

Just as the library's ILS can provide information about the circulation of the library's collection, electronic and networked resource vendors can provide libraries with information describing the use of subscription databases and electronic journals, electronic books, and reference works. As many public libraries subscribe to databases designed to serve students (InfoTrac's Student Edition database and Gale's In Context databases are examples), an understanding of how these databases are used and that some databases may replicate or provide updated content of print material held by the library (Gale's Opposing Viewpoints in Context includes electronic versions of titles from the publisher's print series, including Opposing Viewpoints, Current Controversies, and At Issue) can inform the continued purchase of print resources.

Accessing electronic resource use statistics has historically been a somewhat difficult and even controversial endeavor; however, with the development in 2002 of COUNTER (Counting Online Usage of Networked Electronic Resources), an initiative to set standards for the reporting of electronic resource usage statistics by vendors, this information has become somewhat easier to obtain. Compliant vendors (of which Gale is one) produce reports that include the number of successful full-text article requests made to article databases by month; the total search requests, result clicks, and record views by month; and the total number of denials of database access by month. These data have a number of applications, as the Council on Library and Information Resources (2012) notes: usage data can be computed to determine the cost-per-use of electronic services, which might then affect decisions to continue or drop subscription services, and "turn-away" data (describing unfulfilled searches or failed attempts to use a service) can be used to indicate the number of simultaneous users the library may license and authorize. If a library requires authentication to use resources off-site (i.e., if a library requires a patron to "sign in" with his or her library card to access the library's electronic resources), it may also be able to compare this authentication data to its user database to determine which classes or categories of users access specific resources (CLIR 2012).

Although these data can be useful to libraries considering resource renewal, they can be easy to misinterpret and misuse. "Usage data," advises the Council on Library and Information Resources, "must be interpreted cautiously . . . for two reasons":

> First, usability and user awareness affect the use of library collections and services. Low use can occur because the product's user interface is difficult to use, because users are unaware that the product is available, or because the product does not meet the users' information needs. Second, usage statistics do not reveal the users' experience or perception of the utility or value of a collection or service. For example, though a database or Web page is seldom used, it could be very valuable to those who use it. The bottom line is that usage statistics provide necessary but insufficient data to make strategic decisions. Additional information, gathered from user studies, is required to provide a context in which to interpret usage data. (2012, 3.5.2 "Analyzing and Interpreting the Data," para. 1)

These cautions may have particular resonance for librarians considering the value of electronic and networked resources created and collected for young adults. Because "user awareness" affects the tendency of patrons to use an electronic resource, the visibility of public library electronic resources for young people has the potential to impact their use. Much instruction related to electronic resources takes place in schools, and public libraries may witness shifts in the "popularity" of particular resources that correlate with their introduction during library instruction periods. The tendency for public libraries and public schools to share electronic resources via consortium agreements may also affect the interpretation of usage data, particularly where the identity of the user is concerned. If students have access to subscription databases via the school library's website and the public library's website, and each of these sites requires particular forms of authentication (e.g., students must use their school ID numbers to access databases via the school library's website or use their library cards to access databases via the library's website), student use of these resources may be difficult to account for with any certainty.

Surveys: Finding Out What Users and Stakeholders Want and Need

Many libraries create and administer surveys of their user population to identify user needs and determine whether these needs are being met. When considering a survey to identify the needs of the users of the library's YA collection, it may be useful to consider input from both the primary users of the collection (young adults) and secondary users or stakeholders, including homeschooling parents or caregivers, teachers, and school librarians. Evans and Saponaro (2005) point out that one goal of survey research is identifying and soliciting feedback from library users and nonusers. This can be a tricky goal to accomplish; however, cooperative efforts with local schools and organizations can facilitate the collection of this information. Sarah Ludwig suggests making paper-based surveys available for patrons in the library's teen area, working with high school English teachers to distribute surveys in their classes, and posting polls on the library website (2011, 59). Broadly speaking, surveys conducted for the purposes of needs assessment do not typically require institutional review board approval (which involves institutional review of the survey and its administration methodology with an eye toward ensuring that the data are acquired and used ethically); however, when working with teachers to administer surveys in schools, librarians may have to secure permission of the school principal and district administration.

An online survey may be one of the easiest kinds to administer. The development of a number of free and low-cost survey software packages like Surveymonkey and Zoomerang has allowed more librarians to create and administer online surveys of library patrons. The Young Adult Library Services Assocation's 2008 "Creating Online Surveys" suggests that online surveys consist of five sections:

1. Survey title
2. Brief explanation of the survey and its purpose
3. A deadline describing the amount of time the survey will be "live" and when the survey will be "closed" to respondents
4. The body of the survey, consisting of the survey's questions and queries
5. A thank-you note for participants

YALSA (2008) recommends that when developing the body of the survey, librarians should include no more than fifteen questions; limit open-ended questions, as these can be taxing for survey takers and the results can be cumbersome to interpret; "pilot test" the survey with a coworker or teen to determine its readability; and use prizes as incentives for participation.

An online survey may be the easiest to administer, depending on its location (e.g., posted to the library's website, posted to the library's teen page of its larger website) and how it is administered (e.g., a solicitation to participate is sent to teen library card holders), but it may not result in a high response rate and may not capture the opinions of both library users and nonusers. Distributing a survey through local secondary and high school English classes, as Ludwig suggests, may generate answers and opinions from a more heterogeneous sample of the young adult population and include responses from both those teens who have library cards and use the library and those who do not have library cards and do not use the library. With teacher, school, and district permission, it may be possible to administer the library's survey during class time. If the survey is short and relatively easy to complete, perhaps students can be asked to complete and return it at the end of a class period, thus ensuring a greater response rate from a more diverse group of respondents.

Young adult librarians may also consider surveying educators and school librarians to determine how and if they expect their students to make use of the public library. These surveys can be completed by families in local homeschooling organizations or can be administered to public and private schoolteachers. Bishop (2007) recommends that school librarians conduct surveys of classroom teachers to inform the development of school library collections and suggests that librarians ask teachers about any major units of study planned for the school year and particular resources that students may be required to consult to complete assignments. This approach has utility for the public librarian as well; however, before conducting a survey of local teachers, it is important to meet with the school's librarian to determine the feasibility of this approach. This is an opportunity to introduce the public library as a resource complementary to the school library and to forge a partnership that can aid in the development of a collection that is responsive to student needs but does not replicate the school library's collection.

Considering Library Use Data

Just as demographic and community data allow librarians to describe the library's service population of both existing library users and potential library users, library use data allow librarians to develop a narrower description of the behavior of the "existing library user" segment of the service population. Because these library use data are primarily culled from the segment of the population that does use the library, they do not reveal the information needs and information-seeking methods and motivations of that portion of the population that does not use the library and thus do not represent a true cross-section of the library's service community. Library use data can help determine who is using the library and why and can inform the assessment and development of the library's collection in terms of its current users' needs and wants.

Part 3: Putting It All Together

Evans and Saponaro (2005) suggest interpreting the collected data in terms of what they, following Jonathan Bradshaw, call "social needs," which can be described as "normative," "felt," "expressed," and "comparative." *Normative needs* are based on research and expert opinion and can be considered those that experts identify on behalf of a user population. Normative needs associated with young adults include those culled from library and information science research, described previously: popular culture information and artifacts, school-inspired information requests, and information that answers personal needs and curiosities.

Felt needs, in contrast, are identified by the population or community and may or may not represent those normative needs identified by researchers and experts. Examples of "felt needs" associated with young adults are particular to local populations and may include a need for material in a language other than English or interests in local sports teams or celebrities. *Expressed needs* are reflected in individual behavior and in the library can be interpreted by the activities of users. *Comparative needs* can be identified by comparing the activities of one population with another. Evans and Saponaro offer that circulation can be considered a measurement of comparative need; by comparing the per capita circulation associated with the library's young adult cardholders to the per capita circulation associated with the library's adult cardholders, a comparative image of library use (as expressed by circulation) can be created.

Using the results of the library's needs assessment to identify the categories of social needs of the young adult service population allows us to consider how the collection meets or fails to meet the needs of existing users and note any discrepancies between the library's collection and the unexpressed needs of library nonusers. The results of a needs assessment can be expressed as answers to the following questions:

1. What are the normative needs associated with the library's service community of young adults?
2. What are the felt needs expressed by the library's service community of young adults?
3. What are the expressed needs of the young adult users of the library's collections and services?
4. How do the normative, felt, and expressed needs compare, and at what points do these needs overlap?

To answer these questions, librarians should consider the relationships between "objective" community and demographic data and more "subjective" user data. Table 4.2 lists data sources that may be consulted to answer these questions as well as potential outcomes of such data collection.

The results of a library's needs assessment can tell us how it is meeting the current needs of its users, identify areas of high interest and use by current users, and help us identify segments of the library population that may not be currently served by the library's collection or that face barriers affecting their access to the collection. These results can inform our development of the library's collection in response to current users and help us set service goals that impact collection development. These service goals may involve the development of foreign-language collections to meet the needs of English Language Learners and non-English speakers or the establishment of collections of technological tools like "loaded" e-readers or portable gaming devices to meet the needs of users whose access to technology may be limited. Because patron awareness of

Chapter 4

Table 4.2.   Data Sources and Analysis Suggestions for Answering Needs Assessment Questions

Question	Data Sources	Data Analysis Results
What are the normative needs associated with the library's service community of young adults?	LIS research describing young adults' information needs in general	Typologies of young adult information needs
	Curricular data + input from educational stakeholders (e.g., school librarians, teachers)	Lists of information needs imposed by the curriculum, including assignment goals and required reading
	Demographic information + LIS research describing the information needs of specific populations	Typologies of information needs associated with communities of young adults who belong to specific racial, ethnic, linguistic, and social groups
	Demographic information and educational attainment information + research describing barriers to information access and the digital divide	Barriers to information seeking (e.g., the digital divide, literacy skills) that affect the local population
What are the felt needs expressed by the library's service community of young adults?	Results of surveys of library users and nonusers	Lists of information needs and interests of library users and nonusers
What are the expressed needs of the young adult users of the library's collections and services?	Observational reports of library use	Patterns of library use by specific young adult populations
	Circulation statistics	Areas of high interest in the collection (e.g., popular and sought-after topics, authors, and materials)
	Reference statistics	Areas of information interest among the young adult population

How do the normative, felt, and expressed needs compare, and at what points do these needs overlap?	LIS research describing young adults' information needs + observational reports of library use + circulation statistics + reference statistics	Comparison of theoretical information needs of young adults (LIS research) to expressed needs of young adults
	Curricular data + input from educational stakeholders (e.g., school librarians, teachers) + observational reports of library use + circulation statistics + reference statistics	Consideration of library use in relation to information needs imposed in school (e.g., which school assignments or projects inspire library use)
	Demographic information and educational attainment information + research describing barriers to information access and the digital divide + observational reports of library use + reference statistics	When observational reports describe computer use and reference statistics include requests to use computer resources, use of the library's resources to overcome barriers to information access may be inferred

library resources affects the tendency for patrons to make use of these resources, any new collection development goals created in response to the identification of the normative and felt needs of the population can be considered somewhat risky. Evans and Saponaro (2005) write that libraries tend to be very successful in meeting the expressed information needs of patrons; maintaining and refining collections that meet the expressed and documented information needs of current library users represents a "win-win" situation for libraries. That is, by developing collections that respond to the expressed needs of current library users, the investment that libraries make when purchasing material for these users is almost certain to be recouped in circulation. Libraries that respond solely to expressed needs "risk unbalanced spending," Evans and Saponaro warn, as well as "failure to respond to real, though unexpressed, information needs" (2005, 40–41). Because needs assessment can reveal where and if the library is "overresponding to active users' needs" (Evans and Saponaro 2005, 41), it can motivate us to take considered collection development risks and work to enlarge the library's population of "active users."

SOURCES OF DEMOGRAPHIC, COMMUNITY, AND EDUCATIONAL INFORMATION

Demographic Information

1. U.S. Census Bureau Homepage, www.census.gov: The Census Bureau's website allows users to search for demographic data at the national, state, and town or regional level. A "Quick Search" by state or town provides a population count, broad statistics related to race and ethnicity of the local population, and some educational attainment and language use information.
2. American Fact Finder, www.factfinder2.census.gov: A resource of the U.S. Census Bureau, American Fact Finder provides data in the form of an American Community Survey, an annual survey that produces housing and population information, drawing from over three million households surveyed across the country. Its American Housing Survey provides information about housing, including characteristics of occupants, indicators of neighborhood quality, and numbers of those eligible for and benefiting from assisted housing opportunities.
3. KIDS COUNT Data Center, www.datacenter.kidscount.org: This initiative of the Annie E. Casey Foundation provides data describing indicators of child well-being, including demographic and educational data mined from state and national sources. The website allows users to search by state or by using more narrow geographical parameters.
4. Public Library Geographic Database, www.geolib.org/PLGDBcfm: Created by the University of Florida's School of Library and Information Studies, this database allows users to display demographic data mined from U.S. census data on a map to identify discrete populations in geographic regions.

Educational Information

1. National Center for Education Statistics Data Tools, www.nces.ed.gov/datatools: The "Data Tools" page linked from the NCES homepage provides links to sources of information about public school districts, public and private schools, and public libraries.
2. Common Core State Standards Initiative, www.corestandards.org: The website of the organization responsible for the Common Core State Standards presents information about this standards movement and allows users to download PDF versions of the standards and appendixes.

Library Information

1. IMLS Data Analysis Tools, www.imls.gov/research/library_services.aspx: The IMLS Data Analysis Tools page includes links to two data analysis initiatives: "Public Library Locator" and "Compare Public Libraries." "Public Library Locator" provides searchers with information about individual public libraries' staffing, collections, and expenditures; "Compare Public Libraries" allows users to compare public libraries that serve similarly sized communities, that are situated within the same geographic region, or that are located in communities characterized by similar income levels.

FIVE

Selecting Material for the Young Adult Collection

Selecting material for the library's young adult collection is, as Peggy Johnson notes, "both an art and a science" (2009, 108) and requires the selecting librarian to make a number of decisions that will ideally result in the development of a collection that reflects both the library's service community and its organizational mission and values. As young adult book publishing grows in the print as well as the digital markets, and library collections for young adults expand to include multimedia material in "traditional" and streaming forms, YA librarians face new challenges during selection. Librarians selecting material for young adults face information overload as they sift through reviews, bibliographies, promotional material, blog posts, and electronic discussion lists to determine how best to spend the library's materials budget. Furthermore, today's YA librarians must not only consider which titles to purchase, but also in which formats to select these titles, decisions that require knowledge of the young adult community, its information needs and reading preferences, and its technological connectivity.

The largest ongoing task of selection involves becoming familiar with what practitioners call "the universe of published materials": literary, informational, educational, and entertainment material to meet the needs and respond to the interests of patrons. To remain current with this world of choices, librarians employ a variety of bibliographic and selection resources—professional and trade review journals, promotional materials, listservs, bibliographies and standard catalogs, and awards and "best books" lists—to learn about new titles and remain abreast of publishing trends. Armed with this information, librarians apply and redevelop selection criteria, making choices that affect not only what material is purchased, but also where it will be housed in the library.

91

THE SELECTION PROCESS

The Purposes of Selection

Librarians select materials for library patrons in accordance with the library's mission and to adhere to its collection development policy. Most public library mission statements are broad and describe the library's charge to make a wide variety of material available to a diverse population of patrons; the collection development policy will outline and "operationalize" that mission in the form of policies and procedures that describe and delimit the YA collection. Many of these policies outline the library's intent to maintain collections of material of contemporary relevance, popularity, and interest to its service population; therefore a large component of selection consists of choosing newly published or reissued material for addition to the collection. Because these policies may also detail the needs the collection is intended to meet (e.g., the curricular or educational needs of the library's service population), selection may also involve choosing material to meet newly recognized or established needs or selecting material in new or alternative formats.

Selecting materials for library collections is always a purposeful activity; librarians select new and updated material to maintain relevant collections and meet library users' identified needs and also engage in the retrospective selection of older material to fill gaps in the library's collection or to replace older but still relevant items that are well-used and worn. Evans and Saponaro note that the first task of selection involves identifying "collection needs in terms of subjects and specific types of material" (2005, 70). These needs are broadly described in the library's collection development policy and are more specifically informed by needs assessment and collection evaluation. A significant change in local curricular requirements—the development of an advanced placement program at the local high school, for example, or a new requirement for students in certain science courses to complete competitive science fair projects—can inspire goals for collection development, particularly if the librarian has noted young people's use of the collection to support educational endeavors and an evaluation of the collection reveals a dearth of support material for AP students or science fair competitors. Surveys of library users and an analysis of their requests for specific titles, series, or media may inform collection goals as well. For example, if library users express interest in manga, the librarian may consider developing a collection in that format to meet the expressed needs of readers and requesters.

Selection, thus, is a two-pronged activity involving continuous consideration of new material with an eye toward selecting specific items to update the library's collection, as well as more targeted consideration of new and retrospective material in particular subject areas or formats with an eye toward selecting specific titles, series, or media to meet identified needs (see figure 5.1).

When selection occurs—that is, when requests for material are submitted for acquisition—varies across libraries. Although some libraries may submit requests for material only at specific points in the fiscal year, some acquisitions departments accept requests on an ongoing basis, allowing librarians to select and purchase material to be added to the collection throughout the year. Naturally budgetary allocations will limit the amount of material a librarian may request for purchase, which makes it necessary for all selecting librarians to remain aware of how much of their allotted funds has been spent throughout the year, especially if acquisition is an ongoing activity. With these limitations in mind, Kay Bishop (2007) advises librarians to maintain "consideration files," or lists of suggested, requested, or otherwise relevant items for evaluation and acquisition. Items listed in these files may be considered part of the librarian's "wish list" for the collection and may include descriptions of how and if they would meet the library's goals for its young adult collection. Ultimately, as Patrick Jones, Michele Gorman, and Tricia Suellentrop point out, collection development is not just about buying and acquiring new items; rather, it is a process of "resource allocation" (2004, 97). Acquiring new material is the task of the selector, yet he or she must remain cognizant of the current collection—what it consists of, how it is used, and how it fulfills the library's mission—and consider how each acquisition might enhance or work within the existing collection of material.

Becoming Familiar with the "Universe" of Published Material

Librarians may select materials on a continual basis, submitting requests for purchase to the acquisitions staff on a monthly or even weekly basis, or they may develop "wish lists" throughout the year and refine

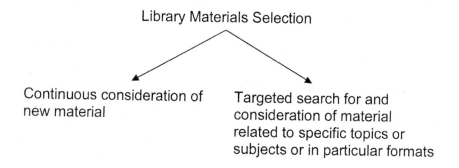

Library Materials Selection

Continuous consideration of new material

Targeted search for and consideration of material related to specific topics or subjects or in particular formats

Figure 5.1. Two-Pronged Selection

these for purchase and acquisition annually or semiannually. Thus, though purchasing and acquisition may occur on a more or less frequent basis, selection librarians strive to remain current with a growing and diverse "universe" of published materials. To this end, YA collection development librarians peruse journals that review and describe new material; consider promotional material describing new series, spin-off series, and companion titles to books in the current collection; read and participate in professional listservs that recommend and discuss books and media for young adults; and examine bibliographies of recommended titles and award winners as they are announced by professional and literary organizations. As librarians learn about new items, they may add these to their consideration files for further evaluation and possible acquisition.

Professional and Review Journals

Many libraries subscribe to trade or professional review journals that include brief reviews and descriptions of books and media and may also include articles and columns describing an aspect of publishing or librarianship or recommend best practices in materials selection, collection development, or library services. These review sources are typically written for book buyers in bookstores or library selectors and may describe materials in a variety of formats for a variety of audiences, or they may be more narrowly focused on the description and review of books and media in specific subject areas, in specific languages, or for specific audiences. Evans and Saponaro state that trade and professional review journals are "of two types: those designed to promote and those designed to evaluate" (2005, 87). Trade journals designed to promote (like *Publishers Weekly*) include notes describing publishers' promotional and marketing plans for individual titles; this information can aid librarians in the selection of material that may be more or less popular or well-known because of its heavy promotion. Trade journals designed to evaluate material consider librarians their primary audience and include reviews that are descriptive and evaluative in terms of library needs and interests. For example, a review of a picture book in an evaluative trade journal may note the book's potential for storytime use.

Subscriptions to trade and professional journals can be expensive for libraries—for example, the cost to subscribe to the print version of *Publishers Weekly* and access its online content is currently more than $200 per year—and although a wealth of general and specific trade and professional journals exist, few libraries subscribe to all of them. Librarians who select material for young adults often consider review sources describing material for young people as well as material for adults: *Publishers Weekly* (a promotional trade journal) and *Booklist* (an evaluative professional and trade journal) are frequently consulted journals that review material for young people as well as adults. *School Library Journal*, which reviews material for young people through high school, and *Voice of Youth Advocates* (*VOYA*), which reviews material published for teens and 'tweens and describes adult titles of interest to young adults, are frequently consulted evaluative titles of particular interest to youth services and young adult librarians.

Libraries may subscribe to review journals in print or electronic form or may choose a subscription that offers access to both forms; each form of access has its benefits and drawbacks. The print form provides selectors with reviews in context and allows for traditional cover-to-cover reading of both reviews and editorial content. Review journals may highlight titles of particular excellence or interest by "starring" or "boxing" review content (i.e., drawing attention to titles and reviews in graphic form); when viewed in print these reviews and titles can be easily discerned from other content. Many review journals organize reviews in terms of audience or format, devoting pages of each issue to reviews of material for preschoolers, school-aged children, middle-grade readers, and young adult audiences as well as to video, audio, electronic, and print materials. This organization helps to facilitate purposeful reading and browsing. Review journal websites provide electronic subscribers with access to current and archival content and facilitate database-like searches for specific titles or for material that meets established criteria. For example, *Booklist* online allows subscribers to search the full text of its current and archived reviews by title, subject (based on *Booklist*'s controlled vocabulary taxonomy), audience, format, Dewey Decimal number or range, grade level, publication date, review status (e.g., "starred"), and award status (i.e., the search can be limited to return only titles that have received awards). This search option is especially useful to selectors interested in filling topical or format "gaps" in the library's collection. Readers of *School Library Journal* can subscribe to the journal in print form or can enhance their subscription by adding access to the publisher's Book Verdict database of reviews; users may use Book Verdict to access *School Library Journal* reviews or, for a larger fee, access reviews from the publisher's other journals and resources, including *Horn Book* magazine, *Horn Book Guide*, and the Junior Library Guild.

Frequency of publication, extent and depth of coverage, utility and relevance of editorial content, and access to prepublication reviews are some of the primary criteria for selecting a review journal or journals. Figure 5.2 describes the nature of these features in several journals commonly used for YA material selection.

Table 5.1. Commonly Consulted Professional and Trade Review Journals

Title	Promo. or Evaluative	Pub. Frequency	Items Reviewed Annually	Prepub. Reviews (Y/N)	Material Reviewed by Audience Type	Material Reviewed by Media Type	Reviewer Status (Professional or Practitioner)	Online Content Available
Publishers Weekly	Promotional	Weekly	~8,000	Y	Children's, young adult, adult	Print books, e-books, audiobooks, comics and graphic novels	Professionals and practitioners	Access to archived reviews available to subscribers
Kirkus Reviews	Promotional	Twice a month	~7,000 mainstream ~3,000 self-published	Y	Children's, young adult, adult	Print books, e-books, comics and graphic novels, iPad book apps	Professional	Access to archived reviews available to subscribers; online access to complete issues available to subscribers
Booklist	Evaluative	22 print issues per year, plus 4 issues of Book Links	~8,000	Y	"The Young," "Middle Readers" (grades 6–8), "Older Readers" (grades 9–12), adult	Print books, e-reference books, videos, audio recordings, audiobooks	Professional	Access to archived reviews available to subscribers via online database

School Library Journal	Evaluative	Monthly	~5,000	Y	Children's, young adult, professional titles	Print books, videos, audio recordings, CD-ROMs, online resources	Practitioner	Online access to archived reviews available to subscribers
Voice of Youth Advocates (VOYA)	Evaluative	6 issues per year	~2,200	Y	Young adult, adult books for young adults, professional titles	Print books, audiobooks, graphic novels and comics, movies and DVDs, e-books	Practitioner	Digital version of journal available to subscribers
Horn Book Magazine	Evaluative	6 issues per year	~80 titles per issue	Y	Children's, young adult	Print books	Professional	Online access to archived reviews available to subscribers
Bulletin of the Center for Children's Books	Evaluative	11 issues per year	~900	Y	Children's, young adult, professional titles	Print books	Professional	Online access to journal available to subscribers

When considering the scope and depth of each journal's review coverage, it is important to note how it selects the material it reviews. For example, the *Horn Book* magazine, according to its website, "reviews books very selectively," printing reviews of only those titles it considers "notable for high standards in plot, theme, characterization and style" (2013, "Review Copies," para. 2); each issue includes reviews of approximately eighty recommended titles. *School Library Journal*, in contrast, includes both positive and negative reviews that recommend or caution against purchasing reviewed material and reviews a larger number of titles in each of its issues. It is also important to consider the paid or volunteer status of the journal's reviewers, as their positions as freelance reviewers or practitioners will probably influence their critical perspective. *Voice of Youth Advocates* and *School Library Journal* both rely on volunteers, who are assigned material to review by the journals' editorial staff and are not compensated for their work. Whereas *School Library Journal* accepts reviews only from librarians who are currently working with young people in libraries, *Voice of Youth Advocates* does not require its reviewers to be currently practicing librarians, but does ask that they have three to five years' experience working with adolescents in a library or an educational capacity (e.g., as a teacher or school administrator). *Kirkus Reviews, Booklist*, the *Horn Book* magazine, and *Publishers Weekly* assign titles to editorial staff or freelance writers for review.

Promotional Materials and Vendor Resources

Publishers of children's and young adult materials often send promotional flyers and catalogs to librarians to alert them to new publications. Although these promotional materials arguably present the advertised publications in a positive light, they can draw selecting librarians' attention to material that may not be reviewed in professional and trade journals and may include information about the publisher's promotional efforts on behalf of an author or title. For example, such material can alert librarians to mass market titles and paperback originals that may not be profiled or reviewed in professional or trade publications. Genre offerings published by specialized imprints (e.g., Penguin's Firebird imprint, which publishes paperback science fiction and fantasy) as well as popular paperback originals and series produced in conjunction with television shows or movies (e.g., Poppy's Glee series of books, based on the popular television show) are among titles that may be popular and requested by young people but are not profiled in professional journals.

Libraries working with vendors may also receive promotional material that highlights vendor-selected and recommended material or alerts librarians to new series and popular titles. Many library vendors have developed promotional catalogs that resemble professional bibliographies; these are included in shipments of material to libraries and are often accessible via the vendor's selection and acquisition database. These resources can be useful, particularly as they describe and promote material that may not be discussed as extensively in professional resources, including popular DVDs of direct-to-video and wide-release movies, chart-topping music in multiple genres, and religious or inspirational titles. Libraries may develop a descriptive profile for vendors to use to select titles for recommendation that target their needs and interests, and promotional material provided by these vendors offers more extensive coverage of current material in specialized formats or requested subject areas.

Professional Listservs

Many YA librarians subscribe to electronic discussion lists (listservs) to learn about new titles, series, and media and to discuss their selection, promotion, and use. The American Library Association sponsors a number of listservs for YA librarians; its Young Adult Library Services Association's "yalsa-bk" list is dedicated to the discussion and recommendation of young adult fiction and nonfiction, its "ya-music" list is devoted to music of interest to and popular among teens, and "ya-urban" inspires discussion among librarians serving young people in urban communities. Many academic centers and local library associations have also established listservs to connect librarians more regionally. "PUBYAC" (http://www.pubyac.com) is a discussion list sponsored by the University of Illinois, Urbana-Champaign that focuses on serving children and young adults in public libraries. "CCBC-Net" (http://www.education.wisc.edu/ccbc/ccbcnet/default.asp) is a discussion list sponsored by the University of Wisconsin–Madison's Cooperative Children's Book Center and schedules topics related to children's and young adult literature for discussion on a bimonthly basis.

Bibliographies and Book Lists

Several professional organizations and publishers compile bibliographies, standard catalogs, and book lists recommending titles of interest or relevance to young adult librarians, and many YA librarians consult these lists when selecting material or evaluating the library's collection. The ALA's Young Adult Library Services Association's lists of award-winning and recommended titles are among the most consulted by young adult librarians, and other organizations, such as the National Council for the Social Studies and the National Science Teachers Association, develop lists of recommended titles in topical areas that promote material for use in social studies and science curricula. These lists of recommended titles are useful for selection because they can expand a librarian's knowledge of the "universe of published materials"; however, as Jones, Gorman, and Suellentrop point out, selecting material for young adults is not just a matter of "ordering everything on BBYA [YALSA's annually compiled list of "Best Books for Young Adults"]" (2004, 98). Rather, YA librarians should consider these lists with a critical eye, selecting—or not—listed material that reflects the needs and interests of the local community. Topical bibliographies and readers' advisory guides, particularly those devoted to reading interests in particular genres and formats, can aid in selecting material in areas in which a librarian may have little experience. Many of these bibliographic resources are produced for library professionals and include descriptions of a genre or format's characteristics and appeal factors, noting "classic" works in a genre or format and suggesting criteria for the selection of material. The following subsections discuss commonly consulted lists and published bibliographies that compile and recommend titles for YA library collections (Note: format- and genre-specific bibliographies and readers' advisory resources are discussed in greater detail later in this chapter.)

Professional Bibliographies

1. YALSA's "Best Fiction for Young Adults": Formerly "Best Books for Young Adults," this more narrowly focused, annually compiled list consists of recommended fiction published for young adults between the ages of twelve and eighteen. According to the BFYA policies statement, material on the list is "selected for [its] demonstrable or probably appeal to the personal reading tastes of the young adult" (YALSA 2010b, "Audience").
2. YALSA's "Popular Paperbacks for Young Adults": This annually produced list of material published for young adults, as well as adult material of popular interest to young adult readers, comprises currently available paperbacks selected for their popularity. These titles are organized around themes (recent themes include "All Kinds of Creepy" [2005] and "Simply Science Fiction" [2004]) that evoke popular genre and reading categories.
3. YALSA's "Quick Picks for Reluctant Young Adult Readers": This annual list compiles titles selected and recommended for young adults "who, for whatever reasons, do not like to read" (YALSA 2009, "Purpose"). This list identifies high-interest titles for leisure or recreational reading, "not for curricular or remedial use" (YALSA 2009, "Purpose").
4. YALSA's "Teens' Top Ten": This annual list is voted on by teens and consists of titles initially recommended by any of fifteen teen book groups participating in YALSA's YA Galley Project, which circulates advanced reading copies of young adult materials to participating teen book groups across the United States.
5. National Council of the Social Studies (NCSS), "Notable Social Studies Trade Books for Young People": This annually compiled list of trade books is selected by a committee appointed by the

NCSS in cooperation with the Children's Book Council and includes recommended material for young people in grades K–8. The annotated list of selections is organized to highlight each title's relationship to the National Curriculum Standards for Social Studies.

6. National Science Teachers Association (NSTA), "Outstanding Science Trade Books for Students K–12": This list of recommended science titles is compiled annually and chosen by a committee appointed by the NSTA in cooperation with the Children's Book Council. Full reviews of each recommended title are published in the association's trade journals and are available online via the organization's NSTA Recommends database (http://www.nsta.org/recommends/).

Bibliographic Resources and Standard Catalogs

1. *Senior High Core Collection* and *Middle and Junior High Core Collection*: These titles, part of H. W. Wilson's Core Collections series, are catalogs of fiction and nonfiction titles recommended by content specialists, reviewed by librarians, and recommended to libraries for priority or supplemental purchase. These catalogs are notable for their scope: titles are recommended for nearly every subject area defined by the DDC.

2. *A Core Collection for Young Adults*, 2nd ed, by Rollie Welch (Neal Schuman, 2010): The second edition of *Core Collection* recommends classic and contemporary fiction and nonfiction titles for young adults in a variety of formats and includes a CD-ROM for librarians who wish to check their current collections against Welch's recommended lists.

3. *Teen Genreflecting 3: A Guide to Reading Interests*, by Diane Tixier-Herald (Libraries Unlimited, 2011): The third edition of Tixier-Herald's bibliography of recommended titles in various formats and genres for young adults can be used to select and assess library collections. This guide includes annotations as well as information on the selection and evaluation of material in particular genres and formats.

4. *Best Books for High School Readers, Grades 9–12* and *Best Books for Middle School and Junior High Readers, Grades 6–9*, by Catherine Barr and John Gillespie (2nd eds., Libraries Unlimited, 2009): Granularly organized and indexed guides to fiction and nonfiction titles assigned to both broad and narrow subject and genre designations that resemble curricular topics and organization rather than DDC controlled vocabulary make this title useful for librarians and teachers.

Annually compiled book lists may suggest new titles to add to the library's collection or may be mined for material to select retrospectively.

For example, a librarian developing a graphic novel collection may consider the latest as well as historical "Great Graphic Novels for Teens" lists when building a collection of graphic novels from scratch. In comparison, published bibliographies are more often used for retrospective selection, as their contents include both contemporary titles and "classics," and their production schedule limits just how contemporary the items listed may be. Typically, authors of published bibliographic resources delimit their recommendations, and because it takes longer to publish such bibliographies than to publish periodicals, the newest titles recommended in one of these resources are typically two years older than the bibliography itself.

Applying and Redeveloping Selection Criteria

Becoming familiar with the always growing world of material produced and published for young people—as well as with material produced for adult or child audiences that may also appeal to young adults—is a large and never-ending professional obligation. Many YA librarians, especially those who are fans and readers of young adult literature and other materials for young people, gladly take on this professional task. In fact, learning about—and reading, watching, listening to, and playing with—material for young adults is probably one of the biggest "perks" of the job. Making decisions about which of this material to select for the library, however, can be one of the toughest parts of the job. Jones, Gorman, and Suellentrop (2004) remind us that when developing collections for young adults, in most cases they are collections of *material for young adults* and not necessarily collections *of young adult material*. As Patrick Jones (2003) and Mary Key Chelton (2006) have asserted, library collections for young adults consist of more than just fiction published for young adults; contemporary public library collections for young adults include multimedia items (audiobooks, CDs, DVDs, video games), graphic novels and sequential art forms, magazines and pamphlets, and fiction and nonfiction published for adults, children, and young adults. When our interests and the interests of the young adults we serve coincide, selecting and acquiring material on their behalf is like living out a fantasy. When those interests diverge, however, we have to make tough decisions about what material to acquire for the library's collection.

The library's mission and its collection development policy outline the criteria YA librarians employ to select and acquire material for young adults. In addition, its composition will be influenced by the following criteria, identified by Jones, Gorman, and Suellentrop:

> The quality and quantity of school library collections;
> The budget, space and staff available;
> Reading interests of YAs in [the library's service] community;
> [The librarian's] own professional values;

What needs that collection should meet; and
The roles the library has chosen for itself. (2004, 109–110)

How the library defines and physically delimits its collection for young adults will inform the composition and nature of any such collection housed in a dedicated library space and of any material for young adults housed in or cataloged in other areas of the library. For example, smaller libraries may dedicate a corner of the library for young adult literature, defining that space as one in which only material published expressly for young adults is housed. Although this library's YA librarian or selector may be responsible for choosing young adult literature and nonfiction to stock this area, he or she may also identify and select adult and children's material of interest to young adults that is housed or cataloged in other areas of the library. Libraries that assign more physical space to the young adult collection may choose to house young adult, adult, and children's fiction of interest to young adults in this area and may shelve high interest young adult, adult, and children's nonfiction there also. The YA librarian may select material housed in this section and may also be responsible for selecting curricular, reference, and supplemental material published for young adults, adults, or children to be housed in other areas of the library. Depending on how each library is used by its young adult population, the selecting librarian may devote the bulk of the materials budget to high interest and recreational material or to curricular and educational support material. Ultimately, librarians charged with selecting material for young adults may find their budgets and responsibilities limited to certain types or kinds of material depending on how the library organizes its collections, acquisitions staff, and program and assigns selection responsibilities.

Whether a librarian selects material produced and published for young adult audiences or adult and children's material as well as young adult material for the library's YA collection, most employ the same general criteria. When choosing material for young people, YA librarians seek to add items that are

1. reflective of the library's mission, goals, and objectives;
2. relevant to user needs and interests in terms of format, content, and subject;
3. accessible to young adult users in terms of language and format;
4. reflective of a contemporary understanding of the world or, if historical, interpretable within a clear historical context;
5. complementary to the library's collection of material in general and, more specifically, to material within the subject area;
6. reflective of the quality standards applied by the library to material of similar format, content, and subject; and
7. reasonably priced given the material's presumed value to the library's collection and users

These broad criteria reflect the considerations Evans and Saponaro identify as primary among selectors: "user population, collection content, collection priorities, materials budget status, primary authors and publishers or producers in the selector's area of responsibility, and review sources and general production levels in the selector's area of responsibility" (2005, 94). To employ these criteria, selectors must take into account the value of the individual items being considered for purchase, as well as the current and anticipated future value of these items within the library's collection. For example, the success of Stephenie Meyer's Twilight series inspired a supernatural romance publishing boom in young adult literature, which in turn inspired Twilight-hungry readers to devour similar and newly published titles. As librarians sought to keep up with reader demand for more books like the Twilight series, they considered a variety of similar titles that, due to budgetary constraints and the necessity to purchase material to meet other user demands, could not all be selected for the library. Thus, librarians had to examine each new Twilight-inspired novel or series for its relevance to user interests and its relationship to the library's collection in general. They had to balance their purchase of single titles against planned trilogies against series with no end in sight, as well as the potential continued relevance of each new Twilight-esque title. Furthermore, they had to balance their accumulated knowledge of young adult literature, publishers, authors, and series against what they understood their clientele wanted and strive to make the most considered and useful purchases within this narrow area of interest without inadvertently creating a collection consisting entirely of vampire romance novels that, the Twilight series excepted, would probably have a limited shelf life.

SELECTING MATERIAL FOR THE YOUNG ADULT COLLECTION

Choosing Fiction for the Young Adult Collection

The young adults for whom librarians develop collections read a variety of literature. Adult novels, classic novels, "new adult" literature, young adult literature, and middle grade or "younger YA" literature are five very broad, primary categories of YA reading and suggest equally broad categories to consider when selecting fiction for young people.

Adult Novels

Mary Kay Chelton has noted that when she began her career serving young adults in libraries in the early 1960s, "the service standards of the era said that YA collections should be 80 percent adult books . . . in part because the goal of YA services was (and still is) to facilitate the transition to adulthood and adult interests while serving the needs of the present"

(2006, 10). Although the fledgling status of young adult literature as a publishing category probably contributed to the service standards Chelton cites, the historical growth of young adult literature and its contemporary boom has in part drawn YA librarians' attention from adult to young adult literature, making this category the mainstay in young adult library collections. Concerns about censorship and the appropriateness of adult literary content for young adults have further discouraged many YA librarians from considering adult novels viable additions to the library's young adult collection. Adult fans of and advocates for young adult literature worry that, as Chris Crowe noted in *English Journal*, if young readers' "only experience with books comes from the stale high school literary canon and popular adult fiction . . . how will they know about a whole body of wonderful literature that has been produced for adolescent readers?" (2002, 101). Although the contemporary popularity of young adult series like The Hunger Games and Twilight has no doubt drawn more attention to young adult literature than it received when Crowe wrote his essay, arguments over prescribing a diet of young adult versus adult literature for teen readers continue.

Research into young adults' reading habits that gives young people an opportunity to discuss their reading preferences notes their tendencies to read widely across formats and genres and to pick and choose from literature published for adults and young adults. A 2009 survey undertaken by the website Teenreads.com revealed that 31 percent of the teen respondents "read adult titles without reservation," whereas 58 percent reported that whether they read adult titles "depended on the book"; only 11 percent of the respondents reported that they did not read adult books at all (Fitzgerald 2009, 23). That the adult authors mentioned most often by teen readers of adult books (see below) are often those who are discussed and interviewed in popular media (e.g., Jodi Picoult), are media personalities (e.g., David Sedaris), or enjoy profits from movies and television shows made from their novels (e.g., Charlaine Harris, James Patterson, Nicholas Sparks) speaks to the effects of these authors' widespread popularity. As much research describing teen reading choices notes that young people have difficulty determining what books to read, it is not surprising that adult titles and authors popular among readers at large are read by teens as well.

The development of the Alex Award in 1988 and its establishment as an official ALA award in 2002 has underscored the importance of adult titles to young adult readers and authorized the place of adult titles in their lives and in library collections for them. The award, named for librarian Margaret Alexander Edwards, is granted annually to ten books published for adults that "have special appeal to young adults" (YALSA 1997–2013a, para. 1) and is granted to both fiction and nonfiction titles. Before the establishment of this award, professional and reviewing journals noted adult titles that might be of crossover interest to young people, labeling these titles with an "A/YA" (*VOYA*) or developing lists of "adult books for young adults" (*School Library Journal*) to aid librarians in the selection of these materials (this practice continues). Noting that adult titles recommended for young adults "may contain mature content and/ or language," *School Library Journal*'s policy for reviewing such titles defends their relevance to young people, arguing that these books may "inspire accelerated students, address the information needs of students in the arts or sciences, reflect popular culture, or speak to the personal interests of teens reading casually or as they seek personal development" (T. Jones 2007, "Adult Books for High School," para. 1). These criteria for the review of adult material can easily be applied to selection of adult material for young adults.

Many adult authors have ventured into the young adult arena and expanded their audience. Adding a mix of adult and young adult titles by these authors is one way to diversify a young adult collection in a way that allows the collection to, in the words of Chelton (2006), "facilitate the transition to adulthood and adult interests." Following are examples of pairings of adult and young adult material by authors who made their names as writers for adults:

1. James Patterson: This author's Maximum Ride series of novels for young readers can be linked to two adult titles that feature the series' characters in secondary roles: *When the Wind Blows* (1998) and *The Lake House* (2003).

2. Robert B. Parker: The author of the Spenser mystery novels for adults also penned a young adult novel featuring Spenser as a young person: *Chasing the Bear: A Young Spenser Novel* (2009). Although Parker's two other young adult novels (*Edenville Owls* [2007] and *The Boxer and the Spy* [2009]) do not feature the fictional private investigator, the classic mystery writer's young adult books could be supplemented by the first adult novel in the Spenser series, *The Godwulf Manuscript* (1974).

3. F. Paul Wilson: This thriller author's Jack: Secret Histories series of novels for young people introduces the hero of the author's adult novels, Repairman Jack, as a fourteen-year-old. Wilson's *Cold City* (2012) is the first of his adult prequels that provide backstory for the Repairman Jack character, who first appeared in *The Tomb* (1984).

4. Peter Abrahams: The adult mystery and thriller author has written a mystery series for younger teens, Echo Falls Mysteries, featuring a female protagonist, as well as the stand-alone young adult mysteries *Reality Check* (2009) and *Bullet Point* (2010).

5. Meg Cabot: The author of the popular Princess Diaries, The Mediator, and Avalon High series, as well as numerous stand-alone young adult novels, has also written a number of light mysteries

and adult romance novels. Her Heather Wells series of mysteries (*Size 12 Is Not Fat* [2005], *Size 14 Is Not Fat, Either* [2006], *Big Boned* [2007], and *Size 12 and Ready to Rock* [2012]) are humorous adult titles that complement her young adult works.

Popular Adult Authors   Following is a brief and certainly not comprehensive list of adult authors of titles that have proven to be popular with and interesting to young people (as indicated in Fitzgerald 2009):

1. Mitch Albom
2. Jane Austen
3. Meg Cabot
4. Agatha Christie
5. Mary Higgins Clark
6. Suzanne Collins
7. Michael Crichton
8. Janet Evanovich
9. John Grisham
10. Charlaine Harris
11. Sophie Kinsella
12. Dean Koontz
13. George Orwell
14. Chuck Palahniuk
15. James Patterson
16. Jodi Picoult
17. David Sedaris
18. Nicholas Sparks
19. John Steinbeck

Sources Recommending Adult Material for Young Adults

1. *Cart's Top 200 Adult Books for Young Adults: Two Decades in Review*, by Michael Cart (ALA, 2013): Retired librarian and current young adult literature expert and *Booklist* columnist and reviewer Cart recommends fiction and nonfiction titles published for adults that also appeal to teen readers.
2. YALSA's Alex Awards: These annual awards are given to ten works of fiction and nonfiction published for adults that may be of particular interest to young people.
3. *SLJ*'s "Adult Books 4 Teens" (http://blogs.slj.com/adult4teen/): Blogging under the auspices of *School Library Journal*, Angela Carstenson and Mark Flowers recommend adult titles for teen readers. This blog—accessible for free online—replaced the regular "Adult Books for High School Students" print column in *School Library Journal* in 2009.

4. *Voice of Youth Advocates* (*VOYA*): Each issue of *VOYA* includes reviews of adult material (listed as "A/YA") that may be of interest to teen readers.

5. *Booklist*'s Editor's Choice: Adult Books for Young Adults: This is an annual list of adult books recommended by *Booklist*'s youth book and media editors for their relevance or appeal to young adult readers.

6. *Teenreads.com*'s "Adult Books You Want to Read" (http://www.teenreads.com/features/adult-books-you-want-to-read): This online column features adult titles reviewed in *Teenread.com*'s sister online publication, *Bookreporter.com*, that may be of interest or appeal to teen readers.

Classic Novels   Classic novels considered works of literature for adults often appear on assigned reading lists and may have a special place in the young adult collection. Although these tried-and-true titles are probably included among the library's adult materials, student versions of them that feature summaries, translations, notes, annotations, and criticism are useful additions to the library's collection for young adults. Although librarians and teachers may look askance at Sparknotes and Cliffs Notes, the Sparknotes' No Fear series (No Fear Shakespeare and No Fear Literature) pair the original text of Shakespeare's plays and literary classics like *The Scarlet Letter* with modern English translations, making these assigned texts easier for less experienced readers to understand. Graphic novel or illustrated adaptations of classic works, like *The Merchant of Venice, King Lear, Beowulf,* and *The Odyssey,* all by Gareth Hinds, or the Classic Canon series published by Seven Stories Press, can also supplement a collection of original works. It is important to note, however, that students are rarely assigned graphic or otherwise adapted literature and, though these versions of classic texts can go a long way in aiding young readers' comprehension of sometimes difficult vocabulary and syntax, librarians with limited budgets should first purchase the original and unedited texts that are required reading to fill students' curricular needs and then try to acquire adaptations to complement and supplement the collection.

New Adult Literature

"New adult" literature is a relatively recent marketing category that is somewhat controversial among young adult literature critics and fans. According to an article in *Publishers Weekly*, the category features titles aimed at reading audiences between the ages of eighteen and twenty-five, and the label "signals content some will consider too mature for teen readers" (Deahl and Rosen 2012, 6). Venerable critic and young adult literature historian Michael Cart (2012) argues that the new adult category is a marketing label that describes "crossover fiction," a category that includes titles published for adults but also read by young adults (like Marcus Zusak's *Book Thief* and *I Am the Messenger*) and titles published for young adults but also read by adults (like Francesca Lia Block's *Weetzie Bat*). Though Cart has noted titles that have achieved success in multiple or unexpected markets, these novels may be distinguished from the latest "new adult" titles based on their intention. That is, whereas Zusak's and Block's books may not have been written for or marketed to overlapping categories of readers, the "new adult" books of today are written expressly for this "in between" audience.

According to the *New York Times*, "new adult" novels "fit into the young adult genre in their length and emotional intensity, but feature slightly older characters and significantly more sex, explicitly detailed" (Kaufman 2012, para. 2). New adult titles feature characters older than the traditionally adolescent young adult protagonist and, according to the vice president and executive editor at William Morrow, Lucia Macro, "the new adult tag speaks more to voice, style and theme" (quoted in Deal and Rosen 2012, 4). Written primarily by younger authors who typically reside on the upper end of the demographic about which they write, new adult titles first emerged in the online self-publishing world, then were taken up by publishers interested in capitalizing on aging young adult readers. Somewhat reminiscent of the "chick lit" and "lad lit" of the 1990s, these "new adult" novels typically feature young and newly independent protagonists—college students or new graduates—who are negotiating their place in the adult worlds of work and romance. According to NA Alley, a website maintained by a group of new adult authors and devoted to discussing the category and marketing their writing, "a novel is considered 'new adult' if it encompasses the transition between adolescence—a life stage often depicted in Young Adult (YA) fiction—and true adulthood" (NA Alley n.d., "What exactly is 'new adult' fiction?," para. 2). According to NA Alley, the "new adult" formula includes several prominent themes ("identity, sexuality, race, alcohol abuse, drug abuse, bullying, empowerment, familial struggles, loss of innocence, fear of failure, etc.") and issues ("living away from home for the first time, military deployment, starting college, engagements and marriages, etc.") that characterize the form (NA Alley n.d., "So what are some common themes," paras. 2, 3).

Like those adult titles read and requested by young adults, "new adult" novels feature content and language that may be considered too "mature" for teen readers; however, libraries that collect adult titles for young adults and shelve or colocate these titles among young adult material should have little trouble stocking this material. The newness of the form precludes the firm establishment of any "classic" authors, although the adult novels of Meg Cabot have been considered crossover examples of the "new adult" genre.

Sources Recommending and Discussing "New Adult" Books

1. NA Alley (http://naalley.blogspot.com/): A blog formatted website created and maintained by a group of new adult authors for promotional and informational purposes, this site includes a page entitled "Catalog of NA Reads" that features new adult titles that fall within the contemporary and speculative fiction genres.
2. A Chair, a Fireplace, and a Tea Cozy's "New Adult: A Recap" (http://blogs.slj.com/teacozy/2013/01/04/new-adult-a-recap/): This blog is published by Elizabeth Burns, who blogs under the auspices of *School Library Journal*, describing the "new adult" form, considering the shelving and categorization of the form in libraries, and listing some titles that may be considered "new adult."

Young Adult Literature

Although varying definitions of "young adult literature" exist in the reading, publishing, teaching, and library worlds, this book defines young adult literature as a publishing category encompassing books written expressly for and/or marketed to an audience of young adult readers between the ages of twelve and eighteen. Young adult literature typically features a protagonist who is the same age as or slightly older than the target reader and exhibits a characteristic narrative voice and tone. Sue Corbett, quoting editor Marc Aronson, observes that the distance between the narrator and his or her fictional experience is key to identifying young adult literature: "A wistful, wiser-now voice of an adult looking back at his youth is the surest way to get a book booted from YA to adult" (2005, 30). This does not mean that young adult novels are devoid of flashbacks; indeed, Maureen Daly's *Seventeenth Summer*, a novel that serves as the arguable prototype for the genre, is told by a narrator looking back on her titular seventeenth summer. Although Angie, Daly's protagonist, is older than seventeen, the first-person narrative still exhibits a kind of naiveté that allows the novel to remain young adult. Literary critics argue that young adult literature is invested in depicting and resolving young people's struggles with institutional authority and control, and this thematic struggle is evident in classic young adult novels like Robert Cormier's *The Chocolate War* and contemporary series like Suzanne Collins's The Hunger Games. Broadly speaking, critics and professionals describe young adult literature as a form of writing invested in capturing an adolescent voice limited by age and experience and describing an adolescent condition characterized by its situation between the trappings of childhood and the freedoms of adulthood.

Because the young adult reader may exist on a broad continuum and be classified, in terms of social and psychological development, as an early, middle, or late adolescent, the body of literature written for this wide demographic includes material written for both experienced and inexperienced readers and in language that may resemble both children's literary and adult literary discourse. Thus, young adult literature describes a broad swath of texts and literatures, not all of which speak to the audience writ large. Novels for younger YA readers may feature characters in middle school and early high school dealing with realistic or fantastic situations familiar to or understandable by less experienced audiences, while novels for older YA readers may feature characters of middle to late high school age facing realistic or fantastic situations familiar to or understandable by more experienced audiences.

In spite of this genre's comparatively short history, critics and professionals have identified a number of "classic" young adult titles that are considered representative. S. E. Hinton's *The Outsiders*, Robert Cormier's *The Chocolate War*, Beatrice Sparks's *Go Ask Alice*, Judy Blume's *Forever*, and Douglas Adams's *The Hitchhiker's Guide to the Galaxy* are examples of classic YA titles published before 1980. More recently recognized classics, like Francesca Lia Block's *Weetzie Bat*, M. T. Anderson's *Feed*, Louise Rennison's Confessions of Georgia Nicholson series, Walter Dean Myers's *Monster*, and John Green's *Looking for Alaska*, represent a newer generation of young adult classic novels. Many of the authors of these classic works have been recognized for their lasting contributions to young adult literature with the ALA's Margaret A. Edwards award, a young adult literary "lifetime achievement" award. Although the majority of the novels cited here are considered realistic fiction, young adult authors writing within more strictly defined generic categories may be considered classic writers as well. Ursula K. Le Guin, Madeline L'Engle, Robin McKinley, Phillip Pullman, Robert Westall, and R. L. Stine, young adult authors known for their fantasy, science fiction, mystery, and horror writing, have produced classic works in these genres, which are described in greater detail later in this chapter.

Authors of "Classic" Works of Young Adult Literature

1. Maureen Daly
2. Paul Zindel
3. Robert Cormier
4. Rita Williams Garcia
5. Christopher Pike
6. William Sleator
7. Jacqueline Woodson
8. Chris Crutcher
9. Gary Soto
10. Aidan Chambers
11. Nancy Garden
12. Sharon Draper
13. Caroline Cooney
14. Cynthia Voigt

15. Paula Danziger
16. M. E. Kerr
17. E. L. Konigsburg
18. Madeleine L'Engle
19. Robert Lipsyte
20. Walter Dean Myers
21. Donna Jo Napoli

Sources Recommending and Discussing "Classic" YA Literature

1. YALSA's Margaret A. Edwards Award (http://www.ala.org/yalsa/edwards): Granted annually since 1998, this honor is bestowed on an author for young adults in recognition of his or her body of work and lasting contribution to young adult literature. The winners, who include S. E. Hinton and Robert Cormier, may be considered "classic" authors of young adult literature.
2. Vandergrift's 100: List of Young Adult Authors and Titles (http://comminfo.rutgers.edu/professional-development/childlit/YoungAdult/100list.html): This list, maintained by Rutgers University professor emerita of library science and youth services Kay Vandergrift, is updated regularly to include young adult literature of historical and contemporary significance. Although, as Vandergrift notes, Vandergrift's 100 is not an exhaustive list of young adult authors and titles, it can serve as a recommended reading list and starting place for those new to young adult literature.
3. *Young Adult Literature: From Romance to Realism*, by Michael Cart (ALA, 2011): The 2011 edition of Cart's 1996 history of young adult literature describes the growth of the literary form and publishing trends such as "crossover" literature; discusses the emergence of literature on the lives of sexual, racial, and ethnic minorities; and includes a discussion of young adult nonfiction.
4. *Literature for Today's Young Adults*, by Alleen Pace Nielsen, James Blasingame, Kenneth L. Donelson, and Don L. F. Nielsen (2013): The ninth edition of this book, which has been used as a textbook in education and library science courses across the United States, provides readers with an introduction to adolescent literacy habits and reading as well as an overview of young adult publishing and literature.
5. *500 Great Books for Teens*, by Anita Silvey (Houghton Mifflin, 2006): The venerable editor's book of 500 recommended titles for teen readers includes both contemporary titles and prototypical examples of young adult literature within a number of genres and thematic categories, including "adventure and survival," "historical fiction," and "war and conflict."

Middle Grade or "Younger YA" Literature

Although many of the classic works of young adult literature recommended and discussed here seem to be pitched to a high school audience, titles written for younger adult audiences—considered "crossover" children's titles or middle grade titles—may be part of the young adult publishing category as well. The eight- to fourteen-year-old members of the middle grade audience in the upper range of childhood and just entering adolescence are called "'tweens" by marketers; in the library they may be readers who select material from both the children's and the young adult collections. In response to the growing population of 'tweens, who, according to *AdWeek* (Chaet 2012), spend $30 billion of their own money and influence up to $150 billion of their family's spending, publishers have been tapping into the 'tween market and developing stand-alone books and series aimed at this audience. Shannon Maughan writes that because 'tweens are the demographic "most closely associated with the societal phenomenon that marketers call KAGOY (kids are getting older younger)," this group offers a unique challenge to publishers (2002, 36). "There is a gap between the sophistication of the issues and images that tweens face in society and the level of maturity that 'tweens possess to deal with such issues and images," Maughan observes (2002, 36). This means that more sophisticated young adult literature may be "too old" for these readers, who nevertheless want to read young adult fiction. Middle grade fiction or "younger YA" literature written for readers on the young end of the spectrum, is a growing publishing category that takes this readership into account.

Younger YA literature typically features characters on the younger end of the spectrum; protagonists may be middle school or junior high school students who are beginning to seek out opportunities for independence. As Patty Campbell notes, "fitting in, or finding a comfortable place in the small world of family and school, is the typical goal of the middle fiction protagonist, while for a YA this venue is to be rejected in favor of the outside world with all its scary possibilities" (2000, 486). Chronicle Books publisher Victoria Rock states that a significant difference between books for younger and older young adults lies in how each handles sexuality and reproduction: "[F]or tweens, [sexuality and reproduction] means getting your period, and for teens it means contraception" (quoted in Maughan 2002, 36). In short, younger young adult literature is, as Campbell writes, "unselfconscious" and "lighter" in tone than young adult literature for older readers (2000, 487). That said, many heady middle grade titles have been honored with a Newbery medal or honor; Lois Lowry's *The Giver*, a 1994 Newbery Medal winner, and Nancy Farmer's *The House of the Scorpion*, a 2003 Newbery Honor and a 2003 Printz Honor book, are often read by and recommended or assigned to students in middle or junior high school who fall on the lower end of the young adult age spectrum. Although these award-winning novels may not be "light," they are less literarily and thematically ambiguous than their older YA counterparts.

Middle grade and younger YA literature may be housed in a library's children's or young adult collections; ultimately, the organization of this material should reflect how young people in this "in-between" age group use the library. Just as some young adult collections contain material for adults that may be colocated in the library's adult collection, young adult collections may house duplicate copies of material shelved in the children's collection. Because the Newbery Award is granted to outstanding material for children, an audience defined by the award as those "persons of ages up to and including fourteen" (ALSC 1997–2013, "Terms," para. 2), and the Printz Award is granted to outstanding material for young adults, defined by YALSA and the awards committee as persons between the ages of twelve and eighteen, some Newbery Award–winning and honor material may also be considered within the realm of middle grade or younger young adult literature, and as was the case with *The House of the Scorpion*, a single book might be recognized by both awards. Thus, copies of the aforementioned Newbery winner and honor books may be found in a library's children's collection with other Newbery titles as well as within collections of required or summer reading in the library's young adult collection. Ideally, middle grade and younger YA books should be shelved where they are most likely to be found by their primary reading audience; however, the library's collection development policy, which should delineate the ages and grades of the young people served by its children's and young adult collections, as well as observed and historical patterns of service to children in the middle grades, will determine where the majority of this material is housed and who is responsible for its selection.

Authors of "Middle Grade" or "Younger YA" Literature

1. Lois Lowry
2. Gary Paulson
3. Avi
4. Jack Gantos
5. Carl Hiaason
6. Ann M. Martin
7. Joan Bauer
8. Kate DiCamillo
9. Louis Sachar
10. Jerry Spinelli
11. Sharon Creech
12. Katherine Applegate
13. Cathy Hopkins
14. Lisi Harrison

15. Cornelia Funke
16. Rick Riordan
17. Karen Cushman
18. Marina Budhos
19. Linda Sue Park
20. Rachel Vail
21. Margaret Peterson Haddix

Sources Recommending and Discussing Middle Grade or "Younger YA" Literature

1. *VOYA*'s "Top Shelf Fiction for Middle School Readers": Published every February in *Voice of Youth Advocates*, this is a list of titles that the journal deems "the best" of material published in the previous year, featuring "themes and subject matter . . . of particular interest to readers aged 11 through 13 or in grades 6 through 8" and that may be considered complementary to the middle school curriculum or especially appropriate as free-reading choices for students in middle or junior high school ("Top shelf fiction" 2012, 541).

2. ALA's Notable Children's Books ("Older Readers"): Each year, the ALSC honors books written for or with special appeal to children in audience categories defined by age or grade, placing these on a list of "notable children's books." Among those titles listed are books for "older readers," which the Notable Children's Books Committee Manual defines as those readers in grades 6–8 or between the ages of eleven and fourteen.

3. *Best Books for Middle School and Junior High Readers: Grades 6–9*, by Catherine Barr (Libraries Unlimited, 2013): The third edition of this bibliography of recommended reading for students in grades 6–9 includes short annotations of fiction and nonfiction titles as well as notes about whether the recommended titles are available in audiobook or e-book format.

4. *Serving Young Teens and 'Tweens*, edited by Sheila B. Anderson (Libraries Unlimited, 2006): This book distinguishes young people in early adolescence, describing library services and recommending fiction and nonfiction resources expressly for this young teen audience.

5. *Readers' Advisory for Children and 'Tweens*, by Penny Peck (Libraries Unlimited, 2010): This readers' advisory resource describes contemporary 'tween publishing trends and 'tween genre fiction and recommends young adult novels for younger YA readers. Peck offers reading recommendations and includes extensive lists of resources for further recommendations.

Selecting Genre Fiction for Young Adults

Genre fiction, literature that conforms to an established style or adheres to conventions of plot, theme, or subject matter associated with a
particular genre, is a popular reading choice for young people and adults
alike. Recognizing reader preferences for various genres, many libraries
have reorganized their fiction collections by genre, shelving mystery, science fiction, fantasy, and romance titles so that patrons can find favorite
and read-alike titles more easily. While professionals continue to argue
over the appropriateness of this form of organization, noting the difficul-
ties inherent in assigning genres to increasingly "genre-bending" literature, genre remains, as Ursula Le Guin asserts, "a method for [beginning
the job of] sorting out and defining varieties of narrative fiction" (2005,
21). Furthermore, as Barry Trott has noted, an understanding of generic
categories and characteristics is a prerequisite for readers' advisors, "for
it is in analyzing genres that we come to understand the stylistic elements
that authors use that will appeal to readers. . . . This knowledge will then
allow us as readers' advisors to connect readers with books they will
enjoy" (Trott and Novak, 2006, 34). The following subsections define and
describe genres of literature popular among young adults, including brief
and representative, but not comprehensive, lists of notable authors and
resources for further investigation and selection in these literary categories. Recognizing the prevalence of the genre-crossing "mash-up" in contemporary publishing for young adults, this section concludes with a
discussion of this phenomenon.

A number of published guides to collecting genre fiction in libraries
and advising readers have been published in the last decade; these sin-
gle-genre guides are excellent resources for both collection development
and reading recommendations. Librarians on a budget, however, may
find broader resources that describe more than one genre of literature
and recommend key authors and texts within each genre just as useful.
The following are representative of such works:

1. *Reading Rants: A Guide to Books That Rock,* by Jennifer Hubert (Neal
   Schuman, 2007): Drawing from her popular Reading Rants website
   (http://www.readingrants.org), Hubert presents annotated bibliographies of recommended books organized thematically and somewhat nontraditionally, focusing on, for example, "The Closet
   Club" (books for LGBTQ teens) and "The Terrible Tweens" (books
   for 'tween readers).
2. *The Teen Reader's Advisor,* by RoseMary Honnold (Neal Schuman,
   2006): Beginning with an introduction to readers' advisory work
   with young people, this book devotes individual chapters to the
   discussion and recommendation of young adult novels in several

forms and genres, including "religion and spirituality" and "social issues."

3. *Teen Genreflecting 3: A Guide to Reading Interests*, by Diana Tixier Herald (Libraries Unlimited, 2010): This third edition of Herald's readers' advisory text features nearly 1,100 annotations and new recommendations. The organization is characteristic of the Genreflecting series and features descriptions and definitions of genres and recommendations for key titles and authors.

Contemporary Realistic Fiction

Although the first young adult novels (then called "junior novels") drew heavily from romance traditions (for girls) and sports reporting (for boys), the rise of the contemporary realistic novel in the late 1960s and 1970s allowed this genre to emerge as the representative young adult form. The 1980s saw the rise of the "problem novel," a genre of fiction that presented accounts of teens facing contemporary social problems like drug and alcohol use and abuse and sexual and domestic abuse in an often formulaic style, eventually leading to criticism of the form. The emergence of more complex and sophisticated narratives in the 1990s resulted in what some have called the "second golden age" of young adult literature, though some critics argued that the realistic fiction of the turn of the twenty-first century was too bleak for readers. At the center of realistic fiction for young adults is the coming-of-age story, a narrative that charts the emotional growth and maturation of the adolescent protagonist.

Opposing impulses may lead readers to realistic fiction. They may seek out realistic novels in an effort to find solutions to their own problems and read about others facing similar challenges, or they may search for realistic stories that diverge from their own experience in an attempt to escape or learn more about the world. Contemporary realistic novels are distinctly more diverse than their 1980s problem novel counterparts and give voice to GLBTQ characters, characters of color, and characters with disabilities; therefore, a library's collection of realistic fiction should represent a spectrum of experiences and ideas. Young adult realism may be tempered with humor, as in the early novels of Ron Koertge, or may involve romance, as characters begin to consider sexual decision making. Novels in verse, like Ellen Hopkins's stories of addiction (*Crank*, 2004) and suicide (*Impulse*, 2008) or Sonia Sones's *One of Those Hideous Books Where the Mother Dies* (2005), in which protagonist Ruby narrates her move to Los Angeles to live with her father after her mother dies, are also gaining new prominence.

Notable Realistic Fiction Authors for Young Adults
1. Jay Asher

2. Laurie Halse Anderson
3. Ellen Wittlinger
4. Chris Crutcher
5. Coe Booth
6. Sharon Draper
7. An Na
8. John Green
9. Paul Volponi
10. Sara Zarr
11. Elizabeth Scott
12. Francisco X. Stork
13. Stephen Chbosky
14. Sharon Flake
15. Jacqueline Woodson
16. Rita Williams-Garcia

Sources Recommending and Discussing Young Adult Realistic Fiction

1. *This Is My Life: A Guide to Realistic Fiction for Teens,* by Rachel L. Wadham (Libraries Unlimited, 2010): This entry in the Genreflecting series recommends contemporary realistic fiction published between 1999 and 2009 for young adults, organizing and grouping annotations into thematic sections for easy reference.
2. *Gay, Lesbian, Bisexual and Transgender and Questioning Teen Literature: A Guide to Reading Interests,* by Carlisle K. Webber (Libraries Unlimited, 2010): This readers' advisory guide recommends and annotates young adult titles that feature both protagonists coming into their GLBTQ identities and protagonists whose sexuality is a secondary consideration. Realistic titles related to GLBTQ identity, genre fiction featuring GLBTQ characters, and graphic novels and manga are represented here.

Romance

According to the 2009 *Teenreads.com* Reader Survey, romance is one of the most popular genres among teen readers. A 2012 *Publishers Weekly* article described growth in this area of publishing for young adults, pointing to the 2009 establishment of the Harlequin Teen line as well as the 2010 creation of Sourcebooks Fire and the 2011 development of Kensington's KTeen romance imprints for teens as evidence of publisher response to this teen interest. While many novels for teens include an element of romance, "pure" romance novels adhere to two primary criteria, outlined by the Romance Writers of America: "the main plot centers around individuals falling in love and struggling to make the relationship work" and these characters, "who risk and struggle for each other and their relationship are rewarded with emotional justice and unconditional love" (RWA n.d., "About the Romance Genre," paras. 3, 4). Teen romances are slightly different from their adult counterparts, as the young adult version of the genre "often combine[s] with coming of age stories, where the process of falling in love is the catalyst for maturing and growing up" (Brannen 2011b). Like adult romances, teen romance novels may be more or less explicit; however, although in adult romances sexual congress is an assumed component or outcome of courtship, teen romance novels do not operate under this same assumption.

Romance novels may appeal to teen readers interested in a primarily optimistic genre; that the protagonists of romance novels are "rewarded with emotional justice and unconditional love" makes these stories incredibly satisfying. Jones, Gorman, and Suellentrop consider this genre "the emotional category that is probably the easiest to match with teens," particularly as young adult romances catalog the "highs and lows" and "trials and tribulations of other teens that may not have the bad skin condition or overprotective parents they find themselves with" (2004, 118, 119). As Jennifer Brannen notes, "romances can be a forum for teens to figure out their own romantic expectations or issues" as well as serve as "virtual test runs for romantic relationships" (2011b). Because young adult romances exist on a continuum between chastity and sensuality, these novels can also provide a certain degree of titillation and even information to curious readers. Romance novels for 'tweens and younger YAs may explore first crushes and first kisses, while romance novels for older young adults may present their characters with more complex physical and emotional challenges. Recent young adult romances have expanded to describe the romantic relationships of GLBTQ characters; David Levithan's *Boy Meets Boy* and Julie Anne Peters's short story collection *Grl 2 Grl* are notable groundbreaking titles in this arena. The supernatural romantic trilogy—made popular by Stephenie Meyer's Twilight—and other romance genre mash-up trilogies like Ally Condie's Matched series have also expanded the genre in length and convention.

Notable Romance Authors for Young Adults
1. Sarah Dessen
2. Meg Cabot
3. Louise Rennison
4. Anna Godberson
5. Melissa de la Cruz
6. Cecily von Ziegesar
7. Simone Elkeles
8. Lurlene McDaniel

Sources Recommending and Discussing Young Adult Romance
1. *Rocked by Romance: A Guide to Teen Romance Fiction,* by Carolyn Carpan (Libraries Unlimited, 2004): This readers' advisory guide in

the Genreflecting series focuses on teen romance and includes annotations of popular titles, discussions of and recommendations of
titles within subgenres like historical romance and romantic suspense, and a list of topical resources.

2. Romance Writers of America's RITA Award for "Best Young Adult
Romance": Granted annually, with this award the association rec-
ognizes a young adult romance novel deemed the best of the year
by the judges.

3. *Romantic Times Book Reviews* (http://www.rtbookreviews.com/):
The online complement to the print magazine reviews romance
literature in all forms and subgenres and features sections devoted
to young adult romance reviews, author interviews, and publishing news.

Fantasy

The enduring popularity of J. K. Rowling's Harry Potter series has
only enhanced existing demand for fantasy novels from young adults.
According to the *Continuum Encyclopedia of Children's Literature*, fantasy, a
genre represented in folktales and folklore and in literature for children,
young adults, and adults, comprises "many kinds of stories variously
featuring talking animals, sentient toys, ghosts, magical powers, time
travel, and lands of make-believe" (Fantasy 2005). Though these stories
and novels involve greater or lesser establishment of the alternative real-
ities or rules that the fantasy genre requires, high fantasy, a term used to
describe "stories of mythic proportions . . . with serious, far-reaching
themes and grand-scale plots that spill over into several volumes" (Fantasy 2005), is what first comes to mind when the genre is mentioned. In
short, however, fantasy is a form of speculative fiction that asks "What
if?" and builds a world in which the answer to this question is fully
realized. The use of or reliance on magic, rather than science, is what
distinguishes fantasy fiction from science fiction, a complementary form
of speculative writing.

Fantasy novels typically invoke mythical archetypes and, as Brannen
notes, may feature characters like "the magician, the witch, the hero/ine,
the mage [and] the necromancer" and "encompass fairy tales and new
worlds, magical creatures and magical realism, humor and darkness"
(2012a). This genre's themes of good versus evil and justice and retribu-
tion contribute to the satisfaction readers obtain from the books in this
category. Sharyn November (2004) has noted a number of tropes associated with fantasy that seem to speak directly to teen readers; for example,
the novels often feature an adolescent or pubescent character who sud-
denly "com[es] into his or her powers, whether intellectual, magical,
physical, or . . . hereditary," an inciting fictional event that can serve as a
metaphor for adolescence (32). The character must then learn to accom-

modate his or her new powers or adapt to a magical situation, plot lines that drive the fantasy and can be read as coming-of-age.

Teen readers' tolerance for lengthy tomes and series is a likely by-product of the popular series, like Brian Jacques's Redwall, that they enjoyed as younger readers, so selectors of young adult fantasy should not be put off by the length of books or series. In addition, many teen fantasy readers enjoy novels written for young people as well as for adults, and because some fantasy authors, like Neil Gaiman and Terry Pratchett, write for both audiences, mixing adult with young adult titles is relatively easy.

Notable Fantasy Authors for Young Adults
1. Tamora Pierce
2. Ursula Le Guin
3. Philip Pullman
4. Robin McKinley
5. Holly Black
6. Jane Yolen
7. Kristin Cashore
8. Rick Riordan
9. Jonathan Stroud

Sources Recommending and Discussing Young Adult Fantasy
1. *Fantasy Literature for Children and Young Adults: A Comprehensive Guide*, by Ruth Nadelman Lynn (Libraries Unlimited, 2005): The fifth edition of Lynn's detailed bibliographic and readers' advisory resource includes annotations of recommended and classic titles as well as thorough explanations of the myriad subgenres associated with fantasy.
2. *VOYA*'s "Best Science Fiction, Fantasy and Horror": *Voice of Youth Advocates* compiles an annual list of the year's best science fiction, fantasy, and horror novels for young adult readers; this list appears in the April issue of the journal.
3. Andre Norton Award for Young Adult Science Fiction and Fantasy (http://www.sfwa.org): Presented annually by the Science Fiction and Fantasy Writers of America (SFWA), this award honors an outstanding science fiction or fantasy novel published for middle grade or young adult readers in the previous year. A list of award winners honored since the award's inception in 2005 can be found on the SFWA website.
4. The Mythopoeic Fantasy Award for Children's Literature (http://www.mythsoc.org): The Mythopoeic Society, an organization dedicated to the promotion, study, and discussion of fantastic and "mythopoeic" literature, grants its Award for Children's Literature to a work of children's or young adult literature and, according to

the organization's website, honors those "in the tradition of The Hobbit or the Chronicles of Narnia."

Science Fiction

Although science fiction and fantasy are often considered in tandem, readers and fans recognize real distinctions between the two genres of speculative fiction. Unlike fantasy, which bases its world building in magic, science fiction is distinguished by its reliance on real or imagined science and technology. Science fiction may be roughly divided into two categories: "hard" science fiction, which focuses on the technical details of the science and technology that inform the fictional world, and "soft" or "social" science fiction, which draws from sociology and psychology and may pay more attention to character development. Dystopian literature, which has been enjoying popularity among young adults, can be considered a type of science fiction as well.

Science fiction novels are often set in the future, in space, or on another planet and may feature robots and clones created by humans or creatures and aliens from other galaxies. Novels in this genre may appeal to readers because, Brannen points out, they "address big issues in an entertaining but serious way. Questions about the environment, human rights, or intellectual freedom can be framed metaphorically or fantastically without losing their power or importance" (2012b). A trope common to science fiction, which November calls "the sudden invasion"—alien arrival, war, or "technology go[ing] berserk"—may be especially appealing to young adults, who may feel that during adolescence, "the world is shaken and made over without your consent, and when there are no easy answers" (2004, 32, 33).

Although science fiction is forward looking, the works of a number of classic authors, such as Isaac Asimov, Robert Heinlein, and Philip K. Dick, remain relevant and influential, despite their publication dates. As in the world of fantasy, many science fiction authors write for young adults as well as adults, and collections of science fiction developed for young adults often include adult novels like Frank Herbert's *Dune* and Orson Scott Card's *Ender's Game*, as well as YA titles.

Notable Science Fiction Authors for Young Adults
1. William Sleaton
2. Scott Westerfeld
3. Madeleine L'Engle
4. James Dashner
5. Douglas Adams
6. Paolo Bacigalupi
7. John Christopher

Sources Recommending and Discussing Young Adult Science Fiction

1. *Anatomy of Wonder: A Critical Guide to Science Fiction*, by Neil Barron (Libraries Unlimited, 2004): Although this resource primarily discusses literature written for adults, this is a thorough introduction to the genre and its subgenres and recommends online resources and science fiction literature for young adults.
2. *VOYA*'s "Best Science Fiction, Fantasy and Horror": See previous annotation.
3. Andre Norton Award for Young Adult Science Fiction and Fantasy (http://www.sfwa.org): See previous annotation.

Horror

Although horror novels may feature supernatural creatures associated with the fantasy novel—vampires, dark witches and wizards, and monsters—the horror genre distinguishes itself as a form of writing meant to evoke a physical, psychological, or emotional response in the reader. Thus, horror novels involve both supernatural and human enemies and, as the suspense is ratcheted up and elements of mystery are inserted into the narrative, may be considered thrillers as well. Patrick Jones identifies a number of elements common to the horror novel for teens: the protagonists are typically teenagers; the supernatural element is often "unspeakable and unexplainable," but, though there might be mentions of black magic, "there is no hard-core satanic activity in these books"; chapters may be short; and, although characters do die in the novels, "with [some] exceptions the body count is not high" (2001a, 9–10). As horror is written to elicit reader response, "gross-out" details, like a description of the desiccating flesh of a zombie, are often included. This is not to say that all horror novels are explicit; gothic horror, for example, is more invested in the psychology of fear and may suggest rather than depict the horrific.

Although not all horror readers relish the "gross-out" factor, fans of this genre appreciate the visceral qualities of the horror narrative. In addition, as Campbell has pointed out, horror novels "connect in a deeply metaphorical way with adolescent concerns about being different, rejected . . . . Revenge for slights is a frequent motif, relating to teens' concern with peer group acceptance. Trust, loyalty, and betrayal are common themes" (1994, para. 6). Other critics have argued that horror novels in general are metaphors for our human fears and social anxieties; if they don't assuage these fears, they acknowledge them. Horror fiction written for young adults may more directly address the "adolescent concerns" that Campbell argues are metaphorical components of the genre; adult horror novels, especially those, like Stephen King's *Carrie* and *Christine*, that feature teen protagonists, do the same in a more or less direct fashion. Because horror readers thirst for literary sensation, many young

adult readers graduate early from adolescent to adult horror and may
even seek out offerings from classic horror writers like Edgar Allan Poe
and H. P. Lovecraft. Including works by these and other classic authors is
one strategy for incorporating "adult" fiction in the young adult collection.

Notable Horror Authors for Young Adults
1. R. L. Stine
2. Christopher Pike
3. Lois Duncan
4. Darren Shan
5. Jonathan Maberry
6. Nancy Holder
7. Carrie Ryan
8. L. J. Smith

Sources Recommending and Discussing Young Adult Horror Fiction
1. *The Suck, They Bite, They Eat, They Kill: The Psychological Meanings of
   Supernatural Monsters in Young Adult Fiction,* by Joni Richards Bodart (Scarecrow Press, 2012): Bodart describes three supernatural
   figures common in young adult literature—the vampire, the
   shapeshifter, and the zombie—and considers representative titles
   written for YA readers that deal with these monsters.
2. Horror Writers' Association's Bram Stoker Award for Young Adult
   Literature (http://www.horror.org): Since 2011 the HWA has recognized young adult novels with its Bram Stoker Award for horror. The organization has also developed a website—linked from
   its main site at http://www.horror.org/yahorror/—devoted to the
   discussion of young adult horror literature in general and featuring interviews with the YA Bram Stoker nominees.
3. *VOYA*'s "Best Science Fiction, Fantasy and Horror": See previous
   annotation.

Mystery

Mystery novels begin with a crime, an unexplained event, or a puzzle
and then challenge their protagonists (and their readers) to determine the
solution. They are typically laced with clues that the protagonist and
reader uncover and then apply to the solution of the mystery. As Brannen
(2011a) notes, although mystery novels may contain "red herrings"—
false clues that mislead the protagonist—the rules of mystery writing
forbid an author to "cheat" a reader. While mysteries written for adults
may feature characters that make mystery solving their careers—police
officers, private investigators, and bounty hunters—the protagonists of
young adult mysteries are typically amateur detectives. In comparison to
adult mysteries, Brannen writes, "YA mysteries usually feature compel-

ling lead characters who find themselves in the throes of plots and peril by seeing things that the adults around them don't" (2011a). When the humanity of the criminal is in question and the narrative suspense is high, the mystery and horror genres overlap in the form of the thriller.

In a classic article for *School Library Journal*, Barbara Moran and Susan Steinfirst describe the appeal of mysteries: "They present puzzles to be solved and wrongs to right . .. The conclusion reassures the reader of any age that there is order in chaos and that, in a disorderly world, justice can triumph" (1985, 116). Mystery readers enjoy competing with the protagonist to uncover hidden clues and solve a mystery in a fictional situation in which "brains frequently triumph over brawn" (Brannen 2011a). Many young mystery fans enjoy the work of a classic writer for adults, Agatha Christie, and this author's works are often found interfiled in young adult collections.

Notable Mystery Authors for Young Adults
1. Joan Lowery Nixon
2. Carol Plum-Ucci
3. Peter Abrahams
4. John Feinstein
5. Christopher Golden
6. Philip Pullman
7. Nancy Werlin
8. Will Hobbs
9. Kirsten Miller

Sources Recommending and Discussing Young Adult Mystery Fiction
1. *Booklist*'s "New Crime Fiction for Youth": This annotated list of newly published mystery and crime novels for young people appears annually in the May issue of the review journal.
2. *VOYA*'s "Clueless? Adult Mysteries with Young Adult Appeal": *Voice of Youth Advocates* compiles in its December issue an annual list of mystery novels published for adults that also appeal to young adult readers.
3. Mystery Writers of America's Edgar Award for Best Young Adult Mystery: Granted annually by the MWA, the Edgar Award honors the best young adult mystery novel published or widely available in the United States in the previous year.
4. Malice Domestic's Agatha Award for Best Children's/Young Adult Novel: Granted annually by the Malice Domestic organization, this prize is given to the Best Children's/Young Adult Novel that falls within the "traditional" mystery category, and like the winners of the organization's adult awards, contains no explicit sex, excessive gore, or gratuitous violence.

Historical Fiction

Although there is some debate about the specific requirements of this genre, all agree that a work of historical fiction is set primarily or entirely in the past, usually in a single historical period or era, and depicts its characters within the historical context of its setting. *Children's Literature Review* (Historical fiction for children 2007) notes that early critics encouraged a definition of historical fiction that specified a historical distance of one generation between author and setting, but more contemporary critics and readers accept that, in the case of historical fiction for young people, a distance of at least twenty years between author and setting is acceptable. The heart of historical fiction lies in its ability to capture and re-create the spirit and culture of the era in which it is set. To that end, authors may attempt to incorporate historical turns of phrase or use antiquated terminology to further portray the historical milieu.

As Melissa Rabey observes, "Most librarians would not think to put historical fiction at the top of a list of fiction genres popular with teens"; the genre's association with school assignments and required reading works against its potential for popularity (2010, 38). That said, the opportunity to experience a historical world, albeit virtually, is as attractive to the genre's fans as the elaborately created and magical realms of fantasy are to its readers. Traditional historical fiction may incorporate elements of other genres, including romance, mystery, and adventure, allowing readers to find a niche within the broad category. The contemporary publication of more "genre-bending" titles and the growing popularity of "steampunk," a genre that depicts a bygone era enhanced by "engineering and technology that is futuristic for that period" (Rabey 2010, 41), expands this often overlooked genre even further.

Notable Historical Fiction Authors for Young Adults
1. Philip Pullman
2. Karen Cushman
3. Ann Rinaldi
4. Kathryn Lasky
5. Elizabeth Wein
6. Ruta Sepetys
7. Judy Blundell
8. Louise Erdrich
9. Karen Hesse

Sources Recommending and Discussing Young Adult Historical Fiction
1. *Historical Fiction for Teens: A Genre Guide,* by Melissa Rabey (Libraries Unlimited, 2010): Part of the Genreflecting series of readers' advisory resources, this book describes subgenres associated with

historical fiction and provides annotations of key titles and read-alike recommendations.

2. *Literature Links to American History, 7–12: Resources to Enhance and Entice*, by Lynda G. Adamson (Libraries Unlimited, 2010): This bibliography recommends and describes historical fiction set in American history from before 1600 to the twentieth century and is notable for its inclusion and recommendation of graphic novels and multimedia resources.

3. The Scott O'Dell Award for Historical Fiction (http://www.scottodell.com/Pages/ScottO%27DellAwardforHistoricalFiction.aspx): Established by author Scott O'Dell in 1982, this annual award is granted to the author of a notable work of historical fiction published within the last calendar year. The award's website includes a downloadable PDF that lists the winners and organizes the titles by era and location of historical setting.

Religious and Inspirational Fiction

Although not technically a genre, works in the categories of religious and inspirational fiction—and Christian fiction, in particular—are often requested by young adult patrons and their families. Not to be confused with "gentle reads," which take care to avoid extreme language, violence, and sexuality, religious and inspirational literature is characterized by its evangelical or affirming religious message; protagonists are typically believers and seek to live their lives enacting their religious faith. Religious or inspirational fiction for young adults often features adolescent characters whose faith is tested in the secular world. These novels may address "edgy" topics, as Melody Carson's True Colors novels do, but offer religious responses to these issues. Christian fiction may be the most visible example of religious and inspirational literature, but literature affirming Jewish and Muslim traditions is emerging in the young adult market.

Religious themes and affirmation can be incorporated in virtually any genre; teens seek out inspirational fiction in familiar or popular genres, looking for both a contemporary read and a spiritual message. Selecting books set in a particular religious context might require more knowledge on the part of the selector who identifies as a religious outsider, because members of religious communities may evaluate religiously themed titles for religious message as well as literary excellence. Consulting members of the community and soliciting recommendations from local churches, synagogues, temples, and mosques is a solid, local first step toward adding this material to the collection.

Notable Religious and Inspirational Fiction Authors for Young Adults

1. Melody Carson (Christianity)
2. Robin Jones Gunn (Christianity)
3. Sonia Levitin (Judaism)
4. Haya Leah Molnar (Judaism)
5. Aliya Husain (Islam)
6. Randa Abel-Fattah (Islam)
7. Rukhsana Khan (Islam)

Sources Recommending and Discussing Young Adult Religious and Inspirational Fiction

1. *Reaching Out to Religious Youth: A Guide to Services, Programs and Collections*, edited by L. Kay Carman and Carol S. Reich (Libraries Unlimited, 2004): This collection of essays describes major religions practiced in the United States (including Buddhism, Hindu, and Latter-Day Saints) and suggests library programs, services, and materials for young people who identify with these religious communities.
2. Association of Jewish Libraries' Bibliography Bank (http://www.jewishlibraries.org/main/Resources/BibliographyBank.aspx): The association posts bibliographies of material for adults, young adults, and children that discuss or address themes and topics related to Judaism and Jewish life on its website and encourages professionals to submit bibliographies of recommended material as well.
3. National Jewish Book Awards (http://www.jewishbookcouncil.org/awards/national-jewish-book-award.html): Presented annually, the National Jewish Book Awards recognize books in more than eighteen categories, including literature for children and young adults, that have significant Jewish content.
4. *The Librarian's Guide to Developing Christian Fiction Collections for Young Adults*, by Barbara J. Walker (Neal Schuman, 2005): This resource provides guidance to those developing collections of Christian fiction and includes recommendations for selection policy writing and lists of award-winning titles.

Urban Fiction

Urban fiction is a relatively new genre of literature that describes, often in gritty detail, the lives of people—typically minorities—in urban and under-resourced communities, making reference to and drawing inspiration from hip-hop culture. Authentic urban fiction is typically written and produced by authors who identify as part of a particular urban minority culture and is published and distributed by independent and often minority-owned presses. The popularity of the genre, especially among people of color, who publishers once erroneously believed were not book buyers, has encouraged the development of urban fiction publishing lines and imprints by major publishing houses, extending the reach of these authors and increasing the availability of urban titles.

Readers are drawn to urban fiction for its high drama, popular culture cachet, and often sensual content. Though urban titles by adult authors like Vickie Stringer and Nikki Turner are popular among young readers, urban novels written expressly for young adults are emerging in the market. These novels feature teen characters growing up in compromising circumstances who must decide whether to continue in The Life or separate themselves from their local communities. Although these novels are written in a vernacular that includes plenty of spicy vocabulary, urban fiction—and especially urban fiction for young adults—is at heart a moralistic genre; truly bad guys get theirs in the end, and virtue is rewarded.

Notable Urban Fiction Authors for Young Adults
1. L. Divine
2. Travis Hunter
3. Babygirl Daniels
4. Darrien Lee
5. Ni-Ni Simone
6. Anne Schraff
7. Sapphire

Sources Recommending and Discussing Young Adult Urban Fiction
1. *The Readers' Advisory Guide to Street Lit*, by Vanessa Irvin Morris (ALA, 2012): Longtime urban fiction advocate Morris describes the genre and its appeal and recommends "teen-friendly" titles and strategies for collecting material in this genre.
2. *Urban Grit: A Guide to Street Lit*, by Megan Honig (Libraries Unlimited, 2010): An entry in the Genreflecting series, this volume describes urban literature and its thematic subgenres, including erotica and prison literature, and includes a list of recommended core titles for adults and young adults.
3. Street Fiction-dot-org (http://www.streetfiction.org): This online resource reviews urban fiction, interviews authors, and includes a section devoted to the discussion and recommendation of titles for young adults.

Genre Mash-ups

Genre "mash-ups," also called novels that bend or cross genres, represent what *Publishers Weekly* has called the "New Black" (Corbett 2012). Paranormal romance novels, which mix horror and romantic tropes, may be the most easily recognizable and ubiquitous mash-up, but steampunk novels, like Scott Westerfeld's Leviathan series, which introduce science-fiction-like speculation to historical fiction, are growing in popularity. In novels that combine genres, elements from each temper and complement the other; for example, as Sue Corbett, quoting literary agent Lucy Carson, notes, "In high concept sci-fi, the love story is what keeps the story 'relatable'"(2012, 24). Thus, readers who may have shunned romance in the past may give a mash-up that blends romance with a favorite genre a try, while readers who balked at historical fiction may find themselves devoted to steampunk.

Readers may be drawn to mash-ups because these novels "push the boundaries of storytelling" (Reynolds 2011) by combining elements of genres and even literary form. Because mash-ups may combine unlikely scenarios and circumstances (e.g., love among the ruins in a dystopian romance), genre-bending titles appeal to teen readers who are "looking for a complex story that sweeps them away from their everyday concerns" (Rabey 2010, 38). The audacious novels published by Quirk Books, which include Seth Grahame-Smith's *Pride and Prejudice and Zombies* and Ben H. Winter's *Sense and Sensibility and Sea Monsters*, as well as fan fiction in the "slash" tradition, can be considered the primary influences on this mixed-up genre.

Notable Mash-up Authors for Young Adults
1. Libba Bray (historical fiction, fantasy, paranormal)
2. Veronica Roth (science fiction, romance)
3. Marissa Mayer (science fiction, fairy tale retelling)
4. Malinda Lo (fantasy, fairy tale retelling)
5. Scott Westerfeld (steampunk)
6. Cassandra Clare (steampunk)

Sources Recommending and Discussing Young Adult Mash-Ups
1. *Fang-tastic Fiction: Twenty-first Century Paranormal Reads*, by Patricia O'Brien Mathews (ALA, 2011): Although this resource does not call itself a guide to mash-ups, it is a reference and advisory text describing material for young adults that includes paranormal content and falls into five categories: soul mate romances, urban fantasy, chick lit, cozy mysteries, and historical series.
2. *Read On: Speculative Fiction for Teens*, by Jamie Kallio (Libraries Unlimited, 2012): Heavy on the fantasy recommendations, Kallio notes that what she calls "speculative fiction" for young adults "[doesn't] follow the rules" and effectively mixes generic tropes like historical fiction and horror. The resource is divided into sections designed to recommend titles according to the appeal factors of story, language, mood, setting, and character.

CHOOSING NONFICTION FOR THE YOUNG ADULT COLLECTION

Informational print resources for young adults are myriad in form and function and are written and designed to answer young adults' information needs and speak to their interests. Young people seek out these resources to aid in completing assignments, learn about topics of interest, be instructed in a new hobby or pursuit, or browse or read cover-to-cover for pleasure. As Ed Sullivan points out, "nonfiction is not just about information . . . for many young adult readers nonfiction serves the same purposes as fiction does for other readers: it entertains, provides escape, sparks the imagination and indulges curiosity" (2001, 44). Literary nonfiction featuring lyrical and even poetic narrative, photo essays and "photobiographies," instructional manuals and how-to-do-it tomes, and series nonfiction should all be considered part of the library's collection for young adults. In spite of their differences in format and style, informational resources and nonfiction written for young adults have two things in common: the extent of their content and the context of this content are based on assumptions about what young people want or need to know, and the structure of the content is purposeful and aims to facilitate traditional reading or information extraction.

Broadly speaking, nonfiction for young adults can be classified in three distinct but overlapping categories: high interest nonfiction, literary nonfiction, and series or reference nonfiction. High interest nonfiction speaks to young adults' extracurricular informational needs and interests and may include how-to books like Christopher Hart's *Manga for the Beginner: Everything You Need to Know to Start Drawing Right Away* (2008), celebrity autobiographies like Eminem's *The Way I Am* (2008), guidance material like *The Seven Habits of Highly Effective Teens*, by Sean Covey (1998), and popular culture–related material like *Glee: The Official William McKinley High School Yearbook* (2012). Nonfiction materials that present information in forms more closely associated with traditional literature, like Marilyn Nelson's *A Wreath for Emmett Till* (2005), which depicts the murder of its titular subject in poetic form, or that blend narrative and graphic images, as Elizabeth Partridge's *John Lennon: All I Want Is the Truth* (2005) does, are representative of literary nonfiction. Those highly structured titles that present primarily curricular information in a way that makes facts and opinion easily extractable are representative of reference nonfiction, much of which is part of nonfiction series, like Chelsea House's Cultural History of Women in America series or the series The Way People Live from Lucent Books.

High Interest Nonfiction

"High interest nonfiction" is a catchall term for nonfiction that addresses topics of cultural, lifestyle, or general interest to young people.

These books may be written as traditional narratives; structured in a point-by-point, expository "how-to" style; or resemble literary nonfiction in their use of song lyrics, poetry, and graphic images. High interest nonfiction is distinguished by its topics: it speaks directly to the contemporary popular culture, leisure, and lifestyle interests of young people with little, if any, didacticism. Those works that are meant to be didactic, like actor Hill Harper's *Letters to a Young Brother: Manifest Your Destiny* (2006) or Amber Madison's *Hooking Up: A Girl's All-Out Guide to Sex and Sexuality* (2005), find their authority in the author's celebrity status, first person account, and direct-to-teens narrative voice.

Although some adults are concerned about the frankness of these titles (like the aforementioned *Hooking Up*) or consider the popular culture focus of high interest nonfiction less than edifying, nonfiction of this type is an invaluable component of a library's collection for young adults. As Jones asserts, this type of "[n]onfiction reading, from the 'Chicken Soup for the Soul' franchise . . . to quickie rock star biographies, helps kids grow by connecting them with their peers and with the world around them" (2001b, 44). Sullivan and others have noted the reluctance of adults to sanction such high interest informational reading; however, as Sullivan notes, "there are a significant number of students who prefer 'the real thing' for their reading" (2001, 45). Reluctant readers in particular may be drawn to titles that have relevance to their own lives and are more direct than literary texts.

Because much of the appeal of high interest titles lies in their currency, collections of high interest fiction for young adults should be contemporary in publication date and topic. For example, if knitting and crafting are popular activities among local teens, *Mary Thomas's Knitting Book* (1972), which features mid-twentieth-century-style illustrations and outdated patterns, is probably not going to cut it. Instead, knitting and crafting books with contemporary cachet, like Shannon Okey's *Knitgrrl 2: Learn to Knit with 16 All-New Patterns* (2006), will attract more attention and get more use. In addition, books about contemporary celebrities, stars, and musicians should be up to date. It is not enough for a library to stock one book about, for example, Justin Timberlake, and consider this topic "covered"; readers want the latest Timberlake title, and if the only J. T. related book available in the library is 1999's *'N Sync with Justin*, by Matt Nutter, this book should be weeded until a more current biography is available. Nutter's 1999 biography may include valuable information about Timberlake's early career, but this information is now both outdated and incomplete.

Finding new and replacement high interest informational reading material can be challenging; Sandra Hughes-Hassell and Pradnya Rodge have observed that "while many journals contain reviews of nonfiction, the real 'pop' stuff often does not get reviewed," leaving librarians and selectors with few—if any—resources for selection (2007, 29). Publishers' and vendors' catalogs that emphasize media tie-in products and popular informational materials can alert selectors to new titles, as can chain bookstores that select and promote nonfiction. YALSA's annual "Quick Picks for Reluctant Young Adult Readers," which includes recommendations of high interest nonfiction as well as fiction, and its "Popular Paperbacks for Young Adults" list, which includes some nonfiction, are additional sources for recommendations. Teens should also be consulted, and their preferences should inform selection.

Literary Nonfiction

Literary nonfiction published for young people is distinguished by its treatment of its subject; it may address topics of high interest to young adults, deal with subjects associated with the curriculum, or address current events, but it does so in a way that distinguishes it from the merely utilitarian. Elizabeth Partridge (2011) argues that the narrative treatment of a nonfiction subject and the presentation of information in a form more associated with storytelling than the expository presentation of facts distinguishes literary nonfiction. Marc Aronson (2006) expands this definition, asserting that the originality of topical treatment is a marker of literary nonfiction. This originality may be expressed in a work's organization and presentation of information, or in the originality of the author's thought. For example, Jim Giblin juxtaposes information in an uncommon way in *Good Brother, Bad Brother* (2005), which pairs the stories of John Wilkes and Edwin Booth, a presentational concept that "existed in no other source" (Aronson 2006, 42). In short, Aronson writes, the point of literary nonfiction "is not just, or even mainly, to give you well stamped-out results. Rather it is to engage the reader in how those results are obtained" (2011, 60).

Selecting literary nonfiction can be difficult, particularly as many of these titles are what Jones, Gorman, and Suellentrop call "'should' reads—books librarians think of as high quality that YAs should read" (2004, 125). These titles may not easily fill a school-inspired information-seeking need or address a topic of immediate high interest, and thus may need more promotion than those books Jones, Gorman, and Suellentrop call "gonna" books (books that young people are "gonna" want to read, no matter what) or "hafta" books, "the books kids need when they have to do homework" (2004, 125). However, for some readers these books are "wanna" books, "books that kids look for when they 'wanna' read a good book" (2004, 125). With its attention to literary presentation and design, literary nonfiction may be read, like fiction, for pure pleasure, and readers who prefer informational rather than fictional topics may turn to literary nonfiction to meet their pleasure reading needs.

As the Common Core State Standards encourage the incorporation of more complex informational texts in the curriculum, literary nonfiction is poised to emerge as an in-demand resource. According to the Common Core State Standards Initiative's "Revised Publishers' Criteria for the Common Core State Standards in English Language Arts and Literacy, Grades 3–12," English language arts programs designed to reflect the Common Core Standards "will need to increase substantially the amount of literary nonfiction they include" (Coleman and Pimentel 2012, 5). The publishers' criteria indicate that, although standard expository nonfiction texts are a key component of the Common Core, literary nonfiction, which includes "the best of nonfiction written for a broad audience, on a wide variety of topics," should be selected as well (Coleman and Pimentel 2012, 5). Adult and young adult nonfiction are among those titles recommended by the Common Core for students and include Phillip Hoose's *Boston Globe/Horn Book* award winner *The Race to Save the Lord God Bird* (2004), Jim Murphy's Newbery Honor book *The Great Fire* (1995), and Russell Freedman's *Freedom Walkers: The Story of the Montgomery Bus Boycott* (2008).

Notable Literary Nonfiction Authors for Young Adults

1. Elizabeth Partridge
2. Marilyn Nelson
3. Marc Aronson
4. Russell Freedman
5. Steve Sheinkin
6. James Cross Giblin
7. Susan Campbell Bartoletti
8. Tanya Lee Stone
9. Phillip Hoose
10. Jim Murphy

Sources Recommending and Discussing Young Adult Literary Nonfiction

1. YALSA's Excellence in Nonfiction for Young Adults award (http://www.ala.org/awardsgrants/awards/117/apply): First granted in 2010, this annual award is bestowed upon a single winning informational title (honors are granted to finalists) published for young adults in the previous year and deemed excellent in writing, presentation, research, and readability.
2. ALSC's Robert F. Sibert Informational Book Medal (http://www.ala.org/awardsgrants/awards/21/apply): This annual award is presented to a single winner as well as selected honor books and is meant to identify a distinctive work of informational literature, written in English by an American author, for children up to age fourteen. Because the audiences for the books awarded the Sibert and the YALSA Excellence in Nonfiction award overlap, the Sibert award may be granted to titles written for a younger YA audience.

3. National Council for the Social Studies Notable Trade Books for Young People (http://www.socialstudies.org/notable): Compiled with the Children's Book Council, this is a bibliography of distinguished informational and fictional texts dealing with social studies topics and written for students in grades K–12. Past lists include fiction and nonfiction for children as well as young adult readers.

4. National Science Teachers Association Outstanding Trade Books for Students K–12 (http://www.nsta.org/publications/ostb/): Compiled annually by the NSTA and the Children's Book Council, this bibliography of science-related titles includes recommended books dealing with science topics for child and young adult readers.

Series and Reference Nonfiction

Series and reference nonfiction titles published for young adults are the workhorses of the library's information resources collection. These books are typically highly structured and curriculum related and are issued in thematic or topical series characterized by a consistent design and treatment of subject. The characteristic designs of individual series make these titles easy to locate on library shelves. Their organization — frequent and descriptive headings, subheadings, and sidebars, as well as indexes that rely on classroom vocabulary — makes the extraction of what Gavin T. L. Brown (2003) calls "verbatim declarations," facts and figures (e.g., the population of certain countries or the dates of specific wars or conflicts) that students are often required to look up and report, expedient. Nonfiction titles in series are not mere collections of facts; rather, they are expository narratives that function to convey information to readers in utilitarian form.

Because series nonfiction is often written to conform to "series templates and readability guidelines set by publishers" (Weisman 2006, 58), these books are often viewed with disdain by librarians and critics. Sullivan, one of series nonfiction's most voluble critics, argues that "series, particularly nonfiction titles, are often quite substandard in quality and substance, and . . . libraries are being charged exorbitant amounts of money for these inferior products" (2000, 42). Sullivan cites two series production practices of which selectors of informational material for young adults should be aware: the tendency for some series publishers to "stretch subject matter to outrageous limits," producing individual installments of series detailing information that "could easily be assimilated into a single concise and comprehensive book," and the "insidious practice of recycling and packaging the same information under new titles," a practice that results in the publication of nearly identical titles sold in more than one series (2000, 42, 43). Avoiding falling prey to these tactics requires a selector to become familiar with series publishers and their lines; although not all publishers engage in these practices, those that do should be avoided.

In spite of reports to the contrary, Kay Weisman writes, "a majority of nonfiction series books are accurate, attractive, well researched, and cover just about any topic a student researcher could request" (2006, 58). Because these books are written in response to changing curricular standards and are marketed and sold to school and public libraries that develop collections to support student research, series nonfiction often includes titles that address curricular topics in a context and language familiar to students from the classroom, making these works more readable and understandable by new, reluctant, or inexperienced researchers. Deciding which series—or series installments—to purchase for the library can be tricky. Kay Bishop advises selectors to "judge each item within a series independently in terms of its value or known needs," warning librarians that often more than one author is responsible for individual titles in a series, which can affect quality (2007, 63). When examining series installments individually, librarians should consider "whether the works function independently of each other, or whether sequential use is required" (Bishop 2007, 63). Series that organize information by date and comprise individual titles devoted to the discussion of specific eras may only be understandable in context, whereas series that organize information in terms of a broad theme (like Facts on File's Issues and Controversies in American History) may be easier to select individually.

It is important to note that many publishers are now making entire series available via database or through e-book platforms, a move that has the potential to impact the way librarians select materials of this type. Douglas Uhlmann notes that e-book platforms offered by series nonfiction publishers "range in size and type . . . with some offering only a few PDFs of print books, and others presenting masses of highly accessorized informational material that may or may not have print counterparts" (2011, 80). The opportunity to lease or own titles, the opportunity to purchase a collection of material rather than individual titles, and the device dependence of the platform are three of many issues to consider when selecting nonfiction series in e-book form. E-book selection is discussed in greater detail later in this chapter.

Sources Recommending and Discussing Young Adult Series Nonfiction

1. *School Library Journal*'s "Series Made Simple": Published in the journal's April and November issues and readable online (http://www.slj.com/series-made-simple/), this frank roundup of nonfiction titles in series features reviews that consider multiple titles in individual series, recommends purchase of notable series, and identifies those series that are less than adequate.

2. *Booklist*'s "Series Nonfiction for Youth": Published in the journal's April and October issues, this column previews series nonfiction published for young people included in publishers' spring and fall lists. The journal also compiles a "top 10" list of the best series nonfiction published for young people in the previous calendar year, featured in a "Top 10 Series Nonfiction" column in the April issue.

3. *VOYA*'s "Series Nonfiction" reviews: Each print issue of *VOYA* features reviews of nonfiction series in a section entitled "Series Nonfiction," basing each review on the examination of two to three titles in the series. These reviews include frank assessments of individual titles and comments on the overall fitness of each series.

CHOOSING GRAPHIC NOVELS, COMICS, MANGA, AND SEQUENTIAL ART FOR THE YOUNG ADULT COLLECTION

Materials that combine image and text to convey information or story are an increasing component of library collections for young people. Graphic novels, comics, and manga are examples of a larger category of communicative media known as "sequential art," a term that describes the arrangement of images and words to present information or tell a story. The comic strips that appear in newspapers can be considered one of the most ubiquitous forms of sequential art; however, comic books, which may tell a short story or relate an episode of a larger narrative, and graphic novels, which may consist of several episodes of a narrative told in comic book form or stand alone as novel-length works of sequential art, are two of the most popular forms of sequential art. Broadly speaking, "graphic novel" is used to describe a format and can include literature and art in a variety of genres and styles, as well as nonfiction and informational resources. Manga, which describes comic books and graphic novels either created in Japan or that adhere to a distinctive style of art and expression associated with Japanese comics and graphic novels, is a popular form of graphic literature often requested by readers and collected by libraries.

Libraries collect graphic novels in response to teen requests, as well as to diversify collections. As Robin Brenner points out, "graphic novels . . . represent an alternative to other formats, not a replacement" (2006, 125). The form's "alternative" status may be the key to its attractiveness; as Brenner and others have noted, graphic novels and comics tend to attract reluctant readers. This is not to say that graphic novels and comics are easy to read; Brenner, citing *The Power of Reading*, reports Stephen Krashen's conclusion that "the average comic book has twice the vocabulary of the average children's book and three times the vocabulary of a conversation between and adult and child" (2006, 125). The linguistic diversity of graphic novels does not guarantee easy readability across the board, however; a brief introduction to graphic novels in a recent issue of *Library Journal* pointed out that "deaf people, those with autism or ADD, and anyone learning a second language may derive special benefit from comics" (Cornog and Raiteri 2012, 53), as readers are challenged to interpret two systems of communication: image and text.

A number of issues unique to graphic novels can make selection and organization of these resources challenging. Graphic novels are published for readers of all ages and, as the Cooperative Children's Book Center notes, "vary widely in quality and content. Some [graphic novels] are mediocre and others are literary masterpieces" (2007, para. 5). Although some publishing companies issue ratings for graphic novel content, these rating systems may vary by publisher and may not align with the age-based and audience-based organization of the library's graphic materials, making selection tricky. This lack of consistent commercial guidance makes the use of review and selection resources even more important for the library just beginning to develop a graphic materials collection. Once graphic novels and materials are selected for the library, organization and shelving may be a challenge. Because not all graphic materials are produced by a single author or artist, shelving graphic fiction by author may result in the separation of titles in series, making it difficult for fans to locate individual installments. Shelving graphic materials according to the Dewey Decimal System, which categorizes all graphic work under the 741.5 call number, or the Library of Congress classification system, which places graphic materials in the PN or NC categories, can be equally frustrating. Christine Pyles recommends shelving graphic novels in a separate area, classifying fictional material first by publisher, then character or series, and then by date, a model that has been "adopted by comic shops for decades and . . . works incredibly well" (2012, 34). Graphic nonfiction material may be assigned a call number based on the topic of the title and interfiled with traditional nonfiction, or be shelved by call number in an area reserved for nonfiction material in this format.

Notable Graphic Novel Authors for Young Adults

1. Neil Gaiman
2. Gene Luen Yang
3. Jeff Smith
4. Barry Lyga and Colleen Doran
5. Ray Fawkes

Sources Recommending and Discussing Young Adult Graphic Novels

1. YALSA's "Great Graphic Novels for Teens" list (http://www.ala.org/yalsa/great-graphic-novels): Compiled since 2007, this annual list includes recommended fiction and nonfiction in graphic form published for young adults, as well as material published for adults that appeals to teen readers.
2. Eisner Awards (http://www.comic-con.org/awards/eisners-current-info): Considered the "Oscars" of comics, the Eisner awards have been granted annually to graphic novels of merit since 1985; since 2008 the awards have included a "Best Publication for Teens" category to honor the best in young adult publishing.
3. *VOYA*'s "Graphically Speaking" column, by Kat Kan: Since 1994, author and reviewer Kan has been reviewing and recommending graphic novels for librarians in *VOYA*. Since 2002, this column has appeared in every issue of the journal.
4. *Library Collections for Teens: Manga and Graphic Novels*, by Kristin Fletcher-Spear and Meridith Jenson-Benjamin (Neal Schuman, 2011): This guide to developing collections of manga and graphic novels for teens provides a brief history of American comics and graphic novels; discusses manga and its popularity; offers tips for collection development, processing, and evaluation; and makes title recommendations.
5. *Graphic Novels Now: Building, Managing and Marketing a Dynamic Collection*, by Francesca Goldsmith (ALA, 2005): This guide recommends strategies for collection development, selection, and organization of graphic material collections and describes processing issues unique to graphic formats.
6. *Understanding Manga and Anime*, by Robin Brenner (Libraries Unlimited, 2007): This guide to graphic materials focuses on the popular manga form and its related anime (Japanese motion picture or television animation), describing unique and common genres, recommending titles, and identifying collection development challenges and issues.

CHOOSING MAGAZINES FOR THE YOUNG ADULT COLLECTION

Researchers describing teen reading interests often cite magazines as a preferred format. Their monthly or weekly publication suggests more timely content; in addition to online sources, these periodicals are sources of current information related to popular cultural topics and figures. Although some teen magazines have moved from print to online, teen magazines still available in print are extended by websites that both advertise the magazine to nonsubscribers and provide online only content to print

readers. As Cathy Hochadel notes, "thanks in part to the use of web
sites . . . [teen magazines] are . . . more sophisticated and cover far more
ground than they did just ten years ago" (2010, 404). Although the number of periodicals published for and marketed directly to teens has de-
creased since the early 2000s, young people remain loyal to the remaining
titles; as of 2011, *Seventeen* magazine was listed by the Association of
Magazine Media among the top thirty-five circulating magazines in the
United States, and *Teen Vogue* was listed among the top eighty-five. *Game
Informer*, a specialty title read by both adults and teens, was listed as the
fourth-highest circulating magazine; while *Rolling Stone*, a music magazine read across audiences, was listed at number 54 (AMM 2011). These
sales trends are reflected in Hughes-Hassell and Rodge's survey of urban
young people, which revealed that young males preferred magazines
about sports, video games, and music, whereas "females chose music
magazines as their favorite, followed by fashion/beauty and video
games" (Hughes-Hassell and Rodge 2007, 25).

The volatility of the teen magazine market makes selecting magazines
for subscription difficult; however, they remain a good investment for
libraries. Although their stapled and glued bindings result in a short life
span, Jones, Gorman, and Suellentrop argue that "if you allow your magazines to circulate, they will often circulate more than any suggestion
from the 'Best Books for Young Adults'," and though they might fall
apart with extreme handling, "with five circulations, a magazine has
served its purpose; five circulations are more than some YA fiction titles
get in a year" (2004, 127). Though sometimes short lived in physical form,
specialty magazines like *Game Informer* and *Shonen Jump* bring contemporary content to library collections that may not be found in other sources.
For example, *Game Informer* previews and reviews electronic games that
may only be available for a short time and offers game-specific tips and
"cheats" for navigating individual game challenges; *Shonen Jump* includes exclusive manga content that may not be published in book form.
Magazines that report on teen celebrity culture, like *Twist* and *J-14*, offer
teens information not included in general interest celebrity magazines
and profile the young stars featured on the Disney Channel and Nickelo-
deon. Unless they make the transition to "adult" entertainment, these
teen stars are not typically profiled in general interest magazines; however, these young actors and actresses have a significant fan base, especially
among younger young adults.

Selecting magazines for the library's collection no longer involves
choosing from a number of general interest titles for teens. As the teen—
and adult—magazine world becomes more specialized and focused on
special interest topics, magazine selection is a process of connecting local
young adult interests to specialty titles. YALSA's "Ultimate YA Bookshelf," which highlights a core collection of "must-have teen materials for
libraries" recommends, at a minimum, the following magazine titles:

Game Pro (no longer being published; *Game Informer* is a good substitute), *Seventeen*, *Rolling Stone*, *Shonen Jump*, and *MAD*. Beyond these "bare bones" titles, librarians should seek out those special interest publications that reflect the needs and interests of their service population.

Notable Magazine Titles for Young Adults

Celebrity

1. *Twist*
2. *J-14*

Fashion and lifestyle

1. *Seventeen*
2. *Teen Vogue*

Manga

1. *Shonen Jump*
2. *Otaku USA*

Music

1. *Rolling Stone*
2. *The Source*
3. *Word Up*

Sports

1. *Thrasher*
2. *American Cheerleader*
3. *WWE Magazine*

Religious affiliation

1. *Sisterhood* (Christian)
2. *Yaldah* (Orthodox Judaism)
3. *New Voices* (Judaism)

CHOOSING AUDIOBOOKS FOR THE YOUNG ADULT COLLECTION

Audiobooks have come into their own since the last decade of the twentieth century. An increase in the ownership of personal listening devices has led to greater demand for a medium that is growing more sophisticated. The "recorded books" of yore have been replaced by "full cast" audio recordings and riveting interpretations of literature by talented narrators, elevating the audiobook from functional to artistic. Though some have wondered if the rise of audiobooks spells the end of traditional reading, recent research and professional writing have described the benefits of audiobooks and noted that, in some cases, listening to a book can aid in traditional reading development. According to Gene Wolfson, "Audiobooks may be used with adolescent readers to improve fluency, expand vocabulary, activate prior knowledge, develop comprehension, and increase motivation to interact with books" (2008, 110). When young people hear unfamiliar words read with expression, their meaning becomes clear in context, and comprehension grows. For example, full-cast audio versions of Shakespeare's plays make understanding the Bard's language—and stories—much easier. Readers who are already motivated to read may find, as do many avid adult readers, that the portability of audiobooks allows them more time to "read" and increases the number of books they can devour. For avid readers and reluctant readers, audiobooks offer a literary experience that has many of the same benefits afforded traditional print readers.

Developing a collection of audiobooks involves determining which of many formats are most accessible to library patrons. Audio versions of books may be recorded on CD, preinstalled on portable listening devices like Playaways, or available to download as audio files. Collecting material in any or all of these formats has benefits and drawbacks. CD recordings of books are perfect to listen to in the car and on long trips can make reading and listening a family experience. Readers may find the multiple CDs associated with a single title too cumbersome, and teens, who may not enjoy a long solo commute to school the way adults do, may not choose these for regular drive-time listening. Furthermore, as the audiobook publishing world slowly moves from CDs to downloadable files, the number and variety of titles to select in this format will inevitably decrease. Playaways, small, portable listening devices that fit in a user's hand or bag, come with the audio version of a single title preinstalled. Readers don't have to fiddle with multiple CDs and can take Playaways almost anywhere; however, the one title per playaway limit means borrowing more than one audio title and juggling multiple players. Downloadable audio files can be borrowed from the library and installed on personal computers or portable devices, a process that may be accomplished from home by visiting the library's digital materials website or online catalog. The transferability of files remains an issue; not all audio files can be heard or accessed with all devices, and sometimes users must download a driver or player to facilitate access and "manage" the rights to the digital content (digital rights management, DRM) (See table 5.2).

Librarians selecting audiobooks look to the library's mission and collection development statements and consider the needs and interests of patrons, just as they do when selecting print material. However, because audiobooks can be more expensive to produce and require technology for access, a number of unique issues affect the selection of material in this form. Although audiobooks are increasing in number, diversity, and availability, Raya Kuzyk, *Library Journal*'s former media editor, notes that

Table 5.2.   Audiobook Formats, Circulation Models, and Selection Issues

Audiobook Medium	Pros	Cons	Circulation Models	Selection Issues
CDs	Familiar media	Limited portable playability	"Traditional" check-outs from library branches	Not all material published in print form is available in "library editions" Library editions may be more expensive for libraries to purchase than consumer editions
Playaways and Pre-loaded devices	Portable Simple device interface	Multiple devices necessary for multiple titles Device— earbuds and battery— requires disinfecting and maintenance	"Traditional" check-outs from library branches	Selection is limited to what is made available by device wholesaler
Downloadable audio files	Portable Patrons may select and download material from home	DRM software can be difficult for users to negotiate and install	Circulation period may be restricted by content provider	Material is limited to that made available by digital wholesaler

"not all titles available in print are available on audio, and many of those that are aren't available for library purchase" (2011, 34). Furthermore, Kuzyk points out, while the number of titles released in print and audio versions simultaneously is increasing, there is still a lag time between reviews of print and audio content that affects these materials' availability and their selection. This means that a library's audiobook collection— in any format—may not be as contemporary as its print collection, and selection may be limited to what has been produced. Librarians must also consider the accessibility of this medium; in communities where electronic gadget ownership is low among young people, audiobooks in formats that require personal devices may be inaccessible to users. All selection decisions are delimited by material availability, but libraries investing in playaways must select from those that the company makes available for library purchase, and libraries that rely on digital audiobook wholesalers to facilitate patron access to downloadable content can only select content based on what the wholesalers make available.

As more libraries develop diverse collections of digital media, including audiobooks in downloadable digital file form, they must establish relationships with digital media wholesalers, "jobbers" that make digital information available to libraries for patrons to access and use. Libraries or consortia enter into contracts or relationships with a digital jobber— Overdrive is currently the largest distributor of such digital media to libraries—which builds a website populated with the library's audiobook selections for patrons to browse and download, which is then linked to the library's online catalog. New material selection may be granted to the digital media wholesaler, which bases its selection of new material on a "profile" created by the library, or may be the responsibility of one or more librarians. Whether this content is selected by the wholesaler or by a librarian, as with book and print materials jobbers, the universe of material from which to select is limited to that made available by the jobber.

Because patrons may only access downloadable media via the library's electronic catalog, digital audiobooks selected for young adults must be promoted to ensure their use. According to OCLC's 2010 "Perceptions of Libraries" report, less than half (42 percent) of young adults aged fourteen to seventeen reported using the library's website. Unless young adult patrons are made aware of this service, it seems unlikely that they will "stumble upon" the library's virtual collection; thus, librarians should make teens aware of digital material in the library.

Sources Recommending and Discussing Young Adult Audiobooks

1. *Audiobooks for Youth: A Practical Guide to Sound Literature*, by Mary Burkey (ALA, 2013): This guide to audiobooks is not a readers' advisory guide, per se, because it does not include an extensive list of recommended titles; however, it does introduce readers to audiobooks—their production, distribution, and benefits to readers and listeners—and offers suggestions for developing collections of audio material for young adults.

2. YALSA's "Amazing Audiobooks for Young Adults": This list of recommended audiobooks for young adults is compiled annually and consists of titles produced in the previous two years (e.g., the 2013 list includes audiobooks released between 2010 and 2012). The annotated list of twenty to twenty-five recommended audiobooks consists of material that might "appeal . . . to any or all potential listeners between the ages of 12 and 18 years old" (YALSA 2008, "Criteria") and may include both fiction and nonfiction titles.

3. YALSA, *Booklist*, and ALSC's Odyssey Award for Excellence in Audiobook Production: Granted annually to the best audiobook

produced for children or young adults, the Odyssey Award honors a single title (runners-up are granted honors) for its technical and aesthetic excellence.

4. *VOYA*'s "Audio Talk" column: Featured in the journal's April, August, and December issues, this column recommends and reviews unabridged audiobooks that appeal to young adult readers and listeners.

5. "The Audies": Awarded annually by the Audio Publishers Association (http://www.audiopub.org/), the "Audies" honor the best audiobooks produced during the previous calendar year in several categories, including audiobooks for teens.

CHOOSING E-BOOKS FOR THE YOUNG ADULT COLLECTION

Electronic books, or e-books, are emerging as the latest additions to library collections; as they become "an established part of library services, it is critical for teen librarians to be aware of what's going on in the world of e-books and how teens are and will be using them" (Braun 2011b, 27). To date, e-book content is available in two forms: as digital files that can be downloaded to personal readers, tablets, or other devices, and as digital content that can be accessed via networked resources like Google Books, Project Gutenberg, EBSCO, and ProQuest and read using a web browser or downloaded to a personal device. This content may be captured in a variety of file formats, each of which may require compatible software to be read; for example, PDF (which requires Adobe Acrobat), EPUB (which some argue is emerging as a universal format; it can be read by most e-reader devices and software), and MOBI (which is only recognized by Kindle readers and Kindle e-reading applications). Like audiobooks, use of these materials requires patron facility with and access to specific technologies. Some libraries have experimented with loaning preloaded e-readers to users, but most e-book content requires readers and users to have access to an Internet- or network-enabled computer or to a device onto which e-book content can be downloaded and read.

The collaborative or singular nature of the agreements that govern a library's acquisition of electronic books will ultimately determine the degree of control a single library or librarian has over selection. Because of the high cost associated with licensing e-book content, many public libraries rely on library consortia to negotiate agreements with electronic content vendors and aggregators and make this content available to library patrons. Although these agreements allow libraries with limited budgets to make e-book content available to library users at a reduced cost to the member library, because the selection of this content is facilitated at the consortial level, individual libraries and librarians may have limited input into the selection process. Furthermore, because agreements regarding content and level of access are negotiated at the consortial level, as Sue Polanka notes, "the unique needs of libraries may not be met through group purchases" (2011, 6).

As with decisions regarding the purchase and acquisition of print and multimedia resources, e-book selection decisions should be made with the needs and access capability of the library's users as well as the library's mission and goals in mind. With regard to patron needs, Anne Behler (2011) advises that librarians contemplating e-book collections first determine which devices and technologies are used by patrons, what library patrons' expectations of e-books might be, and how the library's e-book collection might complement or extend the print collection. Knowing which devices patrons use—and knowing whether such devices are accessible to library patrons—is the first step in e-book collection development; this knowledge allows librarians to determine whether to spend budgetary funds on devices for lending as well as electronic content. Second, understanding how patrons might use e-books is also important: "Whether library users will be doing leisure reading or research will determine a number of decisions, from what vendor is chosen to what digital rights management (DRM) . . . model is appropriate" (Behler 2011, 2). The answers to these first two questions inform the direction of a library's response to the third question, regarding the purpose of the e-book collection. That is, understanding how and why patrons might use the library's e-book collection will help determine whether to include duplicate copies of print titles or unique e-book content. The library's mission and goals for its collection should also affect e-book selection. As Polanka reminds us, "for anyone contemplating purchasing e-books, asking why is the most important question" (2011, 4). Libraries may purchase e-books in an effort to expand their collections or replicate existing collections in an effort to make resources available to users in multiple formats. These reasons for developing e-book collections influence whether a library selects unique material or duplicate copies of existing material.

E-books may be selected in two ways: on a title-by-title basis by a selecting librarian or a library user (PDA), or en masse as predeveloped collections. The title-by-title strategy is probably most familiar to selectors of young adult material and, as Cynthia Cleto notes, "provides institutions with the flexibility to supplement their print catalogs with targeted selections and ease into an e-book strategy slowly" (2008, 47). Collections of e-books to which libraries may subscribe—like EBSCO's eBook High School Collection or eBrary's Schools and Educators Complete—offer libraries an opportunity to lease multiple titles for a fraction of the cost of buying individual titles; however, libraries must resubscribe to these collections to ensure continued access, and if the library chooses not to renew its subscription to this content, it essentially disappears from the library's collection. Options to purchase high-use titles may be available from subscription package sellers, and libraries may choose to phase out the subscription plan to focus on title-by-title development in more focused, high interest areas.

Because to date many of the largest publishers of trade materials either refuse to sell e-books to libraries or restrict access to content via embargoes or by making limited content available for library licensing, selectors of e-books for libraries find their choices delimited. Unfortunately these limitations often affect the ability of libraries to make available to patrons the same range of popular and "front list" titles in e-book form as they might in print form. Because these best-selling titles are among the most requested by library patrons, publishers that do not let libraries lease these titles (or that embargo these titles) restrict libraries' ability to respond to patron demands in a timely manner.

Libraries that choose to subscribe to e-book collections—like the aforementioned High School Collection or Schools and Educators Complete—find that the job of materials selection has already been accomplished by the vendor that makes the e-book collection available to libraries. These collections are limited to preselected offerings from a finite group of publishers with which the vendor or aggregator has negotiated, and although the materials in these collections may be appropriately topical, they may not reflect—on a title-by-title basis—the selection decisions of the local librarian.

CHOOSING MULTIMEDIA MATERIAL (INCLUDING MUSIC, FILM AND VIDEO, AND VIDEO GAMES) FOR THE YOUNG ADULT COLLECTION

Multimedia materials, including music available on CD, movies available on DVD or Blu-ray, and video games created for multiple game consoles, are an important component of the library's young adult collection. Materials in these formats are among the highest circulating in the library and, as Jones, Gorman, and Suellentrop note, "are often a catalyst to get teens in the door of a library" (2004, 135). Because multimedia content is available in formats that may be in flux, and because this content is often tied to popular cultural interests, it is important for library collections of multimedia material to be current in topic and form. Selecting multimedia material requires librarians to consider issues of access and accessibility and be alert to new media delivery and lending methods, particularly as streaming music and video services emerge in the consumer and library marketplaces.

Selecting Music for Young Adults

Music is an important component of library collections in general and a key component of library collections for young adults. Popular music collections appeal to all library patrons, regardless of age; therefore, before selecting music for young adults, it is important to understand how the library selects and organizes its music collection in general. Libraries with popular music collections for "general" use may include music of interest to young adults; if this music is selected by a single librarian, the duty of the young adult librarian may be to ensure that music requested by young adult patrons is a part of this collection. Libraries that house collections of music in separate physical locations—for adults, young adults, and children—may find themselves investing in duplicate copies of popular music titles, just as they may invest in duplicate copies of adult books with young adult appeal and readership for the young adult print collection. Chelton advises "buying and placing YA-interest items [like popular music] in the YA collection in the first place, and exclusively there if only one copy of an item is purchased" (2006, 11), but this may not always be feasible. By ensuring that copies of music produced by artists with more cachet among young people than among adult popular music fans (like Jesse McCartney and One Direction), the library can develop a general popular music collection to reflect the interests of its adult and young adult patrons.

Whether popular music is housed in a general collection or in more than one physical location, librarians selecting music for young adults should do so with significant input from their young adult patrons. Because different genres of music tend to be popular in different communities and among different age groups, consulting the library's teen patrons ensures that the library's YA music collection is timely and relevant. Kate Pritchard (2010) suggests using streaming music sites to solicit critiques of current titles or suggestions for purchase. Streaming websites like Grooveshark, last.fm, and Pandora, which include social networking components and suggest new titles to users based on the playlists they develop, can be used, as Pritchard used Grooveshark, to develop and share playlists and solicit library users' opinions and suggestions. The *Billboard* charts, readable online, may be an additional source of inspiration. The *Billboard* "Top 200" chart lists the best-selling albums each week and includes material from all genres, including Christian contemporary and Latin music. When accessed online, the "Top 200" chart can be sorted by the number of weeks an album has spent on the chart; if chart presence is a signal of popularity, a list of albums that spent significant time on the top of the album chart can serve as a buying guide or checklist.

Music produced by local young adults—recordings of garage bands, show choirs, or a cappella groups—can be an exciting addition to a library's young adult music collection. Music produced locally and consumed in local youth "scenes," like those associated with hardcore, straight edge, and punk, could expand this collection further while acknowledging the creativity in local youth subcultures. Matthew Moyer and Andrew Coulon, who describe a local music collection initiative at the Seattle Public Library, point out that collecting local music allows the library "to offer content that reaches beyond market saturation and exposes patrons to a variety of styles and genres" (2012, 47). If housed in a space dedicated to the young adult collection or reserved for teen use, a collection of local music could complement the general popular music collection used by all patrons. Moyer and Coulon recommend establishing a solid collection development policy for local music material that emphasizes the scope of the collection and acknowledges the continued local use of "outdated" formats like records and cassettes, making exceptions for these materials.

Selecting music for young adults involves considering access and intellectual freedom issues that remain controversial among librarians and the public. Since 1985, the Recording Industry Association of America has been working with record companies to label music with explicit content with a "Parental Advisory" sticker or logo. This sticker (PAL), which reads, "Parental Advisory: Explicit Content," is a voluntary addition to the packaging of physical media and is meant to indicate that the content includes "strong language, sex or substance abuse" to an extent defined by the RIAA as extreme, according to standards established by the association (RIAA 2013, "Guidelines and Requirements," para. 1). The presence of a PAL on a product affects the product's marketing and sales; as the RIAA notes, "a good number of traditional retailers have in-store policies prohibiting the sale of records displaying the PAL logo to those younger than 18" and some digital music providers, which make similar use of the logo, are implementing similar "parental control mechanisms" (2013, "Background," para. 7). Because the PAL is descriptive and, in the words of the ALA, "ha[s] no legal standing," the presence of such a label should not affect a librarian's decision to select the item or place it in an age-restricted collection of material. As the ALA's "Access for Children and Young Adults to Nonprint Materials" states, "Librarians have a responsibility to ensure young people's access to materials and services that reflect diversity of content and format sufficient to meet their needs" (2004, para. 10). Young people's musical tastes and interests are not "limited by subject, theme, or level of sophistication" (ALA, 2004, para. 10), and collections of music selected for young adults also should not be limited.

Sometimes record labels encourage artists to produce edited versions of content that may be otherwise described with a PAL. Edited versions of music content are denoted with a label that reads "Edited Version" and signals to purchasers that some content has been voluntarily edited from the original source. The RIAA notes that the presence of an "Edited

Version" label does not necessarily indicate that all "potentially objectionable" content has been removed from a recording, only that the "sound recording does not include all of the same content contained in the original" (2013, "Edited Versions," para. 1). Edited versions of original music may be considered "expurgated" works; as the ALA advises, "The decision of rights holders to alter or expurgate future versions of a work does not impose a duty on librarians to alter or expurgate earlier versions of a work" (2008a, para. 4). The ALA encourages librarians to avoid expurgated editions "in the interest of historical preservation and opposition to censorship" (2008a, para. 4). Although some adult and young adult patrons may prefer edited versions of content, the library should not base a purchase decision on the existence of an edited version. Recognizing the validity of preference suggests that librarians should try to purchase both the original and voluntarily edited versions of music and allow the decision to borrow or access such material to rest in the hands of library patrons.

Digital Music Content

Just as libraries are accommodating user preference and demand for print and electronic reading material, they are also developing electronic collections of music for patrons to download. Because the ownership of such digital content is somewhat questionable, some libraries have allied with digital music services, like Overdrive, which supplies libraries with e-books as well as downloadable audio and video, that allow users to select and download music from a catalog of choices much larger than those music collections maintained by most public libraries. The current major digital music distributors to libraries, Overdrive, Alexander Street Music, and Freegal, provide libraries and patrons with music in two distinct ways. Overdrive and Alexander Street Music allow libraries to "subscribe" to their collections and facilitate patron access to mp3 files that "self-destruct" and become unreadable after a specified period of time, a lending model that imitates, to some degree, the print model of lending. Freegal provides libraries with music free of digital rights management software, which patrons may download and effectively own. Libraries enter into a "pay-per-download" contract with Freegal, setting caps on the number of downloads allowed through the library's account within the fiscal year or the terms of the contract in an effort to manage the cost of the service. With regard to young adults, Freegal offers the largest catalog of popular downloadable music, allowing libraries access to material from the entire Sony music catalog; Overdrive and Alexander Street offer much fewer popular choices. Though Freegal would seem to be the obvious content provider for YA librarians, the cost of an unrestricted pay-per-download service could be untenable; thus, the limits libraries impose on the number of downloads patrons are allowed within a specific time frame, or the caps libraries place on the number of downloads charged to the library, effectively restrict access.

As libraries and librarians consider the cost and access issues associated with purchasing or leasing digital music to lend to patrons, YA librarians can direct patrons to websites that offer free (and legal) music downloads. The Recording Industry Association of America (RIAA), under the auspices of its Music Matters website (www.whymusicmatters.com), lists online services that offer users opportunities to purchase digital music, subscribe to digital music services, or download music files for free. Each of the services listed is "authorized" by RIAA, meaning that the content owners, producers, and distributors are fairly compensated for the files available for download on each site, making free and low-cost downloading legal. Although the library cannot legally download songs from these sites and then make them available to library users as a way of developing an electronic music collection, YA librarians might consider pointing patrons to the Music Matters site or providing links to the free and RIAA-authorized sites so that young patrons can access and download their own music selections.

When it comes to digital music lending, Mark Flowers (2010) argues, libraries and librarians are "late to the party." "Libraries need to be in the online music business," asserts Flowers. "There is a whole generation of potential library customers, and large portions of a number of other generations, that don't use CDs" (2010, 37). The way young people consume music has changed significantly in the last twenty years. Listeners are no longer tied to albums or CDs, because the advent of digital media has allowed consumers to pick and choose which material to download, keep, and add to personal playlists. This means that the next step for libraries is to develop solutions for digital media so that library collections will be composed of content that reflects not only the needs and interests of users, but also the formats library patrons use to consume it.

Selecting Film and Video for Young Adults

Popular film and video available on DVD or Blu-ray disc for patrons to borrow is among the most popular content available at the library. According to a *Library Journal* report on its most recent examination of trends, "Media Consumption and Library Use," 27 percent of survey respondents reported that "libraries are their primary source for movies" (Enis 2012, 18). Just as music collections attract library users, the opportunity to select and borrow movies—for free!—can attract patrons to the library. Popular video collections that include not only movies created for teen audiences, but also mainstream films and television shows popular among young adults, will "not only make the library a 'cooler' place for teens to frequent, [they] will make us more teen-service oriented and teen-customer responsive" (Jones, Gorman, and Suellentrop 2004, p. 141).

Furthermore, the recent rise in popularity of multimedia literary products for young adults—like Sara Shepard's Pretty Little Liars book series,
which has also been made into a television program, or Kami Garcia and
Margaret Stohl's Beautiful Creatures series, the first novel of which has
been made into a major motion picture—allows the library to emerge as a
one-stop shop for young people interested in accessing their favorite titles in a variety of forms. Although the popularity of streaming video
services like Netflix and Hulu suggests an approaching end to the era of
DVDs and Blu-ray discs, DVDs nonetheless remain a library resource
valued by patrons. Though some libraries worry that commercial streaming services will draw patrons away from the library and its collection of
media, *Library Journal* reports that "a well-curated collection targeting the
local community will keep circulation steady or growing" (2012,
"Monopoly," para. 3). For YA librarians developing collections of film
and video, the "local community" consists of the library's teen patrons,
and a "well-curated collection" consists of material with relevance and
appeal to this population.

Library film and video collections for young adults include teen movies, mass market films, and television series in live action and animated
formats. Teen movies are those mainstream and cult films featuring teen
protagonists that are produced and marketed primarily for an audience
of teens and are typically released with a "PG" or "PG-13" rating. Classic
movies like *Sixteen Candles* (1984), *Ferris Bueller's Day Off* (1986), and
Heathers (1988), as well as newer titles and soon-to-be classics like *Ten
Things I Hate About You* (1999), *Bring It On* (2000), *Twilight* (2008), and *The
Hunger Games* (2012), all fall within this category, though *Sixteen Candles*
and *Heathers* were both given "R" ratings. Mass-market films that
screened to general audiences but that have teen cachet and appeal are
those titles like *The Social Network* (2010) and the *Scream* and *Final Destina-
tion* franchises of films, typically released with "PG-13" or "R" ratings,
that have been viewed and taken up by audiences of adults and young
adults alike. Television series produced for young adults, like *Degrassi:
The Next Generation, Pretty Little Liars, The Secret Life of the American Teen-
ager,* and *Teen Wolf,* are an additional form of content in teen film and
video collections. Typically released in the form of multiple discs that
include a single season of episodes as well as "behind the scenes" footage
and interviews with directors and actors, or as single discs that include
two to four episodes, collections of television series may include dramas
like those mentioned previously, reality shows like MTV's *The Hills,* and
documentary series like MTV's *Real Life.* Television series and teen-tar-
geted or mainstream movies in cartoon or anime form are a second category of film and video material collected for teens. The popular cartoon
series *Ren and Stimpy* and anime series *Sailor Moon* are characteristic of
this content. Animated movies, like *Beavis and Butt-head Do America* (1996)
and *The Incredibles* (2004), as well as those associated with the anime

tradition, like *Howl's Moving Castle* (2004) and *Akira* (1988), exemplify this form.

That many movies that appeal to young adults are released to theaters with Motion Picture Association of America (MPAA) ratings of "PG-13" and "R" makes selection of film and video content for YA collections somewhat problematic. As the ALA notes, "MPAA ratings," like those PALs found on some music products, "are private advisory codes that have no legal standing" (2004, para. 9). While movie theaters may restrict access to films based on their ratings, libraries are under no obligation to restrict access to material based on those ratings. In "Labeling and Ratings Systems" ALA notes that labels denoting a work's rating can be used as directional aids or can be seen as "attempts to prejudice or discourage users or restrict their access to materials" (2009, para. 2). When libraries refuse to allow patrons to borrow material based on its rating, this is considered prejudicial rather than directional. When libraries organize material according to a ratings system, the ratings label becomes a facet of description. For example, a library may collect and shelve material rated "G," "PG," "PG-13," and "R" in distinct areas of the library, which allows users to browse and borrow items that meet their own definitions of appropriateness.

Because the issue of movie ratings is somewhat fraught in libraries, it is important to examine the library's collection development policy before selecting films for young adults. The collection development policy should include language describing the criteria the library employs for selecting audiovisual material; these criteria may be addressed and detailed in a supplemental policy governing the selection of material for young adults or in the library's general policy. Collection development policies that mention movie ratings range from general to specific. For example, the Alachua County (FL) Library District's policy states that "no attempt will be made to label materials as to perceived appropriateness for viewing audiences" and cites the ALA's Statement on "Labeling and Rating Systems" and "Access for Children and Young Adults to Nonprint Materials" in support of this policy (2011, "Audiovisual Materials and Digital Content," para. 2). The Forbes (Northampton, MA) Library's statement acknowledges that material rated "PG-13" and "R" may be purchased for the library's collections of children's and young adult video and points out that "the Movie Ratings System and an explanation of the rating system is posted for parents and caregivers" (2012, "Children's and Young Adult Materials," para. "b"). This statement alludes to the relevance and popularity of "PG-13" and "R" rated movies for young audiences; supports the inclusion of such titles as part of youth materials collections; and by maintaining patron access to an explanation of the movie ratings system, allows patrons to make their own decisions about the appropriateness of materials.

Selecting films and television content for young adults involves considering issues of technological access. Movies and television in physical
recorded form are available in competing formats: DVD and Blu-ray.
DVDs are familiar to most librarians and comprise the bulk of most library media collections. Blu-ray is a newer technology and a competing
format. Developed to allow for the storage, recording, and playback of
high definition video, Blu-ray discs offer viewers high definition picture
quality and superior audio and boast greater storage capacity than traditional DVDs. Blu-ray discs offer higher quality playback, but they cannot
be played on DVD players and may not always be viewable on television
screens that are not equipped to handle high definition. Blu-ray users
must purchase Blu-ray players—which also accept DVDs—or view the
discs through Playstation 3, which can act as a Blu-ray player. According
to a report issued in 2010 by Centris, a market research firm, 17 percent of
American households owned "at least one Blu-Ray device," compared to
88 percent of households that reported owning a DVD player. Although
this discrepancy suggests that Blu-ray discs may not be the best choice for
library media collections, Centris noted that more households that included children and young adults tended to own Blu-ray players, an
observation that has the potential to affect format choices for library collections for young people.

Although library budgets may not cover the purchase of the same title
in more than one video format, it is important to note that because Blu-
ray discs have greater storage capabilities, Blu-ray releases often include
more "bonus" content—director's commentary, interviews with actors,
behind the scenes footage—than DVD releases. The uniqueness of this
content suggests that, in the case of high-demand video, libraries may
consider having dual versions of a single title an asset. For example, the
single-disc Blu-ray version of *Twilight* includes director commentary,
three music videos, ten deleted scenes—five of which feature director
commentary—a documentary, and three trailers, whereas the single-disc
DVD version of the movie includes only five deleted scenes, the music
videos, and director commentary. Making Blu-ray and DVDs players
available to patrons in the library is one way to overcome the access
issue. Viewing stations featuring devices that allow users to watch Blu-
ray or DVD content provide library patrons with the opportunity to access material in forms they may be unable to view at home.

Streaming and Digital Video

The growth and popularity of commercial streaming video services
like Netflix and Hulu have led libraries to consider entering the streaming and digital video arena as well. Streaming video has its benefits and
drawbacks, as *Library Journal* observes: "Streaming's main selling point is
its accessibility and portability—potentially omniscient access to every-

thing. Its downside is also its accessibility—being dependent upon a 'stream' of consistent connectivity (and ample bandwidth)" (Malczewski 2011, para. 2). Thus, while users may access and view streaming video content by making use of a variety of devices—smartphones, computers, or streaming video conduits like the Roku—those users must have access to significant and consistent Internet connections. Cost is also a factor: although libraries can and do point patrons to sites that house freely available streaming video—like Ted.com, where viewers can watch Ted Talks online, and Hulu.com and Veoh.com, where viewers can select among an offering of television content, albeit with some commercial interruptions—premium and uninterrupted content is available to commercial users only through subscription.

Vendors have introduced streaming video subscription packages for libraries that allow them to make streaming content available for unlimited users; however, the available content is typically educational or informational and does not include mainstream popular media. Until such a service is available, libraries are limited in their ability to distribute premium streaming video content. The Ephrata (PA) Public Library piloted an innovative method to deliver popular content to users, establishing a Roku lending service for its patrons. The Roku, a streaming video player, can be hooked up to home television sets and used to view streaming video on the "big screen." Roku users can then subscribe to services—like Netflix or Hulu Plus—that allow them to select from a wealth of popular and educational content that may be viewed without commercial interruption. The Ephrata Public Library purchased Rokus as well as subscriptions to Netflix and Hulu Plus, and it lends the devices to patrons along with a remote control, power cord, and HDMI cable to connect the device to the television. Although the program has enjoyed success, the library also notes some drawbacks; as Matt Enis points out, "Loaning out one Roku for a week could diminish the circulation of other media—potentially multiple DVDs. Streaming movies will require a broadband connection, which many patrons may not have at home" (2012, para. 9). Thus, libraries considering a Roku or streaming video distribution program must also consider patron connectivity; though broadband service is available in most communities, monthly access costs might restrict some library patrons from accessing this service. Ben Malczewski, reporting for *Public Libraries Online*, is optimistic about the eventual development of technologies and services that will allow libraries to facilitate patron access to streaming video: "A library friendly [streaming video] distribution model will come, and by that time many kinks will have been hammered out (conveniently availing room for all the new ones naturally)" (2013, "The Library Anomaly," para. 4).

Sources Recommending and Discussing Young Adult Film and Video

1. *Visual Media for Teens: Creating and Using a Teen-Centered Film Collection,* by Jane Halsall and R. William Edminster (Libraries Unlimited, 2009): This guide provides librarians with tips for selecting and organizing films for teens in libraries and describes popular film genres, offering selection criteria and lists of recommended titles within each.
2. *VOYA*'s "Teen Screen: Video Reviews for Young Adults": Reviews of non-feature films (e.g., documentaries, educational movies, independent films) appear in the April, August, and December issues of the journal.
3. YALSA's "Fabulous Films for Young Adults": Compiled annually, this list of recommended films is composed of ten to twenty-five currently available films that "reflect young adult interests and needs" and adhere to the year's thematic requirement (YALSA 1997–2013, "Procedures"). Since its inception in 1997 as the "Selected DVD and Videos for Young Adults" list, films related to themes like "Coming of Age Around the World" (2009) and "Other Times/Other Places" (2011) have been recommended. The list includes recommended feature films (including some titles rated "R") as well as documentary and nonfiction titles.

Selecting Video Games for Young Adults

Libraries have considered tabletop games and PC games available on CD-ROM part of their materials collections for years; however, it is only more recently that libraries have been making console games available for users to play in the library or to check out to play at home. The ALA's International Gaming Day (formerly National Gaming Day), celebrated in libraries since 2008, has drawn attention to the role of tabletop and video games in libraries, while professional literature describing library programs and collections featuring games has expanded in scope and depth. The benefits of gaming have been noted and touted in library and educational literature: game playing can enhance literacy and critical thinking, as players are required to interpret image and text and make decisions based on these interpretations, and can aid in the development of social skills and enhance a gamer's ability to work in teams. The ALA's "Gaming @ your library" wiki (n.d.) defends the place of video games in a library's collection, arguing that collections of games support the library's mission to provide "cultural, recreational and entertainment materials" and pointing out that gaming programs can attract new users to the library.

Librarians who wish to develop video game collections must consider a number of issues related to access and form. Kym Buchanan and Angela M. Vanzen Elden identify the primary questions libraries must consider before selecting games and making them available to users:

> Will the games be part of the general collection, a review/curriculum collection, or only available for library staff to use for programming? If they are part of the general collection, will the systems circulate as well as the games? Will the library create a gaming lab? Will the games be mostly single-player, multi-player, or both? Will the library buy games for multiple consoles (e.g., Nintendo Wii, Microsoft Xbox 360), or just one? From where will all of these games and systems be purchased? (2012, 26)

How the library answers these questions ultimately affects the degree of access to video games in the library's collection. For example, libraries that offer video games for unrestricted circulation provide library users with greater access to their game collections than those that make games available for patron use only during special programming or "game nights." Similarly, a collection that includes material only playable on one type of console restricts access to that material for users who do not own that console, while a collection that includes games playable on multiple consoles offers expanded opportunities for users and collections that offer users the opportunity to borrow consoles as well as games expand access even further.

Considering Consoles and Compatibility

Whether libraries develop collections of video games to be used solely in the library or develop lending and "house" collections of video games to be circulated and used exclusively in programming, librarians must first determine which gaming systems will be supported by the library. Shawn McCann (2009) identifies three criteria libraries may use to determine which gaming systems to purchase and support: cost, popularity, and audience. When considering cost, libraries must take into account not just the cost of purchasing a gaming console, but also the cost of accessories and the average cost of compatible games. For example, the Nintendo Wii basic console—featuring one standard and one "Nunchuk" controller and the Wii Sports and Wii Sports Resorts discs—costs approximately $130.00; additional standard controllers, which are necessary to allow more than one player to play at the same time, cost up to $40.00 each; and the Nunchuk, which must be plugged into the standard controller, costs up to $20.00 each. In comparison, the Playstation 3 costs up to $300.00 and includes one controller; extra controllers may cost up to $40.00 each. Although cost is definitely a factor when considering initial purchase, the popularity of a console should inform a library's choice as well. McCann encourages librarians to temper considerations of popularity with availability, as the number of available games playable on each console differs. For example, a number of "exclusive" games exist that can only be played on one brand of console: "Halo" and "The Gears of War" are exclusive to Xbox, and the "Mario" and "Zelda" games are exclusive to Nintendo (Shanklin 2012, "Exclusives"). When considering audience, McCann advises libraries "targeting young gamers, families, or even older patrons just beginning to play games" to give preference to the Wii console, which may be easier for beginners to control and offers access to a comparatively larger number of games rated for young audiences (2009, 73). The Xbox 360, in comparison, "appeals to a more avid or 'hardcore' gamer audience" and features rich graphics and a catalog of popular, albeit more mature, games (McCann 2009, 73).

Backward compatibility—the ability for new versions of games to be played on older consoles—will also affect the library's selection of consoles. Because new gaming consoles appear on the market regularly, in the past many new consoles were constructed to allow gamers continued access to the games purchased for earlier versions. For example, Nintendo Wii users can use that console to play games created for Nintendo's Game Cube, and Xbox 360 users can play some games created for the original Xbox using the new console. A presentation given by Electronic Arts CFO Blake Jorgensen at the 2013 Goldman Sachs Internet and Technology Conference suggested that backward compatibility may soon be a thing of the past. As gaming consoles allow Internet connectivity, companies that produce exclusive games may require consumers to download compatible versions of games originally developed for earlier generation consoles. This will undoubtedly affect a library's collection of games for lending, as older discs will become increasingly incompatible with patrons' newer systems. This phenomenon may lead to the development of game distribution systems not unlike those associated with streaming video, which allow consumers to subscribe to a service that facilitates their access to online games. The Wii Virtual Console, which when connected to the Internet links users to the Wii Shop Channel, where players can download games created for older Nintendo consoles in versions compatible with the Wii, may represent the future of game acquisition. Until this future is realized, Buchanan and Vanzen Elden advise libraries developing game collections to "integrate both the system and its games into their collections to ensure that the games can be played for a long time" (2012, 29).

Considering Public Performance and Digital Rights Management Issues

Before selecting individual titles and planning for in-library gaming programs, librarians must consider the legal and digital rights management issues that affect library lending and programming practices. For example, libraries hosting video game programs that involve group play and game performance may be breaking licensing and copyright laws. The ALA's "Librarian's Guide to Gaming" cautions that although a 1996 court decision (*Allen v. Academic Games League of America*, 89 F.3d 614) ruled that playing a video game in public does not constitute a "public performance," individual game EULA/TOS (end-user licensing agreement/terms of service) "may supercede this decision, and state that public performance is not allowed" (ALA n.d., "Games and Public Performance," para. 1). Some video game companies, however, do encourage public game performance; the "Librarian's Guide to Gaming" cites Nintendo and Red Octane as two companies that support public game performance in libraries in particular. Although circulating games is not illegal, digital rights management issues can complicate games circulation. Libraries loan video games to patrons with the assumption that the game will not be installed and pirated, a tacit agreement that libraries, librarians, and users recognize is often breached. As the "Librarian's Guide to Gaming" points out, a game's EULA should indicate whether a game may be circulated and, furthermore, should note whether DRM software limiting the number of installations has been placed on the game disc.

Selecting Individual Games

Just as an understanding of literary genres can inform the development of fiction collections, an understanding of video game genres can aid in the development of balanced and diverse game collections. As Matthew Roach writes, "video games are another way of telling a story"; however, the genres that describe video games "are not related to the type of story told, but rather to the type of game to be played" (2010, 44). Scott Nicholson, author of *Everyone Plays at the Library* (2010), has developed a model of game genres called "SNAKS" that describes games in terms of their archetypal experiences: games may involve Strategy, Narrative, Action, Knowledge, or be inherently Social in nature. Strategy games, like "Civilization," tend to be slower and require the player to plan and consider outcomes before making any moves and, Nicholson claims, are not the best to play in teams. Role-playing games of all types, like "World of Warcraft," may be considered Narrative games, and, as Nicholson advises, because of their complexity, are good for "long-term, repeated sessions" (2009). Action games, like "Mario Kart" focus on "dexterity, hand-eye [coordination] [and] reflexes"; exist more often as console games; and tend to be "flashy," "loud," "exciting," and "fast-paced" (2009). Knowledge games emphasize trivia or educational knowledge and can be played individually or in teams. Social games, like "Dance Dance Revolution," are what Nicholson calls "party games" and can involve a lot of players engaged as competitors or audience members. In addition to these SNAKS genres, Roach identifies additional genres of "Racing," "Fighting," "Shooting," and "Sports" games, each of which requires the player to race, fight, shoot, or control a sports team or player.

The development of a rating system for video games has raised public awareness of the sometimes violent and gory content of popular games and has complicated public library selection practices. The Entertainment Software Rating Board (ESRB) has created what Liz Danforth calls the most "widely used and largely well-regarded" rating system for electronic video games (2010, 36). The ESRB's ratings, which exist on a continuum between "E" for "Everybody" and "M" for "Mature" (see chapter 3 for a chart describing these ratings), suggest what the ESRB considers to be appropriate age categories for audiences, and include "content descriptors," like "Alcohol Reference" or "Blood and Gore," that point out the particular content that influenced the categorical age rating (ESRB, n.d., "Content Descriptors"). Games with ESRB ratings "E" and "E10+" (which suggests the appropriateness of a game for everyone ages ten and up) are seldom problematic in libraries, but games with a "T" rating, indicating an audience of gamers ages thirteen and up, and an "M" rating, indicating an audience of gamers ages seventeen and up, are more problematic. The ALA points out that like PALs and MPAA ratings, ESRB ratings are a private ratings system and "cannot be mandated or enforced by any government or agency of government, including a publicly funded library" (2010, "Rating Systems," para. 2). Danforth suggests aligning library policy regarding the selection and organization of games with "T" and "M" ratings with any policy describing the library's selection and organization of "PG-13" and "R"-rated material, citing "professional ethics" which "place[] a high expectation on us to handle all parts of our collection evenhandedly" (2010, 36).

A number of resources suggest core collections and popular games for libraries (see below), but libraries developing game collections for young adults should first consult their teen patrons to determine which gaming consoles are most used in the community (a measure of local popularity that will affect the development of system-exclusive game collections) and to solicit suggestions for popular titles. The library's collection of popular print material may be an additional source of inspiration. Demand for books and series that exist as crossover media—books written to continue stories based on premises outlined in video games and books from which video games have been developed—may be popular in game form as well. Rollie Welch (2008) points out several popular titles that may exist in multiple forms in libraries: *Doom*, the novelization of the movie based on the video game; *Resident Evil*, a title that describes a video game series, a paperback series of novels based on the game, as well as several movies; and *Halo*, a video game series that has inspired paperback and comic book novelizations.

Sources Recommending and Discussing Video Games for Young Adults

1. YALSA's "Top 50 Core Recommended Collection Titles" (http://
    wikis.ala.org/yalsa/index.php/Gaming_Lists_&_Activ-
    ities#Top_50_Games_for_Library_Programs/Top): Compiled for
    the YALSA wiki, this list of fifty games recommended for libraries
    includes a brief description of each game and notes its ESRB rating
    and the console or system with which it is compatible.
2. *Game On! Gaming at the Library*, by Beth Gallaway (Neal Schuman,
    2009): Gallaway's guide to gaming offers tips for librarians devel-
    oping game collections and considering library programming in-
    volving games and includes guidance for selecting games and
    writing collection development policy.
3. *SLJ Teen*'s "Music and Game Reviews from Young Adults": The
    review journal's free electronic newsletter (for subscription infor-
    mation, see http://www.slj.com/slj-newsletters/) features monthly
    reviews of popular music and video games by young adult review-
    ers.

SELECTION CHALLENGES

Selecting material for the library's young adult collection is ultimately a
process of resource allocation. Guided by collection development policies
meant to reflect the library's mission, goals, and objectives, selecting librarians must determine how to spend the library's increasingly limited
funds in a way that best reflects its institutional goals for service and
information provision. As librarians consider the wealth of material and
media that may be selected on behalf of library patrons, they must balance budgetary restrictions against library user needs and demands. Sad-
ly, library budgets are one of the primary delimiters of library collections;
smart selectors are aware of this and strive to make every purchase count.
As library collections expand to include e-books as well as physical
tomes, digital rights management (DRM) conflicts threaten to limit library collections as well. DRM applies to "any system used by producers,
publishers, and vendors to embed technological controls on what users
can do with electronic files—ebooks, movies on DVDs, and other media,"
including restrictions or limitations on use of materials purchased by
libraries that attempt to protect that digital material from being copied,
shared, or otherwise altered (DCWG 2012, 1). It challenges a number of
traditional library practices, such as the "first sale" doctrine, which allows libraries to lend books acquired legally for circulation and, by establishing set limits on the life of a digital item, can curtail library attempts
to preserve information (ALA 1997–2013). These DRM issues affect consumers of digital content, but they have perhaps a greater deleterious

effect on library patrons, who look to libraries to provide access to material they might not otherwise be able to afford. Much in-demand electronic content—like e-books—is available to consumers but not to libraries, a contemporary fact of business life that limits what libraries can provide to patrons and effectively restricts patron access to the universe of electronically published material.

While library budgets and stringent DRM circumscribe library collections, censorship remains a threat to the library's collection for young adults as well. Most of us, as part of our professional education, are made aware of common threats to intellectual freedom; book challenges and attempts to remove or ban library material are easily recognizable attempts to censor information or literary expression. More difficult to identify are the censoring impulses that come into play when we make the decision to purchase or overlook a particular title for the library's collection. While Lester Asheim's famous 1953 essay, "Not Censorship, but Selection" (published on the ALA website at http://www.ala.org/offices/oif/basics/notcensorship) acknowledges that both library budgets and space considerations force librarians to "reject" titles during the selection process, he argues that this rejection, when authorized by a librarian who approaches selection with a "positive" orientation ("seeking [the] values in the book as a book" rather than "seeking for vulnerable characteristics wherever they can be found"), exemplifies the principles of fair selection rather than censorship. Unfortunately many librarians charged with selecting material for young people do, in the interest of protecting a "vulnerable" population, choose not to select material that exhibits those "vulnerable characteristics" that prompt debate about a title: use of profanity, depictions of violence, and depictions of sexuality are three common literary flags that urge rejection. This practice is known as self-censorship and is defined as the rejection of material in fear of its potential to incite debate or complaint among members of the community. Moving material published for young adults to the adult area of the library, placing labels on library material that suggest an age range for "appropriate" readership, and restricting access to library material constitutes self-censorship as well; as Deborah Lau Whelan (2009) has reported, this practice is widespread among YA librarians in public and school libraries.

Library collections for adults as well as young people should reflect, as Asheim has written, "the librarian's view of what readers want and need, whether the librarian likes it or not. The librarian's bias is that the collection should be unbiased" (1983, 180). Whelan, quoting the ALA's Office for Intellectual Freedom's deputy director, Deborah Caldwell-Stone, writes, "If a book is age appropriate and there are students who would benefit from reading it," the potential for a work to be controversial should not negatively affect its selection (2009, 30). Although Caldwell-Stone argues that the "age appropriateness" and "beneficial" nature

of any item outweigh its possibly controversial contents, these terms—
"age appropriate" and "beneficial"—can become censor's weapons as
well. While the term "age appropriate" suggests that there are absolute
and encompassing age-based landmarks for understanding, as readers
and professionals, we know that this is not the case. Furthermore, while
books and media may benefit a reader in tangible and intangible ways,
many avid readers seek out books without obvious "benefits"; light and
easy titles—"beach reads"—or sensational mystery and horror titles are
escapist pleasures. In a 1983 essay that revisits his 1953 "Not Censorship
but Selection," Asheim argues that librarians should strive to achieve
balance in their collections, acknowledging that varying definitions of
"balance" exist among different members of communities. To apply this
advice to selecting material for young adults, YA librarians should consider the plural definitions of "age appropriate" and "beneficial" and
employ these descriptors thoughtfully rather than restrictively. Asheim's
concluding statements point out the challenge of this task of achieving
balance, underscoring the importance of selection practices that are
guided by professional standards rather than personal ideologies:

> [T]he librarian's responsibility is to identify interests and to make judg-
> ments with the entire collection and the entire community in mind, not
> just that part of it with the largest constituency or the loudest voices or
> the most intimidating threats. It sounds easier than it is, but that is true
> of all responsibilities. To make decisions, to make them for sound rea-
> sons, and to be able to defend them when they are questioned are
> characteristics of professional judgment that I like to think go with the
> librarian's territory. (1983, 184)

Following Asheim, library collections for young adults should reflect selection practices that acknowledge the entire collection and the entire
community. That these collections are usually created to serve primary
populations of library users who are not typically part of the library's
"largest constituency" or authorized to speak with "the loudest voices"
means that young adult librarians invested in the creation of balanced
collections that reflect what users want and need—"no matter what the
librarian thinks"—must listen to the voices of the primary users of these
collections, even when the "loudest ones" threaten to drown them out.

SIX

Acquiring Material for the Young Adult Collection

Materials selection is a multistep, multifaceted process that requires an understanding of the library's priorities for selection as well as familiarity with its procedures for acquiring material. The library's priorities for selection are established in its collection development policy and, in public libraries, typically balance two approaches to selection: the "just in case" model and the "just in time" model. The "just in case" model is familiar to many librarians and places the majority of the institution's selection decisions in the hands of collection development librarians, who, based on their interpretations of patron needs and interests, evaluation of the current collection, and understanding of how patrons use the collection, select material to meet current and anticipated demand. The "just in time" model, which is gaining in popularity, looks to the library's patrons to suggest material and involves the acquisition of library material following the explicit request of the patron. As both of these models impact how the library acquires material for its patrons, librarians tasked with selection must become familiar with the institution's acquisition processes before making selection decisions.

THE ACQUISITIONS PROCESS

Materials selection and acquisition are distinct but related processes within the larger framework of collection development and maintenance. Materials selection is the process of identifying materials to add to the library's collection, whereas acquisition is the process of locating, procuring, and processing these materials so that they may be made available to library patrons. The degree to which these processes overlap or fall under the purview of a single librarian depends on the organizational structure of the library or library system as well as its collection development policies. In small libraries or school libraries, the librarian or school library teacher may be responsible for both selection and acquisition of materials. In larger libraries or library systems, individual librarians or groups of librarians may select materials and then pass their requests to acquisitions staff, who work with publishers' and vendors' representatives to acquire the requested material. In some library systems, librarians may be hired to select material in a specific subject area, in a particular format, or for a certain audience on behalf of all branches in the library. These librarians work with the acquisitions staff to facilitate the ordering, processing, and distribution of materials. This system, called centralized selection, may be used to develop core collections to be housed at individual library branches and may or may not involve the use of discretionary funds that allow local branch librarians some selection input.

Acquisitions librarians are primarily responsible for ordering library material and maintaining relationships with vendors, who may provide all or some of the following to libraries: print materials, audiovisual materials, e-books, and electronic resources and databases. These librarians negotiate prices and contracts with vendor representatives and facilitate the purchase or rental of material as requested by librarians charged with materials selection. Under the auspices of a library's acquisitions department, libraries negotiate approval plans, blanket orders, standing orders, and firm orders. Approval plans are agreements libraries make with vendors or publishers to send material to the library for examination by selectors, who may then choose to purchase or return the material that has been shipped for approval. Blanket orders are agreements between libraries and vendors or publishers to purchase material en masse; the library may agree to purchase all titles in a publisher's series or all titles produced by a particular publisher. Libraries may also agree to purchase material sent by a vendor that reflects the parameters of an agreed-upon subject area under a blanket order. Standing orders are agreements a library has made with a vendor or publisher whereby the vendor or publisher sends that library material that adheres to previously negotiated and agreed-upon parameters; libraries may list popular series and authors in standing order agreements and receive new installments of series or the latest titles from particular authors automatically. Firm orders are requests for individual titles to be sent to the library by a vendor or publisher. These orders may be for one-time-only purchases or for specific titles requested by selectors.

These plans and acquisition forms are the outcome of what Peggy Johnson (2009) refers to as "micro selection" and "macro selection." Micro selection is the process of ordering titles for a library's collection on a title-by-title basis and results in the development of firm orders. Librarians and selectors engaging in micro selection may examine review sources—periodicals that review and recommend material for purchase by libraries and bookstores—professional bibliographies, and standard catalogs and select individual titles to be added to the library's collection. Macro selection describes the process of ordering titles for library's collection "en bloc or en masse" and, according to Johnson, is generally "managed through mass buying plans—standard orders, blanket orders, or approval plans—or the acquisition of large retrospective collections either through purchase or gift" (2009, 121). Macro selection is also used to facilitate library purchase or lease of electronic resources and e-books; as Johnson notes, the macro selection of electronic resources and e-books involves "acquiring access to an extensive package of titles from a single publisher or aggregator" (2009, 122). Most libraries acquire and select material on both micro and macro levels, as micro selection allows for the selection and acquisition of individual or particular titles of local interest, and macro selection involves automatic selection and acquisition of popular or frequently consulted or requested resources.

Patrons may also inspire or drive selection and acquisition decisions in libraries that allow for patron-driven acquisition (PDA). The frequently cited "80-20 Rule," which suggests that 20 percent of a library's collection drives 80 percent of its circulation, as well as studies that have noted increases in the use of ILL services for a "large number" of "'ordinary' titles that collection development practices did not predict would be needed" (Nixon, Freeman, and Ward 2010, 120), have inspired increasing numbers of libraries to develop policies allowing for the purchase of such "ordinary" ILL requests. Under this PDA model, patron ILL requests that meet criteria established by the library (cost, availability, and publication date are typical parameters) are automatically purchased. This model of selection and acquisition has been applied most recently to the selection of e-books in libraries. Unlike PDA triggered by ILL requests, PDA associated with e-book acquisitions begins with librarians, who request a selection of records for titles that may be listed as e-books in the library's catalog. Patrons may select and explore these titles and, following an agreed upon period of use, trigger the library's purchase of the title. As Josh Hadro describes the process in *Library Journal*, PDA is "automated and seamless to the user, who is unaware of the transaction" (2010, para. 5). This automaticity has been criticized by some librarians, who express concern that patron-driven purchases could divert money from budgets that otherwise would be used to select material of less immediate but nevertheless enduring value. However, as Hodges, Preston, and Hamilton (2010) concluded in their examination of PDA of e-books in an academic library, this model of acquisition supports the library's role to provide information requested by its patrons. "The library of the electronic age," they argue, "should provide both the option to 'give [patrons] what they want now'"—the "just in time" model, "and to acquire items that may be needed later"—the "just in case" model (2010, 221).

VENDOR- AND "JOBBER"-FACILITATED PRINT MATERIAL SELECTION AND ACQUISITION

Acquisitions librarians and those tasked with selecting materials frequently work with vendors or "jobbers," wholesale distributors of media to libraries. These vendors serve as intermediaries between libraries and publishers and facilitate the discounted purchase of material from multiple publishers and producers. In addition, vendors offer a number of services to libraries, including cataloging and "shelf-ready" processing of materials (e.g., books ordered through vendors may include plastic jackets, spine labels, and security devices that would otherwise have to be applied by library staff), book leasing, and collection development. Libraries using vendors' collection development services develop "profiles"—descriptions of their collection priorities by audience (e.g., children, young adult, or adult) or type of book (e.g., best sellers, well-reviewed titles)—which are then used to generate customized lists of recommended titles or establish the parameters of standing and blanket orders. Catalogs of recommended material (like Baker and Taylor's "Graphic Novels" catalog) are also developed by vendors to aid selection. Many vendors have developed databases of available titles that include the review and awards information that selecting and acquisitions librarians use to select material for purchase. These databases, like Baker and Taylor's Title Source and Follett Library Resources' Titlewave, not only facilitate acquisitions but also, when local collection data are shared with the vendor, allow librarians to develop customized reports describing their collections for evaluation and assessment purposes.

Many selecting librarians rely on vendor databases to inform their selection of materials. These databases allow librarians to search a vendor's stock of materials from multiple publishers by subject and limit this search by age, grade, or reading level and review status (e.g., the results of a search may be limited to only those titles that have received "starred" or "boxed" reviews), expediting the process of searching for titles to fill gaps in the collection. Following a search for titles, librarians may develop lists of their selections, which may then be passed on to the acquisitions librarian or to the vendor as firm orders for material. This process certainly streamlines selection, but it is important to remember that the material included in a vendor's database does not represent the universe of material produced for young people; the results of any vendor database search are limited to those materials from publishers with which the vendor has prior sale agreements. Furthermore, vendors may promote material they have purchased and stocked in bulk in an effort to maintain a revolving inventory and secure a profit.

The nature and extent of the job of the librarian tasked with materials selection are affected by the agreements the library has already negotiated with vendors and wholesalers, as well as by the workflow arrangements the library has established for selection and acquisition. Whether a librarian is charged with selecting material and communicating those selections to the library's acquisitions staff or is responsible for both selection and acquisition, it is important for that selecting librarian to be familiar with any existing blanket, approval, or standing order agreements the library has established with vendors, so that duplication of selection effort can be reduced. Furthermore, because these agreements are subject to change, it is important for selecting librarians to remain current with the latest contracts as well as with the profile developed by the library that communicates its collection priorities to its vendors. The following information about the library's agreements with vendors should be kept in mind when developing firm orders for individual titles:

1. *Approval plans*: If the library has negotiated an approval plan with a vendor or vendors, which publishers have been targeted? What are the parameters for the subjects of the material selected by the vendor and sent to the library for approval? What other parameters (e.g., grade or reading level, publication date, review status) has the library set to delimit its approval plan?
2. *Blanket orders*: What series (e.g., Greenhaven Press's Opposing Viewpoints) or publishers' imprints (e.g., Capstone's Heinemann Raintree) comprise the library's blanket orders?
3. *Standing orders*: Which author's latest material (e.g., Meg Cabot, Walter Dean Myers) and which series' newest installments (e.g., Beautiful Creatures) are sent to the library automatically? What award-winning titles are automatically sent to the library (e.g., Printz Award and honor books, Stonewall Award and honor books)?

An understanding of which material will be automatically sent to the library for approval or for addition to the collection is key to developing firm orders for individual titles that are purchased to fill more specific needs or reflect newly popular reading choices. In addition, as standing orders, blanket orders, and approval plans represent purchase or approval to purchase agreements libraries have made with vendors, it is important to understand what percentage of the library's budget is earmarked for these automatic or near-automatic purchases and how much may be left for firm orders for individual titles.

E-BOOK ACQUISITION

As libraries and publishers debate the definition of "ownership" with regard to intangible electronic content, a number of business models that describe e-book purchase and lease programs and outline the terms of electronic content licensing and use have emerged to guide acquisitions. Although these business models are in a state of flux, the following are the most commonly used:

1. *Single User or "One Book/One User" Model*: Libraries purchase licenses to lend individual e-book titles to one user at a time, a model that most closely approximates the print model.
2. *Multi-User Model*: Libraries purchase licenses to lend individual e-books to more than one user at a time.
3. *Unlimited User Model*: Libraries purchase licenses to lend individual e-books to unlimited simultaneous users.
4. *Subscription Model*: Libraries purchase subscriptions to collections of electronic books (like EBSCO's High School Collection) that may be accessed by an agreed upon or unlimited number of simultaneous users. Suspension of the subscription suspends patrons' access to the titles in the subscription collection.

Depending on the model or models that govern a library's agreement with a vendor or content provider, a library may "own the title in perpetuity (perpetual access) or use the content for a designated period of time (subscription)" (Polanka 2011, 4). For example, a library may purchase a license to lend an e-book for an established number of times, after which the library must repurchase the license to continue lending the item. Each of these models has its benefits and drawbacks, and as a way of mitigating the inevitable drawbacks, Sue Polanka advises libraries and librarians to "select models that offer more control of content," noting that public domain and open access materials provide libraries with the most control, whereas perpetual access models allow greater control than subscription and short-term loan models (2011, 5).

Libraries may work with a number of providers to acquire e-books; as in print acquisitions, they may purchase or lease e-books directly from publishers; through aggregators, which provide content from multiple publishers as well as a platform for libraries and their patrons to search, order, and download content; or through wholesalers, which distribute content from both publishers and aggregators. Ultimately, e-book selection is limited to those titles publishers make available to libraries, aggregators, and wholesalers, and depending on the publisher, the lists of available electronic material may be noticeably skimpier than the lists of print material.

While some models of e-book acquisition are reminiscent of those associated with print material acquisition, e-books also present new options for acquiring materials. Libraries may place "firm orders" for single or multiple titles with publishers, aggregators, or wholesalers, or negotiate "standing orders" for electronic material with wholesalers and aggregators in much the same way as they do for print material. Librarians may also negotiate PDA or "pay-per-view" options with aggregators and wholesalers, two forms of e-book acquisition that are less familiar to libraries. PDA is typically an acquisitions model offered by aggregators, who provide access to a selection of e-book material via an interface accessible to library users; once a title has been accessed a predetermined number of times, they charge the library for the electronic version of the title and the license to lend it. This form of acquisition ensures that all e-books purchased by the library under this agreement are actually used; however, this model also shifts the locus of control for selection to patrons, a move that has generated some professional ire. Pay-per-view agreements require libraries to pay fees to aggregators or wholesalers to make content available for patron use, then pay for content as it is accessed and used by patrons.

PROCESSING AND ORGANIZING MATERIAL

Once acquisitions plans are established and firm orders are submitted, YA librarians have to consider the regular delivery of material selected for the library's collection. Typically, print and tangible media that have been ordered are delivered to the library and its technical services department, where the contents of each shipment are checked against the original order and the packing slip to determine whether the shipment is complete and usable (i.e., to ensure that damaged material is noted and returned). Depending on the library's organizational structure, this new material may be accessioned—given an identification number or barcode—and cataloged by the technical services staff, an offsite or central processing facility, or the selecting librarian. These initial activities result in the downloading, copying, or development of cataloging records for each new item (or the addition of a duplicate copy of an item to an existing cataloging record) and the assignment of a circulation-related status (e.g., "In processing," "Available," "On hold") to each item once it is "checked in" to the library's system.

When placing firm orders for print or tangible media, librarians may add "notes" to the order form that indicate to the acquisitions and technical services staff where the material will be housed in the library and that note any subcollection of material that the item in question might belong to. For example, duplicate copies of a fiction title might be ordered when that title is placed on a required summer reading list, and these additional copies may then be organized on shelves designated for summer reading titles. To ensure that patrons can find these items, the library's technical services staff should be instructed to indicate in the holdings record that these items belong in the summer reading collection. It is especially important to consider the location of items ordered to meet the needs of the library's young adult patrons when this material is housed in multiple places in the library. For example, some libraries house high interest nonfiction for young adults in a designated young adult space and shelve research and curricular-related material in a general nonfiction collection that includes informational titles selected for both adults and young adults, or in a youth nonfiction collection that includes informational titles selected for children and young adults. Determining where, exactly, material should be shelved in the library (information that is conveyed to the library's patrons via the library's catalog) can be tricky, especially when considering titles, like Steve Sheinkin's *Bomb: The Race to Build—and Steal—the World's Most Deadly Weapon* or Marc Aronson's *Witch Hunt: Mysteries of the Salem Witch Trials*, that may be both high interest and curricular. This decision can be made before placing an order for an item and remade following acquisition. Arguably, every item the library orders is selected for a purpose, and this purpose might suggest where in the library the item should ultimately be housed. If an item is selected primarily to meet the curricular and educational information needs of young adult patrons who, in the hypothetical case of the library that shelves high interest young adult nonfiction in a designated young adult area and interfiles curricular and reference material in a general nonfiction collection, look to the general nonfiction collection to answer educationally inspired information needs, this item should be shelved with general nonfiction. If, however, the item was selected with the high interest needs of the local community in mind, it might be better shelved among the high interest nonfiction. Once the item arrives, however, it might prove to be more or less appropriate in a different area of the library. A surprisingly eye-catching cover, conversational style, and narrative form of organization might encourage a librarian to switch a title purchased for curricular support to a high interest collection.

Electronic material—e-books and digital content files—is acquired and processed in a slightly different manner. As noted previously, libraries may negotiate the lease of electronic content with publishers, wholesalers, and aggregators, each of which may make this content available to libraries in different ways. Aggregators, like the commonly employed OverDrive, offer libraries electronic content for lease, host this material, and make it available via a central platform. While aggregators provide libraries with MARC records to include in their ILS, patrons must visit the aggregator's platform—which is typically linked from the library's website or the item record—to download the material. Libraries may lease titles directly from publishers and wholesalers; however, these companies may not provide an interface or platform to facilitate patron downloading of files, making access challenging. As Michael Kelley notes about the current e-book lending situation in libraries, "At present, e-book library transactions most often occur among discrete distributor platforms that are not fully integrated with library ILSes and which oblige patrons to jump to a different interface that leaves them segregated from the rest of the library's catalog and collection" (2013, para. 10). Although organizations like Readers First—a coalition of libraries working to develop consistent content access requirements for e-content providers so that library users can search and browse a single library catalog that includes all of the library's print and digital content and manage downloads, circulation records, holds, and requests via this comprehensive catalog—are working to develop agreeable solutions and standards for libraries, vendors, wholesalers, and aggregators, the current state of e-book acquisitions requires libraries to direct patrons to multiple access points to borrow or view electronic material.

THE CHANGING FACE OF ACQUISITIONS

As libraries develop collections in response to user demand and access capability, professional journals and commentators argue that libraries are shifting their collecting and acquiring philosophies from "just in case" collection development to "just in time" acquisition. The increasing opportunity for library patrons to drive title acquisition through PDA, particularly as it emerges as a viable acquisitions model for e-books, is one of the likely motivators of this paradigm shift that has the potential to dramatically affect the library's traditional selection and acquisitions model. The likelihood of PDA "taking over" the duties of the library selector has been compromised by the limitations publishers have placed on the universe of published material made available to libraries to lend to patrons or for patrons to select to be added to the library's collection. PDA driven by interlibrary loan requests has the potential to affect the library's acquisition of print resources to a greater extent; however, just as PDA of electronic content is delimited by libraries and librarians who circumscribe the content patrons may request for purchase, ILL-driven PDA is similarly limited, albeit by patron knowledge of the universe of published material.

Electronic resource management is an increasingly larger component of library acquisitions and technical services work as libraries incorporate greater digital content within their collections, and this shift in service orientation will probably affect the way libraries acquire and process materials for patron access. The contemporary library world is in a state of flux, as libraries, publishers, wholesalers, vendors, and content aggregators develop business models that allow libraries to provide patrons with the information and content they desire while protecting the rights of content creators and copyright holders. As Kari Schmidt has observed, "much of the change to accommodate e-books has been reactive, as technical services has had to respond to shifting prices and access models without a clear plan to move forward" (2012, 306). It is likely that any "plan to move forward" will involve the development of discovery tools, which allow libraries to facilitate access to material and collections. Noting that "the library is a major venue of book discovery" but allowing that "no one is sure how discovery works in the e-book world," the Connecticut State Library's Advisory Council for Library Planning and Development (ACLPD) identified "discovery" as one of the next major issues for libraries to address (2012, 3). "Publishers value the library's role in the discovery of physical books, but our role in e-book discovery (and, indeed, the mechanics of e-book discovery generally) remains unclear," the ACLPD's E-book Task Force White Paper concluded (2012, 3).

Whether libraries continue to invest in "just in case" or "just in time" collections, libraries and librarians will need to develop strategies and tools that facilitate patron discovery of existing—or potential—titles and information. While the brick-and-mortar library has relied on the OPAC as well the library's physical architecture—its shelves and display areas—and its staff, who provide readers' advisory and respond to reference questions, to facilitate discovery, the digital library must accomplish these aims in a virtual space. Libraries and librarians need to develop new strategies for promoting materials in the digital library and for conveying the contents of the collection to patrons. This task may be particularly challenging for librarians serving young adults, whose patrons, as Bob Holley has written, "don't usually choose the materials in the collection . . . [they] don't arrive in the library with lists of what they want to read or what they need for their school assignments" (2012, 2). Though young library visitors may be interested in popular or well-known individual titles and series, they may rely more on the physical organization of the library to suggest appropriate titles to fulfill assignment needs or reading requirements for separately shelved and distinctly labeled summer reading titles or educational biographies.

"Except for the large public research libraries," Holley argues, public library users "arrive with the goal of having their questions answered just then or of taking something interesting home to read from what is currently available" (2012, 3). Patrons may certainly "arrive" at a virtual library and chat with or e-mail a reference librarian to have their questions answered "just then," but making that "something interesting"—or, in the case of young library patrons who need information resources to meet school-imposed deadlines, "something useful"—available and accessible to young adult patrons will continue to drive selection and acquisition decisions. Though the means of acquiring material—and the form of the material itself—may change, selection and acquisition will continue to involve making decisions about format and access that have increasing importance to the library—and patron—of the future.

SEVEN

Collection Assessment, Evaluation, and Weeding

While libraries engage in needs assessment to determine the needs and interests of the local service population and aid in the selection of material, they also undertake measurement, assessment, and evaluation projects to review and maintain these carefully selected collections of material and ensure that they meet those identified needs and interests. Weeding or deselection—the removal of material from a library's collection—often occurs in tandem with measurement, assessment, and evaluation and is an important outcome of these practices. G. Edward Evans and Margaret Saponaro note that assessment and evaluation "completes the collection development cycle and brings one back to needs assessment" (2005, 315). Collection development is never finished; as libraries document and respond to growth and change in their service populations with new collections and services, they must also assess and evaluate these collections to ensure their continued relevance. The American Library Association's interpretation of the "Library Bill of Rights," entitled "Evaluating Library Collections" (1981) identifies collection assessment and evaluation as an integral part of the collection development process:

> The continuous review of library materials is necessary as a means of maintaining an active library collection of current interest to users. In the process, materials may be added and physically deteriorated or obsolete materials may be replaced or removed in accordance with the collection maintenance policy of a given library and the needs of the community it serves. Continued evaluation is closely related to the goals and responsibilities of all libraries and is a valuable tool of collection development.

175

Collection assessment and evaluation involves reviewing the collection in light of the library's service goals and what needs assessment tells us about the population the library serves. This process provides librarians with needed information about the collection and its use as well as a lens through which to consider and reconsider how the collection reflects and meets user needs and inspires further needs assessment activities, weeding, and selection.

Review of library collections involves three distinct but related activities: measurement, assessment, and evaluation. Kay Bishop states that measurement represents the "process of identifying extent or quantity" (2007, 142). When libraries measure their collections, they may identify and count the number of books in the whole collection, in a special collection, or in a specific subject area. Libraries may also measure use of their collections and count circulation, reserves and holds, and ILL requests from patrons and other libraries. These activities provide libraries with data that they then use to assess and evaluate their collections. *Assessment* and *evaluation* both describe the use and interpretation of data for specific decision-making purposes. As Peggy Johnson defines these terms, data for "assessment" purposes are collected "to determine how well the collection supports the goals, needs, and mission of the library or parent organization," whereas data for "evaluation" purposes are collected to "describe collections either in their own terms or in relation to other collections and checking mechanisms, such as lists" (2009, 226). By measuring the collection and applying the resulting figures to assessment and evaluation, libraries can determine a collection's utility, a concept Johnson defines as "how effective the collection is at satisfying the purpose for which it is intended" (2009, 225). Most public libraries articulate the purpose of their collections in their mission statements and assert their collections' role in meeting the informational, cultural, recreational, and entertainment reading and information needs and interests of their service populations. Thus, assessment and evaluation in public libraries typically involves determining how effectively collections reflect and respond to the needs of patrons.

Many libraries engage in collection assessment and evaluation on a regular basis and consider this part of the strategic planning process. Although the library's young adult material may be assessed and evaluated within the context of a greater collection assessment and evaluation project, it is often useful to conduct a separate assessment and evaluation of the young adult collection. This activity—and the data that result—are an important form of advocacy for young adults. Because young adult library services are still somewhat new in libraries—YALSA (2012a) notes that only one in three libraries employs a young adult specialist—it is clear that advocacy remains the key to their development and maintenance. Data collected during a young adult collection assessment and evaluation that describe how the collection meets the needs of its teen users, document the circulation of YA material, and demonstrate how the collection supports the library's mission can be used to advocate for more resources expressly for young adults. Furthermore, this information can be used to make decisions about the future direction of the library's collection for young adults, as it points out areas of strength and weakness and suggests paths for topical and format development. Evaluation and assessment also benefit the librarian who engages in these activities. As Sheila Intner has written, collecting data and evaluating and assessing the library's young adult collection helps to "build[] your knowledge, vision, credibility and status in the institution," particularly as the process of inventorying and assessing the library's collection of material for young adults helps a librarian "get to really know [her] collection[]" and, with this knowledge, develop the "confidence to justify making whatever claims to fame or challenges for more resources . . . and to back them up with hard facts" (2003, 346, 347).

MEASUREMENT, EVALUATION, AND ASSESSMENT

Measurement, evaluation, and assessment represent data collection (measurement) and interpretation (evaluation and assessment) processes and activities that can be viewed as both related and cumulative. *Measurement*, the process of collecting data for descriptive, evaluative, or assessment purposes, is a fundamental component of evaluation and assessment. *Evaluation* involves the comparison of local measures describing the library's collection and its use over time or the comparison of local measures describing the library's collection and its use to external measures of collection size, depth, breadth, extent, and use. *Assessment* involves the application of these comparisons to determine what these data reveal about how the library is meeting its service goals and objectives. Thus, whereas evaluation can be broadly considered a process of comparing measures, assessment can be considered a process of comparing measures (evaluating) for a specific purpose.

Measurement

Measurement is a significant component of evaluation and assessment. Fortunately, contemporary integrated library systems (ILS) make measuring library collections easier than ever before. A library's ILS can provide librarians with data on the use of the collection—circulation measures—as well as its breadth and depth—collection measures.

Circulation Measures

1. The percentage of total circulation represented by young adult material

2. Frequently circulated material (e.g., subject classes that circulate with comparative frequency or frequently circulated titles)
3. User classes (e.g., "youth" or "adult") responsible for circulating young adult material

Collection Measures

1. Total number of items in the young adult collection
2. Number of unique items in subject and format areas of the collection (e.g., number of unique graphic novel titles or the number of unique titles in the 900s)
3. Percentage of the collection devoted to fiction, nonfiction (in whole, or by Dewey Decimal or Library of Congress class), and multimedia formats
4. Average age of material in the entire collection or in specific subject areas (e.g., the average age of the library's fiction collection)

In addition to the data provided by the ILS, libraries may also collect and consider other measures of the collection and its use. They may be quantitative (resulting in data that can be analyzed statistically) or qualitative (resulting in non-numeric data that must be interpreted) and may be collected by measuring shelf space, counting and recording the use of material within the library, or surveying patrons.

Although the circulation and collection data that the library's ILS can make available are useful in their objectivity, as Bishop (2007) points out, these quantitative measures are not evaluative on their faces. That is, though circulation data may tell us how many times items were circulated and may even suggest the broad demographics of the patrons who borrowed these items, this information does not indicate how effectively the collection met these patrons' needs and how, in Johnson's terms, the collection functions to "satisf[y] the purpose for which it is intended." Measures of available shelf space, counts of material used within the library, and survey results are similarly limited in their utility. Until these measures are interpreted and considered in the comparative terms required by evaluation and assessment, they remain descriptive—and useful as descriptive measures—but not evaluative.

Evaluation

Evaluation is a comparative activity; libraries collect data that measure the collection and its use and compare them to external benchmarks or standards. For example, libraries may compare the number of volumes in their young adult collections to the number of volumes in such collections curated at peer libraries as a way of setting goals for optimal collection size, or they may compare the size and content of their young adult collections to those housed at local junior high and high school libraries to determine areas of overlap. In addition, libraries may compare the contents of their collections to those recommended in professional bibliographies and core collections and catalogs. These kinds of comparison, Evans and Saponaro (2005) argue, although useful, have the potential to be misleading, as the worth and utility of comparison are predicated on the assumption that, in the case of peer comparison, there is "a close approximation of needs among the comparative groups" and that, in the case of bibliographic comparison, "standards or norms [exist] that approximate optimum conditions" (316). Although these caveats are important to note, Joe Matthews (2007) has observed that external standards for collection size are still considered and used by some states, and the tendency to judge libraries by the comparative sizes of their collections remains pervasive.

Assessment

Evaluation can be defined as "the judgment as to the value of X, based on a comparison, implicit or explicit, with some known value Y" (Evans and Saponaro 2005, 315); in evaluation, the "known value Y" is generally thought to represent a recognized quality standard. Assessment, in comparison, articulates its own "Y" value and asserts that this value is representative of the library's achievement of its mission and goals. If the aim of assessment is, as Johnson (2009) suggests, to determine how the library is meeting its goals with its collection, these goals must be defined and articulated—operationalized—so that they may function as the "known value Y" against which the current collection is compared. Assessment begins with this articulation of goals in measurable form and involves the comparison of measures describing the library's collection and its use to measures of value and quality established by the library to represent the attainment of these goals.

Criteria for assessment—the "known value Y"—should reflect the library's mission and can be drawn from the collection development policies that articulate the library's goals for the collection related to its mission. These policies describe its criteria for materials selection, linking them to the library's mission and suggesting how materials selected using these criteria fulfill the mission. Developing and articulating these criteria for evaluation is called "operationalization," a process in which a measure is identified, created, or assigned that corresponds to a particular evaluative criterion. For example, many public libraries state in their missions that they intend to serve the informational, educational, and recreational reading and information needs and interests of their service populations; to that end, they develop criteria for selecting print and nonprint materials that reflect these needs and interests. These criteria may refer to sources used to guide selection or other factors that impact selection, including popularity, quality, reputation of the author, and patron requests. Each of these criteria may be operationalized so that the library's collection can be assessed in terms of how it reflects them. For example, if the library's mission is to collect material for its patrons that reflects their interests, and these interests include popular material, a library may assess its collection to determine what proportion is composed of such material. To do this, the library would develop a standard for popular materials measurement (the "known value Y") against which its collection ("X") could be compared. To develop this standard, the library may choose to create a list of best-selling books published during a particular time period and compare this list to the library's existing collection of material published during the same period. The resulting overlap—how much of the library's existing collection is comprised of best-selling material and what percentage of best-selling material is housed by the library—could provide an evaluator with a measurement of the library's commitment to selecting popular material, a goal for collection development that reflects the library's mission.

In short, assessment is the application of evaluation techniques for specific purposes. To determine whether it is meeting its goals, the library may develop measures that represent these goals and evaluate its collection using these measures (as in the example above) or may consider external measures and standards to represent its goals and evaluate its collection. The difference between assessment and evaluation, here, lies in how the library defines its goals in terms of its collection's resemblance to professional or other standards. For example, libraries that make "quality" a criterion for materials selection may define "quality" material as that which has been recommended in professional bibliographies or has been granted literary or publishing awards. With this definition in mind, the library may assess its collection for inclusion of "quality" material and compare the contents to, for example, lists of award-winning books. The resulting measure—what percentage of award-winning books are housed by the library—may suggest the library's commitment to collecting for "quality."

These examples that describe how a library might assess its collection to determine its commitment to collecting "quality" or "popular" material demonstrate the process of operationalization, the translation of evaluative criteria into measurable terms. In each example, the library used one criterion to determine popularity or quality: percentage of best-selling books collected (popularity) and percentage of award winners selected (quality). Best practices would dictate, however, that the library develop more than one measurable criterion for evaluation; as Evans and Saponaro remind us, "the value of an item or a collection fluctuates depending on which yardstick one employs" (2005, 315). For example, whereas the percentage of best-selling books collected by the library might indicate its commitment to collecting popular material, the operationalization of "popular" in terms of the best sellers list is somewhat limited and perhaps even biased. To be sure, best-selling titles represent the popular reading choices of many library patrons; however, there are many titles, authors, and series that may be locally popular but do not appear on best-seller lists. To evaluate its commitment to popular materials collection more completely, the library may wish to develop other metrics that indicate popularity. For example, it may look to circulation to determine which titles, authors, or series circulate with the greatest frequency as a means of identifying locally popular material. The percentage of material in the collection identified as locally popular may provide the library with a different, but complementary, metric of popularity.

METHODS FOR MEASURING, EVALUATING, AND ASSESSING THE LIBRARY'S PRINT COLLECTION

Because measurement data are so readily available through the library's ILS, many libraries request regular reports of circulation and collection information and use them to guide shelf-reading and weeding projects and to inform regular reports describing the collection and any trends in circulation. Although these data are useful for descriptive purposes, libraries look to other methods of data collection to evaluate and assess their collections: collection centered or user centered. Collection-centered techniques examine the collection and involve collecting data describing the size, breadth, depth, scope, and age of the collection. User-centered techniques focus on measures of collection use and involve collecting data describing circulation, in-house use, and patron experiences. These can be considered measurement techniques resulting in data that can be applied to evaluation or assessment projects.

Collection-Centered Techniques

List-checking

List-checking is comparing the library's collection to standard lists or bibliographies. It describes whether the library's collection includes recommended titles. When engaging in list-checking, librarians typically examine a small sample of the entire collection or a subject or format area, depending on the standard lists or bibliographies employed and the purpose of the activity. Following are common lists and bibliographies used by libraries to measure their young adult collections:

1. *Middle and Junior High Core Collection* and *Senior High Core Collection*: Published by EBSCO and H. W. Wilson, these regularly issued catalogs recommend core titles for purchase and retention. Libraries may check portions of their collections against the catalogs' lists

to determine coverage in subject areas or to assess the breadth of fiction collections.

2. *Best Books for Middle School and Junior High School Readers, Grades 6–9* and *Best Books for High School Readers, Grades 9–12*: Published by Libraries Unlimited, these regularly issued bibliographies of fiction and nonfiction describe titles considered "best books." Libraries may check portions of their collections against these bibliographies to determine coverage in subject areas or to assess the breadth of fiction collections.

3. *Core Collection for Young Adults*, by Rollie Welch (Neal-Schuman, 2011); *Core Collection for Children and Young Adults*, by Rachel Schwedt (Scarecrow, 2008); and *Core Collection for Young Adults*, by Patrick Jones (Neal-Schuman, 2008): Each of these bibliographies recommends "core collections" of young adult fiction and nonfiction, including both classic and contemporary titles. The recommended nonfiction titles tend to be more recreational than curricular in nature. Libraries may check their collections against these bibliographies, particularly when considering the status of their collections of "classic" material.

4. *Fantasy Literature for Children and Young Adults: A Comprehensive Guide*, by Ruth Nadelman Lynn (Libraries Unlimited, 2005); *Historical Fiction for Young Readers (Grades 4–8): An Introduction*, by John Gillespie (Libraries Unlimited, 2008); and *The Librarian's Guide to Developing Christian Fiction Collections for Young Adults*, by Barbara J. Walker (Neal-Schuman, 2005): These topical bibliographies of recommended material by genre or literary type are just three examples of bibliographic resources devoted to the recommendation of specific types of books for the young adult audience. Librarians may use these to evaluate genre and special format collections and to help make weeding and selection decisions.

These publications are common, large bibliographic resources used for list-checking and selection, but librarians may also look to lists of recommended or required titles developed by local schools, topical bibliographies created by professional associations (like YALSA's "Best Fiction for Young Adults" or "Popular Paperbacks for Young Adults"), or lists of award-winning titles to check their collections. Public libraries may also compare their collections to the holdings of peer libraries or local school libraries to determine areas of overlap or to recommend titles.

What List-Checking Tells Us   List-checking results in one measurement of a library's collection in comparison to a standard, which makes this an evaluation process. If a library chooses to use these professional lists as benchmarks reflecting its goals for collection development, this becomes an assessment process. Depending on the lists used to check the collection, the outcomes of list-checking may include the following:

1. A measurement of the depth of the library's collection of Printz Award winners, achieved by determining how many of the Printz Award and Honor books the library houses in its collection. If the library values its collection by the depth of its inclusion of Printz Award (or any other award) winners, the degree of overlap either demonstrates the achievement of the library's goal of collecting award-winning titles or suggests the need for more development of award-winning material.

2. A measurement of the breadth and depth of the library's collection of fantasy fiction, determined by comparing the contents of the local collection to the core collection suggested in Lynn's *Fantasy Literature for Children and Young Adults*. If the library considers it important to broaden and maintain its collection of fantasy material, a comparison of its list of fantasy titles to those named by Lynn can reveal fantasy subgenres not represented in the current collection and suggest a collection development goal.

3. A measurement of the completeness of the library's collection of summer reading titles assigned by the local high school. By comparing the list of required titles to the library's collection, a librarian can determine which the library currently collects and which may need to be purchased if it wishes to support this summer reading assignment.

Exemplary list-checking measures like those listed here are only valuable if the library assigns them value as it operationalizes its goals. For example, if the library's mission is to facilitate patron access to a collection that includes material of literary quality, and the library considers literary awards—like the Printz Award—indicators of quality, then the completeness of its collection of Printz Award–winning material can be considered evidence of its progress toward this goal.

However, there are a number of caveats associated with list-checking for measurement, evaluation, or assessment purposes, and the preceding examples can be used to illustrate these. Libraries selecting a list to use for comparison must recognize, as Johnson warns, that "any list prepared by an individual or group reflects the biases or opinions of its compiler(s)," which means that any list's validity "rests on the assumption that those titles in the resource list are worthy and that the library needs them to satisfy patrons and support programs" (2009, 242). Thus, although comparing the library's collection of fantasy material to the list of core fantasy titles suggested by Lynn (as above) may be a worthwhile endeavor, it is only meaningful if the library considers Lynn's an expert and definitive benchmark. The publication date of Lynn's—or any—source used for list-checking can affect the validity of this method as well. As Matthews notes, professional bibliographies tend to have a "short life expectancy," and as these bibliographies are delimited by space and creator bias, comparable books held by the library that are not included on these lists may be sufficient for the library's and its users' needs (2005, 114). Libraries using lists to assess the collection do this with the assumption that the "selected list reflects goals and purposes that are similar to those of the checking institution" (Evans and Saponaro 2005, 320); thus it is important that any list used as a basis for collection assessment reflect the institution's goals and objectives.

Despite these criticisms, list-checking remains a useful method for identifying gaps in the collection, particularly in areas of the collection dealing with subjects with which the librarian is unfamiliar. It is best, however, that this method of assessing the collection be combined with other methods, to allow for a clearer picture of how the library's collection meets the needs of its users.

Direct Analysis

Direct analysis, also known as "shelf-scanning," is the process of assessing the physical collection in situ. This analysis may be undertaken by the librarian or by an expert hired to examine the whole collection or a particular subject, audience, or format area of the collection. The librarian or expert scans the shelves to "draw conclusions about the size, scope, depth or type of materials . . . and the significance of the collection; the range and distribution of publishing dates; and the physical condition of materials" (Johnson 2009, 242). As Evans and Saponaro (2005) note, an outside evaluator does not base his or her reports and analysis on professional opinions of the collection alone; the evaluator also solicits opinions from the library's service community, a method of data collection that "provides the evaluator with a sense of what the users think about the collection" (2005, 321). Evaluators may also survey the library staff to determine their opinions of the collection, and any significant differences in patron and staff opinion are noted. If the librarian or expert tasked with examining the collection is asked to draw conclusions about how it meets the goals of the library, this can be considered assessment. If asked to draw conclusions and make recommendations based on his or her expertise alone, the expert's direct analysis can be considered evaluation.

What Direct Analysis Tells Us   Direct analysis of the collection provides the library with the impartial opinion of an "outsider"—a subject or collection expert with no stake in the library's collection—whose analysis is not influenced by the sense of "ownership" that might otherwise bias a local evaluator. The outside expert's close examination of the collection should reveal areas that need to be updated or further developed, highlight how it meets the needs of library patrons, and point out opportunities for user- or collection-centered development. The value of the outside expert's opinion lies in its impartiality; a "fresh" set of eyes on a collection can reveal issues that familiarity causes librarians to overlook.

This does not mean that an outside expert's opinion is completely objective; like any evaluator, the outside expert approaches the task with personal and professional values and preferences that ultimately influence his or her analysis.

Although "pure" direct analysis involves the employment of an outside expert, librarians apply this method of analysis on a regular basis when they undertake weeding projects to maintain the library's collection (see below for more on weeding). When they apply direct analysis to collection maintenance, librarians examine books on the shelves to assess their physical condition and make judgments about their relevance and contemporary appeal. Following established guidelines for age and condition, the librarian considers whether each item on the shelf should remain in the library's collection, be replaced with a new or updated copy, or be removed.

Comparative Statistics

The comparative statistical approach involves the collection and comparison of measures of collection size and expenditures over time or in correspondence with similar data collected by peer libraries. Libraries may compare the size and diversity of their collections to those housed in similar libraries, contrasting the total number of volumes, unique titles, and formats collected by the library to the same figures for a peer institution. The value of a library's comparison of these measures to those collected by a peer library lies in the congruence between measures; for comparisons among peers to be considered effective, both libraries must "agree on the definition of each statistical component and implement identical measurement methods" (Johnson 2009, 244). The Institute of Museum and Library Services and OCLC offer services to aid libraries in the comparison process. IMLS's "Compare Public Libraries" tool (see https://harvester.census.gov/imls/compare/index.asp) allows libraries to compare descriptive measures collected via the annual Public Libraries Survey. The free service permits them to compare themselves to libraries in similar geographic regions; of similar size; with similar organizational characteristics, operating budgets, and staffing; featuring similarly sized collections; and offering similar services. The OCLC's WorldCat Collection Analysis service (see http://www.oclc.org/collectionanalysis/default.htm) allows libraries to compare their collections against the holdings in WorldCat and with those of other WorldCat member libraries. The WorldCat Collection Analysis service allows libraries to identify areas of strength and weakness in their collections, potential gaps, and areas of uniqueness in terms of collection content.

What Comparative Statistics Tell Us   Comparing collection size, format diversity, and budgets among libraries results in the evaluation of one library's collection in terms of another. If the comparison library is considered superior, the library conducting the evaluation might use the results of comparative statistics to set goals for increasing the volume of its collections so that it more closely resembles the size of the comparison library, or for diversifying the number of formats it collects so that its collection more closely reflects the peer library's diversity of format. The assumption that underlies the use of comparative statistics in libraries seems to be that "more is better." Libraries comparing themselves with institutions in similar geographic regions or that serve similarly sized populations typically consider the large size and diversity of a collection to be an objective measure of excellence. Although size and diversity may be one measure, it is not a definitive one that can be captured by descriptive collection statistics alone. The tendency to view descriptive collection statistics through a "more is better" lens makes these data effective supports for lobbying activities that argue, for example, for increases in subscription services and targeted purchasing. The uniformity of these data and the ease with which they can be collected also allow libraries to engage in an internal and historical comparison that charts and tracks changes in the collection's size and diversity.

When librarians examine historical collection data, noting growth and changes in the library's collection over time and considering these changes in terms of the library's mission and goals, this process of statistical comparison may be considered assessment. Here, statistics describing the size of a collection, its age, or its diversity may be viewed as objective measures of a library's collection development activity, and as they represent the library's progress toward its goals, they can help document a library's achievement of its stated goals.

User-Centered Techniques

Circulation Analysis

As noted previously, the advent of electronic integrated library systems has made the collection of circulation and collection data much easier. In addition to facilitating access to shelf lists and reports describing holdings by subject and format, the ILS can provide reports of circulation patterns and trends, identifying areas of high circulation; organizing circulation information by user group (e.g., "youth" or "adult"); and listing recalls, reserves, and renewal requests. As Johnson notes, circulation data can provide us with many useful measurements, including "how many items are checked out each month, what areas are most heavily used, and what areas get little or no use" (2009, 248). Because the data generated by the ILS in circulation reports are objective, Evans and Saponaro (2005) point out, this measurement method can be considered a useful check on other measures of the library's collection.

Libraries use circulation data to compile a number of measurements, among which are three that are considered key:

1. *Circulation per capita*: The number of books circulated in relationship to the number of people in a library's service area during a specified period of time, expressed in a ratio of books per person
2. *Turnover rate*: The number of times each item in the library has circulated during a period of time, determined by dividing the total number of loans during that period by the total number of books in a library's collection
3. *Use factor*: The ratio of circulation to holdings, described as a percentage of a library's circulation in comparison to the percentage of the collection composed of the target material (e.g., graphic novels represent 30 percent of the library's circulation and account for 25 percent of the collection)

These statistics provide us with descriptive measures that demonstrate how the library's collection is used; however, unless these measures are compared against a standard or a goal set by the library, they remain descriptive and not evaluative. Thus, many libraries collect measures of circulation to identify trends in the use of particular areas of their collections (descriptive measurement), for the purposes of comparing measures of collection use over time or comparing the size and makeup of the collection to professional standards (evaluation) and to demonstrate the library's progress toward meeting its collection development and circulation goals (assessment).

What Circulation Analysis Tells Us The circulation statistics described here—circulation per capita, turnover rate, and use factor—are representative and descriptive measures that are essentially fictions. Circulation per capita describes the average number of materials each member of the population borrowed from the library if each member of the population actually used the library; turnover rate describes the average loans for each item in the library, assuming that circulation is even across the collection; and use factor describes circulation as a figure proportionate to the size of a portion of the collection. These statistics are useful, however, because they provide us with a numeric image of how the library's collection is used and allow us to track increases or decreases in circulation over time, identify areas of periodic or consistent high use in the collection, and advocate for more resources to develop the collection.

Circulation numbers are probably the most common statistics reported by libraries; however, they are often also the most misunderstood. Although stakeholders may consider high circulation numbers a sign of library effectiveness, several outside factors unrelated to the quality of the library and its collection can influence circulation figures. The location of the library, its proximity to bookstores and other materials centers, the literacy level of the community it serves, the size of its collection, and

Table 7.1.   Interpreting Circulation Statistics

Circulation Statistic	What This Figure Tells Us	How This Figure Can Be Interpreted
Circulation per Capita	Average number of materials borrowed by each member of the library's service population; a measure of circulation in terms of population size This figure can be parsed to account for circulation in collections defined by audience, subject, or format (e.g., 2.2 adult materials circulate per capita and 1.5 YA materials circulate per capita).	• High circulation per capita indicates high use of the collection and suggests its relevance. • Low circulation per capita can suggest the need for more materials, a need that may be further justified by examining ILL statistics.
Turnover Rate	Average number of times each item in the library has been borrowed within a specific period of time; a measure of circulation in terms of the collection's size This figure can be parsed to account for circulation in collections defined by audience, format, or subject (e.g., YA fiction turns over 2 times per year, whereas YA videos turn over 4 times per year).	• High turnover rate in specific subject areas or formats may indicate a need for more material. • Historical peaks in the turnover of items in specific areas of the collection may indicate the influence of a school assignment. • Persistent increases in the turnover of items in specific subject areas or formats may indicate a new or growing reading or information interest among the population.

Use Factor	Percentage of circulation represented by a portion of the collection defined by audience, subject or format in comparison to the percentage of the collection comprising the same material; a targeted measure of circulation in terms of collection density	• Percentage of circulation attributed to YA materials indicates the comparative interest of patrons in this collection. • When use factor is high (e.g., percent circulation attributed to YA material is comparatively high, and percentage of the collection described as YA is low), more material may be needed to respond to demand. • When use factor is low (e.g., percent circulation attributed to YA material is comparatively low, and percentage of the collection described as YA is high), the collection may require weeding.

even the availability of parking can influence library circulation in a positive or negative direction. Even if a library takes these external influences on circulation into account, circulation statistics still do not completely evince library quality. Because these data do not reflect in-house use of library materials and only report user "successes" (i.e., circulation data document a user's success at finding library material), their value for evaluation and assessment is less clear. Furthermore, as Evans and Saponaro (2005) argue, circulation data do not reveal how and if the checked-out item was used by the patron who borrowed it and, similarly, they do not tell us whether the user found the item valuable or useful. Thus, while circulation data can reveal areas of high use in the library's collection and support the purchase of duplicate copies of in-demand and highly used individual items, their value for determining the quality of a library's collection is limited.

In-House Use Studies

Because circulation statistics do not reveal the full use of the library's collection (e.g., these statistics exclude the use of noncirculating material, such as reference texts), many libraries consider circulation in combination with "in-house use," measures of the use of materials within the library. Measuring in-house use of library materials can be challenging, as many of the methods that gauge this use rely on the cooperation of library users. Libraries may conduct studies of in-house use by asking patrons not to reshelve books and then counting the number of items left on shelving carts or study tables; however, as Matthews has warned, "this method will underreport actual use because the library's customers will return items to the shelves, even when asked not to" (2007, 132). An observation study, conducted following the instructions described in chapter 4, may provide a closer estimation of in-house use. Following an established protocol, librarians may observe library use with the intent of documenting and counting the number of materials used but not borrowed by library patrons. As Johnson cautions, libraries conducting observation studies must take care to "time the study appropriately, so that data do not reflect use in peak or slow periods" exclusively (2009, 249). Like measures of library use based on circulation, studies of the in-house use of library materials reflect patron successes rather than their failures and neglect to document those instances when patrons were unable to find the material they wanted.

What In-House Use Tells Us   Studying the in-house use of library materials can be advantageous, particularly considering the use of non-circulating material, like reference books, current copies of periodicals, and technological equipment reserved for in-library use only. In-house use studies provide measures that complement circulation statistics. Studying the noncirculating material patrons use and leave behind and observing patrons in the library allows us to measure the following:

1. *Use of reference books, periodicals, and circulating materials*: If patrons are asked not to reshelve materials after use, the reference books, periodicals, and circulating items left on carts or study tables can give us a sense of which print resources library users consult regularly and suggest areas or formats of high interest and use in the collection.
2. *Use of technological resources*: Observational studies can demonstrate when and how patrons use the library's technological resources, including wi-fi, public access terminals, and databases.
3. *Use of technology equipment*: If the library offers patrons laptops, tablets, or electronic readers to use in the library, keeping track of their use can demonstrate their popularity and, if need exceeds demands, suggest a need for additional equipment.

Just as researchers and practitioners have noted external factors that affect circulation, similar internal and external factors may affect the tendency for library patrons to use materials within the confines of the library building. The breadth and depth of the library's reference collection may draw users to this feature, and the availability of computer workstations and technology equipment can affect in-house use of the library as well; availability of comfortable seating, a helpful library staff, and library card ownership also affect this type of library use.

ILL Analysis

Measurements of interlibrary loan usage can help librarians document the search "failures" that circulation and in-house use measurements overlook and can point out areas of the collection that may require deeper or further development. Although interlibrary loan use would appear to be a measure of patrons' use of other libraries, as Johnson notes, "items requested through inter-library loan represent a use of the collection because the requester has checked the collection, found the item lacking (either not owned or missing), and has decided he or she still needs it" (2009, 251). Just as librarians may examine circulation figures to determine areas of high use in the library's collection, they may consider interlibrary loan statistics to be equivalent indicators of areas of particular and unsatisfied needs. For example, repeated interlibrary loan requests for specific titles—or for titles that offer particular kinds of informational or educational support (e.g., academic versus popular support)—may be evidence of a class assignment or curriculum demand and should be considered when developing the collection. Interlibrary loan statistics may be best considered in conjunction with circulation statistics. As Bishop (2007) points out, when examining the use of interlibrary loan for requests in particular subject areas, these figures should be compared with circulation figures to determine whether these requests are related to heavy use of that section of the collection or the interlibrary loan requests reflect a true lack of library material.

What ILL Statistics Tell Us　Although ILL statistics demonstrate when, where, and how often patrons request material from other libraries, these measures may not always be indicators of a library collection's "failure." Among libraries participating in consortia, ILL statistics may demonstrate the strength of the consortia's collection to meet the needs of patrons. Following the lead of academic libraries, public library members of consortia may rely on collaborative collection development practices that discourage significant duplication of resources in favor of developing more diverse and unique collections in individual libraries. Public libraries may examine ILL, circulation, and collection measures to determine how collaborative collection development impacts individual library collections and their use. For example, Leslie Button, Rachel Lewellen, Kathleen Norton, and Pamela Skinner's (2012) report describing a cooperative collection development project that had a goal of reducing the number of duplicate titles among the academic library members of a small consortium cited collection and circulation statistics to demonstrate the project's effectiveness. Following implementation of cooperative collection development, each library reported an increase in the percentage of unique titles purchased for each collection, a decrease in duplicate copies of material purchased across libraries, and a modest increase in circulation attributed to resource sharing, figures that demonstrate the success of the program in terms of its goals.

Considering interlibrary loan statistics as a measure complementary to circulation measures and measures of in-library use can illuminate how patrons use the library and its partners in consortia; however, depending on the culture of the library, this figure may be biased against young adult library patrons. That is, whereas adults may feel free to request materials via interlibrary loan, young adults may not know about the service or may have time-sensitive, school-related demands that make it impracticable for them to wait for requested material to arrive at the library. If interlibrary loan is a service offered through the library's ILS, these statistics might be best considered in terms of user class (e.g., "youth" or "adult") and may be analyzed to determine the comparative use of this service by young people and adults. This examination of interlibrary loan statistics by user type can reveal particular weaknesses in the collection as well as particular uses of the library by young people. For example, frequent requests for college level or technical texts by young people may reveal students' use of the library to support advanced placement or technical course demands and may suggest topical areas of local development to support this use.

MEASURING, EVALUATING, AND ASSESSING NETWORKED RESOURCES AND THEIR USE

In many public libraries access to networked resources—subscription databases and resources available locally and remotely through the library's computer network—is facilitated to varying degrees by consortia, groups of libraries and institutions that work together to negotiate contracts with electronic resource providers at competitive costs. Statewide library agencies, using monies provided by the Library Services and Technology Act and administered by the Institute for Museum and Library Services, may also provide public and school libraries with access to networked and database resources. Above and beyond these resources provided by state agencies or made accessible via consortial agreements, individual libraries or library systems may provide further resources to patrons, adding additional subscription resources or licenses to the library's collection of electronic and networked resources. Procured by individual libraries or library systems or made available under the auspices of consortial agreements, public libraries make the following types of networked resources available to patrons (described in Johnson 2007, 46):

1. online databases facilitating access to full-text periodical content (like EBSCO and ProQuest)
2. online reference sources (like Britannica Online or Facts on File)
3. streaming video collections

4. commercial search engines (like Nettrekker)
5. e-book collections
6. online tutorial services
7. software (e.g., Microsoft Office)

Library patrons may access the web-based resources within the library or remotely; the degree of access patrons have inside and outside of the library is dictated by the terms of the agreement the library, system, consortium, or statewide agency has forged with individual networked service providers and the library's technological capacity.

Librarians operating within consortia may have limited individual input into the complex process of electronic resource negotiation and procurement, which makes the local measurement, evaluation, and assessment of electronic and networked resources processes that would seem to have little impact on consortium or state agency selection activity. Because the agreements into which consortia enter do include licensing and resource-sharing agreements related to young adult or student-centered databases and resources, however, it is imperative that YA librarians in member libraries measure, evaluate, and assess these resources selected for young people. Furthermore, because the library's networked resources are characterized not only by the services to which libraries subscribe and the content these services allow patrons to access, but also by the infrastructure that supports patron access to them, evaluation of the library's networked resources involves the consideration of not only what patrons may access, but also how this access is facilitated (or limited) within and outside of the library. Thus, the process of measurement, evaluation, and assessment of the library's networked resources involves

1. measuring, evaluating, and assessing the library's technological infrastructure;
2. measuring, evaluating, and assessing the networked information content the library makes available to its patrons; and
3. measuring, evaluating, and assessing the use of networked content.

Measuring, Evaluating, and Assessing the Library's Technological Infrastructure

The library's technological infrastructure consists of the systems—including devices, workstations, networks, and cabled and wireless systems—that allow patrons to access electronic and networked resources. Just as the library's architecture and shelves, spinners, racks, and display tables facilitate patron access to print resources and are a component of the library's physical infrastructure, the technological systems, tools, and devices maintained by the library facilitate patron access to the library's electronic resources and are part of its technological infrastructure. Because the networked resources to which the library subscribes require technological tools to facilitate their use (e.g., devices with web browsing capability to view web-based databases and resources; applications for PDF, EPUB, and other publishing formats to allow download and access to any full-text provided by networked resources; and media players that allow users to play video or listen to audio files), it is especially important to consider how the library's technological infrastructure supports its young adult patrons, for whom the library may be one of few free technological access points in the community. Although the young people who make use of the library's technological infrastructure—its wireless connectivity and its public access workstations—may have access to mobile technologies, have access to computers in school, or live in households that own computers, competition for these resources at home and at school can be high, and, as the Institute of Museum and Library Services funded 2010 *Opportunity for All* report, describing the use of technological tools in public libraries, demonstrates, the public library's computers are "still of critical importance" to teens (Becker et al. 2010, 38).

Measuring the Library's Technological Infrastructure

Because the majority of young adults who access the Internet in public libraries use library computers to do so (Becker et al. 2010, 38), taking stock of the library's technological infrastructure by considering the nature and extent of the devices and resources available to young adults is a key factor in the assessment and evaluation of the library's networked resources. Many public libraries reserve computers for the exclusive use of young adults, which ensures teen access to technological tools required to access online resources. An inventory of the devices, hardware, software, ports, and wireless "hot spots" available for young adult use functions as a starting point for evaluation and assessment; when considered against measures of networked content and use (see below), it can help to determine whether teen use of the library's subscription and networked resources is hindered or aided by its infrastructure.

The library's technological infrastructure is a critical component of its networked resources; thus, the evaluation and assessment of networked resources for young adults begins with an inventory of the tools and access opportunities the library provides or reserves for exclusive use by young adults. This inventory may include the following:

1. *Number of youth public access workstations*: Number of public access workstations reserved for exclusive use by young adults (in the library's young adult room or section) and/or the number of public access workstations reserved for their use during periods of high youth library traffic (e.g., during after-school hours or on the weekends)

2. *Age of public access computers*: The age of the computers designated for use by the public as well as the library's upgrade cycle, the library's predetermined schedule for replacing computers

3. *Youth public access workstation software*: Software packages (e.g., Microsoft Office, iWork, Open Office, Adobe), Internet browsers (e.g., Chrome, Firefox), and media software (e.g., Flash player, QuickTime) available at each public access workstation reserved for use by young adults

4. *Peripheral technology available for young adult use*: The number of zip drives, headphones, web cameras, microphones, or other external hardware available for young adult use

5. *Device availability*: The devices—tablet computers, e-readers, or laptops—available for exclusive young adult use or, absent exclusive devices, for use by all library patrons including young adults, including any restrictions on this use (e.g., in-library use only, no installs or downloading)

6. *Youth public access workstation Internet connectivity and restrictions*: The speed of Internet access at each station as well as any restrictions on Internet use (e.g., use of filters or restricted access to services like chat, e-mail, or games)

7. *Plug-in access availability*: Number of Ethernet ports and electrical jacks available in the library's young adult room or section and/or number of Ethernet ports and electrical jacks available in the library for young adult use

8. *Wi-fi access availability*: Speed and availability of wireless access to the Internet, including whether this service is available when the library is closed

A description of the technological tools and services libraries make available to young adults for their exclusive use represents what John Bertot (Bertot et al. 2001) calls "extensiveness"—measures of how much of a service a library provides. These measures are what evaluators call "inputs," measures or descriptions of what an institution provides or makes available with the resources it is given. Measurements of extensiveness are often reported to state agencies and library stakeholders as a way of demonstrating how the library allocates its funding reserved for technology tools. As with any measurement, these measures of the library's technological infrastructure are descriptive, not evaluative, and until they are compared against a standard or benchmark or interpreted through an established lens, they merely describe the technological resources the library makes available for young adults.

What Measures of the Library's Technological Infrastructure Tell Us Inventories and counts of the library's technological resources provide a quantitative picture of its infrastructure. These measures may be compared to professional and locally established benchmarks or, if col-

lected over time, may be considered evidence of the historical development of the library's technology services. It is important to note, however, that these benchmarks are emerging and subject to change, as libraries
and professionals work to develop best practices for technology provision in the face of what seems to be overwhelming demand for service
and access.

The rapid development and expansion of technology services in libraries has challenged professionals to establish benchmarks to employ
in the evaluation of the library's technological infrastructure. Reports like
the annual Public Library Funding and Access Study and *Opportunity for
All* (Becker et al. 2010) have described the library technology landscape
and noted that although the library's technological resources are among
the most highly used, libraries struggle to meet growing demand for
services. Two newly created benchmarks for libraries to use when considering the strengths of their networked resources and technology facilities—the ALA's Office for Information Technology Policy's "The Library
in the Networked World: The ALA Self-Assessment Tool" (n.d.) and
"The Library Edge" (available at http://www.libraryedge.org/), an initiative supported by a number of professional organizations, including the
ALA and the Urban Libraries Council—are freely accessible tools that
may be applied to the evaluation of the library's technological infrastructure. Although both resources describe additional points of evaluation
for a library's technology programs and services, several of their benchmarks can be applied directly to the local assessment of the library's
technological infrastructure in terms of the measures shown in table 7.2.

Benchmarks like these allow librarians to "understand best practices
in public access technology services for their communities and determine
what steps they need to take to improve their technology services" (Library Edge 2013, "Benchmarks and Resources," para. 1). As indicators of
best practices, these benchmarks help librarians set goals for resource
improvement and, in the words of the self-assessment tool, help librarians to "outline a vision for the future that libraries can strive toward"
(ALA Office for Information Technology Policy n.d.). Because benchmarks are optimal guidelines and suggest a "vision for the future," librarians may wish to assess their progress toward this vision by comparing
measures describing the library's technological infrastructure over time,
noting, for example, increases in the number of public access terminals
reserved for young adult use, the expansion of bandwidth and wireless
accessibility, and the establishment of device-lending programs.

For YA librarians, assessing the library's progress toward the goal of
making Internet and electronic resources available to its entire community involves considering the parity of resources available to adults and
young adults in the library. A comparison of the library's young adult
technological services to its adult services may reveal service discrepancies and support an argument to enhance the library's technological

Table 7.2. Exemplary Benchmarks for Assessing the Library's Technological Infrastructure

Measurement	Suggested Benchmark	
	ALA Self-Assessment Tool	Library Edge
Number of youth public access workstations	Low ratio of users to equipment; wait for computer use is minimal	The library has sufficient number of device hours available on a per capita basis.
Peripheral technology available for YA use		The library provides peripheral equipment that allows patrons to complete tasks, including headphones, printers, and scanners; multimedia equipment; video-conferencing equipment; and presentation equipment.
Device availability		Internet-enabled devices with extended session periods are loaned within the library and for use outside the library.
Connectivity	Highest speed connection available at all workstations and for wireless connections; all branches are networked	The library meets or exceeds the minimum bandwidth capacity necessary to support public user demand (recommended: each public Internet user is allotted at least 500kbps upload and 1mbps download of network bandwidth capability).
Wi-fi access availability	Wireless service available (see above for recommended connectivity standard)	The wireless network signal extends to all public areas of the library.

infrastructure to allow for equivalent access opportunities. Because the number of young adults in a library's service population is typically a fraction of its adult service population, a prima facie comparison of the library's technical infrastructure supporting resources allocated for adult and young adult use does not prove or disprove equality of access. Instead, libraries may compare the number of resources available in proportion to the population (population total/number of workstations) or the number of resources available per 1,000 persons (number of workstations/population total * 1,000), as in table 7.3.

Here, although young adults are served by only one-fifth of the public access workstations, because they are only a fraction of the sample library's population, their proportional access to public library workstations is greater than that of the adults in this community.

The number of workstations available per 1,000 persons in the library's population is a figure commonly reported to state agencies and is used for comparison in the Public Libraries in the United States Survey; calculating this figure allows libraries to evaluate their technological infrastructure—albeit in terms limited to the number of workstations available—against peer libraries to set service goals. Individual libraries, library systems, or state agencies may use this figure, or a figure describing the population per workstation, to set goals for access as well. For example, the Florida Library Association's minimum standard for the number of public access workstations is 1 for every 3,000 members of the population (2012, 25), and the South Carolina State Library's "Technology Standards for South Carolina Public Libraries" state that the public library should provide one computer for every 1,500 members of its population (2005, 7).

Although state library agencies like the Florida Library Association and the South Carolina State Library have developed standards and benchmarks for libraries to use when evaluating their technological infrastructure, these standards are notably general and do not include mention of special services or provisions for young people. The Young Adult Library Services Association's "National Teen Space Guidelines" (2012b) comes closest to suggesting best practices for technology service provision specifically to young adults. Although the guidelines do not include quantitative benchmarks, the publication suggests a number of technological resources that should be prioritized or available for exclusive use by young adults in designated spaces. YALSA's guidelines suggest multi-

Table 7.3. Sample Comparison of a Public Library's Young Adult and Adult Technological Infrastructures

Young Adult Infrastructure		Adult Infrastructure	
Workstations reserved for young adults	5	Workstations reserved for adults	25
Young adult population	1,200	Adult population	20,000
YA population per workstation: 240		Adult population per workstation: 800	
YA workstations per 1,000: 4.16		Adult workstations per 1,000: 1.25	

media items selected during traditional collection development (e.g., video games, music, audiobooks) as well as resources associated with the library's technological infrastructure, including:

1. downloading stations for in-library use;
2. circulating hardware (like laptops, mp3 players, and e-readers);
3. stationary and portable technologies for use in the library;
4. access to "current and emerging platforms and tools, including but not limited to social networking and photo-sharing sites, user-driven communication tools for tagging and review sharing, audio and visual production technologies, and interactive Web services"; and
5. wireless capability.

These guidelines emphasize the importance of technological resources in the lives of young people and position the library—and the library's young adult services—as a central provider of these resources for its patrons.

Measuring the Library's Networked Information Content

The library's networked information content for young adults—including academic and student databases, links to online homework help or tutoring resources, and electronic reference texts—is an increasingly important component of its collection. Although the most recent Pew Internet report (Purcell, et al. 2012) describing high school students' research habits concluded that young people rely primarily on Internet search engines rather than databases and other electronic resources to complete assignments, the implementation of the Common Core State Standards across the United States, which require students to read and consider complicated informational texts, is likely to turn teachers', librarians', and students' attention from the open web to networked resources. Furthermore, as school library budgets are squeezed and schools increasingly rely on external funding, school libraries—the site of many students' first introduction to informational, educational, and research texts—are turning to digital forms in greater numbers (Krueger 2012). Thus, as students are introduced to digital resources in school and given homework and other assignments that require Internet access and networked information to complete, the public library's networked resource collection becomes an important source for them.

Librarians interested in evaluating and assessing the library's networked information content must first develop an inventory of what resources have been selected for and made available to young adults. This inventory includes not just details of the thematic content of subscription databases and digital reference tools, but also information on in-house and remote accessibility of these resources' content. Because state library agencies and consortia negotiate subscriptions and access on behalf of multiple libraries and library systems, availability or duplication of these resources in school libraries as well as the local public library is especially important for young adult librarians to note, as students may visit the public library to gain access to resources introduced in school. The extent of each resource may be further described in terms of the content it makes available to users. Although many evaluators consider the availability of full text to be the primary measure of a networked resource's value, as Sam Brooks (2006) has argued, this is not the only descriptive measure that can be applied to the evaluation and assessment of networked resources. The following metrics, suggested by Brooks and the Arizona State Library, Archives and Public Records "Collection Development Training Guide" (2013a), and documented in Karla Krueger's useful 2012 *School Library Media Research* article, provide a more complete description of the contents of a networked resource:

1. *Full-text availability*: Which resources are available in full-text form, and to what extent is full text available (e.g., if the full text is available, how retrospective is this full-text coverage)?
2. *"Active" full-text titles*: What percentage of the full-text titles (e.g., magazines or journals) is actively collected and maintained by the database?
3. *"Inactive" titles*: What percentage of full-text titles or titles indexed by the resource has ceased publication?
4. *Special features*: What special features—video, audio, or image files—are made available through this resource?
5. *Subject coverage*: What subjects (e.g., general reference, biography, health) are covered by the resource?
6. *Audience*: What audience (e.g., high school or middle and junior high students) is addressed by the resource?
7. *Reviews & recommendations*: Is the resource listed or recommended in a standard bibliography (like Wilson's *Core Collections*), and has it been reviewed or recommended in professional journals?

Information like that listed may be uncovered by examining the title lists of databases and electronic resources made available by vendors, as well as promotional information and contracts negotiated by libraries.

As noted previously, the library's subscription and licensed resources may be counted, listed, and described in terms of their access requirements (e.g., in-library use only, remote access). The extent of each resource may be further described in terms of the contents it makes available to users and, if specified, the audience to whom the resource is directed. This information, presented in a table (e.g., see table 7.4), makes it easy to determine the subject coverage afforded by the library's collection of networked resources and, if necessary, prioritize resources for weeding or retention.

Table 7.4. Sample Comparison of Three Databases

	Remote access permitted with library card	Collected at high school or secondary school	Type of resource	Subject and audience	Full text availability	Active full-text titles (%)	Inactive titles (%)	Special features	Recommended in core collections or review journal
Gale Virtual Reference Library	X	X	E-reference	General reference grades 6–12	X full text of selected reference resources	N/A	N/A	Text translation; audio version of text available	M/JHCC; *LJ*'s "Best Overall Database," 2012
Britannica Online Public Library Edition	X		E-reference	General reference grades K–12	X Full text of selected reference resources	N/A	N/A	Mouseover Spanish translation available	
Opposing Viewpoints in Context	X	X	Database of e-book, periodical, media, and web content	Current events and controversies, grades 9–12	X 80–85% of full text of selected e-book resources; full text of some periodicals with limited backfiles	~77%	~23%	Multimedia content including audio and video	*Booklist* starred review (5/1/2012)

The contents of databases and electronic resources can be compared us-ing freely available services, like the Academic Databases Assessment Tool (ADAT), designed by the Center for Research Libraries, which allows libraries to compare the content of fifteen bibliographic databases and nine full-text databases, or comparison services offered by vendors like Serials Solutions or EBSCO. These comparison services indicate where database content overlaps and allow for the comparison of search and access features (see table 7.5).

Although knowledge of unique and overlapping content is key to the consideration of networked resources, as Brooks has noted, comparison services tend to describe only "surface" data and may not indicate whether the full-text content of competing databases is truly comparable. For example, Brooks notes, "reports from these comparison services may show that Journal X is available in full text in Database A from 1922 to the present, while the same journal is available in full text in Database B from 1995 to 1998, but will classify this journal simply as a title in common to both databases," effectively equalizing two resources that offer very different ranges of full text coverage (2006, 28). Differences in the ways in which different networked resources identify titles and sources indexed or included in their databases may also lead to faulty comparisons "because competing vendors don't standardize their database coverage lists" (Brooks 2006, 28). That said, when considered in terms of use (see below), these comparisons can suggest the unique value of specific vendors' interfaces, organization, and content.

What Measures of the Library's Networked Resources Content Tell Us

Collection-centric measurements of networked resources provide descriptions of what is currently available to library users in terms of these resources' content, full-text availability, and inclusion of special features. This inventory allows librarians to better determine whether there are topical "holes" in the collection that may suggest the need for more specialized resources and, when budgetary changes require libraries to reconsider resource subscriptions, can help librarians to determine which resources may be redundant.

These descriptive data may also be used to compare resources to one another or to compare the library's networked and print resources for the

Table 7.5.   ADAT Comparison of Two Databases. Accessed March 13, 2013

	Overlap Titles	Unique Titles	Total Titles
Academic Search Complete	1,702	9,750	11,452
Wilson OmniFile Full Text, Mega Edition	1,702	1,519	3,221

purposes of evaluation. As a form of list-checking that involves the comparison of more than one title list or the comparison of an electronic title list to a list of print periodicals, reference titles, or monographs collected by the library, an evaluation of the extensiveness of the library's electronic resources is not without bias. Although comparison of the extensiveness of one electronic resource to another may reveal differences in title selection and coverage, unless one is considered a standard against which the other is measured, the worth of this evaluative method is limited. As others have argued about the utility of the list-checking method in the evaluation of print resources, these measures may be best evaluated against measures of resource use (see below). When considered in terms of the library's goals and objectives, however, these measures might better inform assessment. For example, if the library's goal is to make many diverse resources available in full text to patrons in print and online, both onsite and remotely, the value of an electronic resource may be a function of the extent of the full-text availability of its resources. If the library's goal is to make a core collection of resources available to patrons in multiple formats, duplication of content across the library's print and electronic resource collections may be a measure of its value.

Measuring the Library's Networked Resource Use

Though networked resources may be compared to one another and their contents considered in terms of the library's print collection to determine the scope, breadth, and depth of the entire collection to determine how, where, and to what extent the library offers the same or comparable material in print and digital form, use is an additional determinant of networked resource value. Measuring the use of electronic resources for evaluative purposes can be a complicated process. As Jill Grogg and Rachel Fleming-May have noted, "the murky terminology that has plagued evaluation of print-based materials usage has not improved significantly in discussion of electronic resources usage" (2010, 8). That is, although librarians and consortia may have increased access to standard numeric measures of electronic resource use, these measures are similar to circulation statistics and, though descriptive, cannot be considered evaluative measures per se. Thus, while projects like COUNTER (Counting Online Usage of Networked Electronic Resources) and SUSHI (Standardized Usage Statistics Harvesting Initiative) have provided librarians, publishers, and vendors with standards and best practices recommendations for defining and reporting electronic resource use data, these data alone cannot be considered evaluative. How and if library patrons use the information they view online or download from databases remains the central and difficult-to-solve problem of electronic resource evaluation and assessment.

E-metrics, measures of the library's electronic resource collections and their use, are considered the primary informants of use-based resource evaluation and assessment. Provided by compliant electronic resource vendors, e-metrics can provide information related to accessibility, electronic collections, and the use and users of these services. Although many of these measures are used at the consortium level to support decisions about resource selection and funding, librarians may consider some of them as they affect local collection development and reflect locally expressed information needs. COUNTER (Release 4, 2012) argues that the following statistics may be used to measure the use of networked resources—including databases and electronic books—in libraries:

1. number of sessions or logins to an online service or networked resource
2. number of searches, result clicks, and record views per month, per database
3. access denied by month, database, and category
4. total searches, result clicks, and views per month, by platform (e.g., content aggregator like EBSCOHost Integrated Search)
5. number of successful e-book title requests by month and title
6. number of successful e-book section requests by month and title
7. access denied to content items by month, title, and category
8. access denied to content items by month, platform, and category
9. total e-book searches by month and title

These measures describe not only how many users have accessed the library's subscription resources (number of searches, number of title requests), but also how many have succeeded in identifying and downloading content from these resources (number of full-content units examined), and they can be employed to determine the resource's cost per use. Cost per use, calculated by dividing the number of times a resource has been used by the total cost required to provide access to this resource, is a commonly used but sometimes misinterpreted metric. To determine cost per use, a librarian, library, or consortium must define *use*, which can be described three ways: number of sessions, number of searches, or number of full-content units examined. Though some critics argue that measures of use associated with counts of the number of sessions or searches initiated by patrons are the "virtual equivalent of door counts and circulation statistics and contribute little to our understanding of the role of the library and information sources in the life of the user" (Grogg and Fleming-May 2010, 8), the number of full-content units selected by users may more closely approximate a measure of use.

Cost per use is only one measure of the efficiency of a library's networked resources; the resources' capacity to meet user demands may also be considered measures of efficiency. The following statistics, provided by resource vendors, may be used to measure efficiency in these terms:

1. *Number of turnaways*: The number of times access to a resource has been denied to a user because the maximum number of licensed users has been reached
2. *Peak simultaneous users*: The highest number of users accessing a single resource during a specified period of time

The e-metrics described previously allow librarians to determine "whether the library has enough capacity to meet user demands for licensed resources," a figure that may be indicated by a prevalence of turnaways when the number of users requesting a service exceeds the number of simultaneous users allowed in the library's license (Bertot et. al. 2004, 32). It is important to note that the use of student databases tends to peak during the school year; thus, the number of turnaways, as well as the number of peak users, will likely ebb and flow throughout the year, making a single descriptive statistic (e.g., the average number of turnaways, the average number of peak users) a poor indicator of whether the library's subscription databases can be considered efficient. If the library's subscription databases have been selected to meet the educational needs of users, it will be important to examine the number of turnaways and peak usage figures on a more frequent basis to determine, for example, if the number of simultaneous users allowed by the resource license should be adjusted to meet user needs.

Librarians may also examine transaction logs to determine the proportion of users who access a networked resource in the library or from a remote location. To do this, they may wish to scrutinize the reports recorded by proxy servers, those servers that are used to authenticate off-site use of networked resources. Rewriting proxy servers, like OCLC's EZproxy, record remote requests for access to resources that require authentication, distinguishing requests by the IP address of the user's workstation. These requests are recorded in a system's transaction log file and may be exported for analysis using other programs.

What Measures of the Library's Networked Resource Use Tell Us

Just as measures of circulation provide us with quantitative data that describe one facet of how the library's collection is used, networked resource usage data provides librarians with similar information regarding the use of networked resources. Basic usage data—number of sessions, searches, result clicks, and record views and number of successful requests for full-text data or media files—provide librarians with a general picture of networked resource usage. The number of database sessions is, as Grogg and Fleming-May (2010) note, akin to the library door count, and may demonstrate interest in a resource but not necessarily its use.

The number of searches particularizes the session data, and as this figure is typically smaller than the number of sessions recorded, it may indicate a more purposeful visit to the library's networked resources collection. The Association of Research Libraries suggests that the number of searches demonstrates which "databases . . . are most heavily used, areas of user interest, [and] database popularity" (2001, slide 20). The number of full-text or other media requested by networked resources, the ARL argues, is analogous to the circulation counts of print material, a measure that further distinguishes heavily used databases and networked resources. Many libraries and consortia rely on usage statistics to assign a cost value to networked resources; cost-per-session, cost-per-query, or cost-per-full-text-request can be calculated to determine the comparative cost-per-use of the library's resources.

Measures of networked resource efficiency complement basic measures of use, allowing librarians to consider whether and when networked resources are being taxed (as determined by the number of peak users and the number of turnaways), measures of periodic resource popularity that may be mapped to curricular demand and used to help identify pervasive patterns of use. Thomas Peters (2002) encourages librarians to consider e-metrics over time, examining resource use throughout the year and comparing this use to that recorded during the previous year. By considering basic and peak usage statistics in a historical context, Peters writes, librarians "can begin to identify long-term trends in the adoption, diffusion and use of these e-resources" (2002). This technique may be particularly relevant to young adult librarians, who may correlate the high usage of particular resources with scholastic demand or to the introduction of particular resources in the school library media curriculum.

Young adult librarians should pay attention to trends in the use of networked resources selected expressly for young people, but it is important to note that use of these resources is not limited to young adults. That is, though students may be users of student versions or "junior editions" of networked resources, adult patrons may select these resources as well, especially if these resources have special features absent from "adult" databases that make material more accessible to struggling readers or non-native English speakers. Similarly, young adults may use networked resources selected for adults as well as for students, which discourages the equation of student resource use statistics with actual student use. Thus, though examining patterns of use associated with networked resources selected to meet the informational needs of young adults is revealing, it may be just as important to consider the use of these student-centered resources in comparison to the use of the library's greater collection of resources.

Evaluation and Assessment of Networked Resources

The evaluation and assessment of networked resources involves the consideration of multiple measures: the library's technological infrastructure, the content of its networked resources, and their use. The measurements, considered in tandem or isolation, contribute to library and consortial decision making about the perpetuation or dissolution of library contracts with electronic materials providers.

Because evaluation involves the comparison of measures of content, infrastructure, and use against standard benchmarks or peer institutions, libraries can combine the measures described previously to develop a comparative image of the library's collection of networked resources. Comparing patterns of use associated with specific networked resources across members of a consortium can illuminate areas of unique interest or need among specific populations served at particular locations and support decisions to discontinue subscription to a resource at the consortial level or contribute to arguments for the local selection of more specialized resources. Libraries determining the efficacy of their technological infrastructure for young adults may also consider how usage of networked resources may be affected by the availability of technologies and compare local measures of networked resource use to those collected by libraries with more robust infrastructures, then apply the results to an effort to lobby for more workstations or technological tools reserved for young adult use.

As the library considers how its networked resources collection reflects its mission and goals to make information accessible to its service population, it may wish to take into account how the contents of this collection reproduce or expand its entire collection. If the library's goal is to make comparable information and resources available across media, the print and networked collections should be somewhat comparable in scope and depth. If, however, the library looks to its networked resources to expand the collection, determining the diversity of the library's networked and print collections should be a goal of assessment.

MEASURING, EVALUATING, AND ASSESSING E-BOOK COLLECTIONS AND THEIR USE

As patron demand for e-books increases, libraries struggle to select, acquire, organize, and lend electronic books and to evaluate this newly developing service. Like networked resources, e-books require technology to use, and in the interest of making this content available to all patrons, most libraries have expanded their collections to include e-books for download as well as preloaded readers for patrons to borrow. Selection and acquisition of e-books may be accomplished in a number of ways and result in the development of diverse collections of material selected by consortia, vendors, and individual libraries and made available via multiple online portals. The extent of a YA librarian's influence on the content of the collection and its evaluation depends on how a library selects its e-books. The librarians at institutions that rely on consortial agreements to secure licensing for e-books may have little or no input into selection, whereas librarians at institutions that negotiate their own licensing agreements may be much more active participants in the selection process. To date, libraries, vendors, and publishers are engaged in what *Library Journal* has called an "unresolved tug of war" over pricing, access, and digital rights management, a conflict that has to some degree limited the ability of individual libraries to select and acquire material to meet unique local needs. Understanding how the library's collection of e-books meets—or fails to meet—patron needs and reflects patron interests is increasingly important, as libraries test new models of selection and acquisition and balance local demand against tightening budgets.

Measuring the Content of E-book Collections

As with the evaluation and assessment of networked resources, the evaluation and assessment of the library's e-books begins with a description and measurement of the resources available through this collection. The library's e-books may be measured, evaluated, and assessed as discrete collections of material or considered within the context of the library's whole collection. When e-book collections are considered in isolation, they can be described and measured in much the same way as print collections of material are; a virtual inventory of the library's e-book collection can provide librarians with the raw number of e-book materials selected for young adults, the distribution of titles across the fiction and nonfiction collections, and the average age of the whole collection (or subcollections of material in specific subject areas). Inventories may then be checked against lists, catalogs, or bibliographic resources to evaluate their extensiveness, and they may be compared to inventories of print material in subject and format areas. These collections may also be described in terms of their form; e-books may be available to patrons in EPUB format, a nearly universal digital format; in PDF; or in formats optimized for specific mobile or e-reading devices.

What Measuring the Content of E-book Collections Tells Us

As the library's e-book collection represents a facet of the institution's greater collection of material, it can be evaluated and assessed in terms similar to, but distinct from, those applied to the library's print collection. A number of factors distinguish the e-book from the print collection and affect our interpretation of measures of content in ways that distinguish its evaluation and assessment. First, e-book collections in libraries are limited in content, because various publishers refuse to sell or lease e-book material for library use; thus, the extensiveness of any e-book collection is not a function of how this collection represents the universe of published material, but rather of how this collection represents or reflects the limited universe of e-book material available to libraries. Second, many e-book collections are developed by consortia representing geographically and demographically diverse libraries and populations, making their comparison to local collections developed to meet observed local needs difficult. Third, libraries or consortia that allow for patron-driven acquisition (PDA) may find that their inventories reflect diverse standards associated with the demand of that fraction of patrons who borrow e-books, rather than professional standards suggested by bibliographies or standard catalogs.

Because the library's e-book collection may be more limited than its print collection, and because its selection may be influenced by consortial agreements rather than local concerns, as Alene Moroni notes, "getting away from the scorekeeping evaluation of the collection is a good idea" (2012, 26). Rather than assessing and evaluating the collection in terms of how many items are available, librarians may consider how the collection extends or duplicates the library's print collection and reflects the library's mission and goals for its e-book collections. In addition, Moroni advises, e-book collections should still be "subject to the same standards as those . . . appli[ed] to physical collections," including age and relevance (2012, 27). Just as material in the library's print collection becomes outdated and irrelevant, material in the library's e-book collection also ages and becomes obsolete. A virtual "direct analysis" of the library's collection, particularly in subject areas like science and medicine, which date quickly, is a relevant method for assessing the library's e-book collection in terms of its goals of making current and valid information accessible to patrons.

Measuring the Use of E-books

Vendors and aggregators that facilitate e-book licensing and lending in libraries provide consortia and libraries with circulation and use data similar to the information provided by the library's ILS. These data, which may be more or less explicit than those provided by the library's ILS, depending on the providing vendor or aggregator, can provide librarians with statistics indicating the number of loans, high circulating titles or subjects, patron holds on individual titles, and titles acquired through PDA. Some vendors may also provide librarians with more granular statistics describing use of e-book materials, including figures that describe the use or access of subdivisions of a title: sections, chapters, or definitions.

What Measuring E-book Use Tell Us

Statistics describing the circulation of the library's print collection demonstrate areas of high use and interest in the library's collection; similarly, circulation and use statistics reported by e-book vendors point out high interest and in-demand titles, authors, and subject areas in the library's collection. A number of factors affect the assessment and evaluation of the library's e-book collection, distinguishing the consideration of its content from the consideration of the content of the library's print collection, and the same is true of circulation statistics. Although circulation statistics associated with the library's e-book collection do demonstrate its use, this use is circumscribed by a number of factors that differentiate e-book from print material circulation. First, the limited number of electronic titles available to library patrons has a negative effect on e-book circulation. According to the 2012 *LJ* "Survey of E-book Usage in Public Libraries," "the paucity of titles available" in library e-book collections ultimately "deter[s] users from checking out books" (75). Second, because library users sometimes have to view a digital catalog separate from the library's ILS to browse and download material, use of the library's e-book collection may be limited to those who know about the service and the methods for finding and borrowing electronic material. Third, the availability of e-book readers among members of the community naturally affects e-book circulation and, in communities where the digital divide remains wide, e-book circulation will reflect this divide. Thus, e-book circulation statistics represent the interest and use of that segment of the library's user population with the knowledge and tools to find and download material from among the library's collection of electronic items, a fact that makes the application of standard library circulation statistics like circulation per capita somewhat irrelevant.

Although e-book circulation statistics may not be comparable to those associated with the print collection, these figures do provide libraries and librarians with information about patrons who use this service. These virtual library patrons may represent a new population of library users with needs and interests that both coincide with and diverge from those of traditional library patrons. Kristen Kruse's (2011, 135) brief review of studies comparing the use of electronic and print versions of the same titles demonstrated that high use of print resources or e-books does not predict comparably high use of the same title in a complementary format, suggesting that readers and information seekers may have different motivations for accessing and borrowing e-books. While popular and bestselling titles, as David Gray and Andrea Copeland observe, may always be "desired in both print and electronic formats" (2012, 338), library users may turn to print or electronic texts to meet different needs, which suggests that the value of e-book circulation statistics lies not in their comparison to print statistics, but in their solitary investigation. This hypothesis should inspire libraries that allow for PDA to consider the selections of patrons whose choices inspire the acquisition of material in electronic form. As these lists of PDA titles overlap with or diverge from those in the library's print collection and those requested by patrons through ILL, librarians can develop a clearer picture of the distinct (or not) e-book user and develop electronic book collections that reflect this population's needs and interests.

PUTTING IT ALL TOGETHER: THE COLLECTION EVALUATION AND ASSESSMENT PROJECT

Libraries engaged in collection evaluation and assessment consider several measurements of their collections and their use before drawing conclusions about the fitness of the collections that can then be applied to new collection development goals. These measurements may be collection centric and describe the scope, breadth, depth, and age of a whole collection, of topical areas of the collection, and of collections of nonprint and electronic materials, or they may be user centered and describe how particular areas of a collection are used by patrons within and outside the library building. Taken together, collection-centered and user-centered measures complement each other and, when applied to established standards and benchmarks and considered in terms of the library's mission, goals, and objectives, contribute to evaluation and assessment.

Because of the work involved in the compilation, comparison, and analysis of collection and user data, libraries often undertake large-scale collection evaluation projects within the context of even larger strategic planning projects that involve the assessment of the library's collection development practices. These projects, from start to finish, involve the consideration and reconsideration of the library's mission, goals, and objectives; the measurement of patron of needs, often in the form of needs assessment; and the measurement, evaluation, and assessment of the collection in terms of the library's mission, goals, and objectives. Such collection evaluation and assessment projects serve a number of purposes: for example, the resulting increase in knowledge about the collection and its use allows librarians participating in collection evaluation and assessment projects "to better understand the extent to which the collection meets the goals and mission of the library" and facilitates their adjustment and revision of "collecting and managing activities to increase congruence between collection and mission" (Johnson 2009, 254). Though this process is time consuming, Evans and Saponaro argue, "only after completing the task does the staff know the collection's strengths and weaknesses" (2005, 334). This process benefits the librarian as well; as Johnson suggests, through collection evaluation and assessment librarians can demonstrate "financial and professional accountability" as well as the "responsible stewardship of resources" (2009, 254).

Outside of the context of such large-scale evaluation projects, librarians can use measurement, evaluation, and assessment techniques like those described in this chapter to answer questions about the library's young adult collection and its use. Librarians wishing to determine, for example, what topical areas of the collection or which materials in which formats are most often used by library patrons undertake comparatively smaller evaluation projects, collecting data that drive or inspire the further development of sections of the library's collection. Table 7.6 is a matrix of common questions that spur evaluation and assessment activities as well as a description of data that support their investigation.

Measurement, Evaluation, or Assessment Question	Collection-Centered Data	Use-Centered Data	Results and Interpretation
Measurement Question: What topics or subjects represent areas of high use in the library's nonfiction collection? *Why do you want to know?* Areas of high use in the library's collection may indicate topics of interest or need among the service population.		*Circulation data:* lists of most highly circulated books in nonfiction. *Circulation data:* turnover rate of items in the collection by subject area. *Circulation data:* "use factor" (percent of circulation in subject areas divided by the percent of the collection represented by subject area collections)	Although circulation data can provide us with a list of the most highly circulated titles, it is useful to consider these titles in terms of the turnover and the use factor of the books in the subject collections in which they reside. For example, if Barron's *AP United States History* is highly circulated, "use factor" and turnover rate of comparable items in the library's test preparation collection (DDC 371) will indicate whether AP US History test guides are high-use resources.
Assessment Question: How does the library's collection of fiction reflect the library's goal of collecting award-winning material? *Why do you want to know?* The library's commitment to collecting award-winning titles is reflected by the percentage of the collection devoted to these titles. In addition, the extent of the library's award-winning collection,	*List-checking*		This assessment question requires the librarian to define "award-winning material" in terms of the scope of the awards the library makes it a goal to collect. Is an award-winning collection one that includes National Book Award winners and honor books? Pura Belpre winners and honor books? Stonewall Award winners and honor books? Once the awards are identified, the fiction collection should be checked against lists of winners of the selected awards. The percentage

measured in number of awards represented, and completeness of this collection, measured in terms of the depth of the collection reflecting each award, shows its commitment to collecting material of this type.

Evaluation Question: What resources in X subject does my library hold in common with the local high school, and how often are items in this area—duplicate and unique—used by patrons? *Why do you want to know?* Overlap of the public library's collection with the school library's collection is not necessarily a bad thing; students may expect to see books introduced in the school library on the shelves of the local public library as well.	*List-checking*	*Circulation data*: circulation of titles in common *Circulation data*: circulation of individual titles in the subject area held by the local library *Circulation data*: turnover rate of items in this section of the collection	of award titles collected is an indicator of the depth of the awards collection (e.g., the library collection features 60% of books that have won the Printz Award), and the percentage of the whole collection represented by award-winning books (e.g., 15% of the library's fiction collection is award-winning titles) is a measure of this commitment. Furthermore, the completeness of the library's collection of books that have won individual awards (e.g., does the library maintain a collection that includes books that have won ALA awards in at least the last 5 years?) suggests the depth of this collection. Checking the library's nonfiction collection against the school library's nonfiction collection in the same subject reveals titles in common as well as the breadth and depth of both collections considered in tandem. High usage (represented in terms of raw circulation and turnover rate) associated with items in common suggests the popularity of shared titles.

These examples are representative of small-scale evaluation projects that YA librarians may undertake to inform the further development of topical areas of the collection or to support the establishment or further development of collections of material in specific formats.

WEEDING LIBRARY COLLECTIONS

Although large-scale collection evaluation and assessment projects may only be undertaken periodically—perhaps once every five to ten years— librarians engage in smaller measurement, evaluation, and assessment tasks throughout the year. For example, many libraries report measurements of circulation and use to consortia and state library agencies on a regular basis and make these statistics available to librarians. These statistics are often used to inform, in part, a major collection maintenance activity associated with evaluation and assessment: weeding. Weeding or deselection is the process of identifying and removing unused, obsolete, or deteriorated materials from the library's collection. When informed by circulation and use statistics, the need to weed is, as Matthews asserts, "based on the reality that most items now being borrowed were previously borrowed in the recent past . . . and very few items that are now borrowed have sat on the shelves for a long period of time" (2005, 135). Librarians weed collections for reasons beyond circulation, as well. As Donna J. Baumbach and Linda L. Miller note, weeding is the "act of reevaluating items in the collection and removing any that are inaccurate, out of date, misleading, inappropriate, unused, in poor condition, or otherwise harmful to students" (2006, 3). Their definition of weeding highlights the necessity of ridding the library of material that is no longer current: outdated material that fails to include, in the case of science and medical books, the latest treatments and discoveries related to disease, or, in the case history and the social sciences, reflects antiquated thinking and bias, has the potential to mislead or perhaps even harm users. Arguably, library users expect the library to contain material that is accurate and up to date and reflects current thinking; these users do not necessarily check an item's publication date or engage in an extensive process of information evaluation, instead assuming that the library exercises a kind of quality control. Younger users with less experience in information seeking and assessment may be at an even greater disadvantage; these students, who, Baumbach and Miller (2006) note, have been taught to rely on the library for information, may accept outdated information as truth and act on erroneous facts or reproduce inaccuracies and biases in school assignments and reports.

Many librarians recoil at the idea of removing material from the library's collection. As Gail Dickinson remarks in her often-cited article defending weeding, "Crying Over Spilled Milk" (2005), "visions of headlines such as 'Librarian Trashes Precious Books' and scores of parent protesters guarding the dumpster can turn even the most determined [librarian] into an equally determined procrastinator" (24). Because weeding involves not only removing material from the library's collection, but also contributing this material to waste or recycling services, librarians worry that it is akin to book burning. Indeed, less scrupulous libraries and librarians do weed material that challenges their own beliefs and perspectives in the name of "weeding the collection"; however, when the activity is undertaken with the goal of maintaining the condition of the material and the accuracy of the library's collection and adheres to professional standards, weeding is a key element of collection development and maintenance. As the ALA states in its "Evaluating Library Collection" statement (excerpted at the beginning of this chapter), during the collection evaluation process, "physically deteriorated or obsolete materials may be replaced or removed" from the collection; however, "this procedure is not to be used as a convenient means to remove materials that might be viewed as controversial or objectionable" (1981). Instead, this procedure guarantees the maintenance of a collection that is both "active" and "of current interest to users" (ALA 1981).

The library and its collection derive a number of benefits from weeding:

1. *Space*: By removing inaccurate, outdated, or obsolete material from the library's shelves, weeding frees up space and makes the physical retrieval of library material easier for users.
2. *Circulation*: Weeding results in an increase of circulation as it draws patron's eyes to overlooked material. Because the library's shelves are less crowded, it is easier for users to find (and borrow) what they want. Furthermore, as the size of the library's collection decreases with weeding, the circulation turnover rate increases.
3. *Appearance*: When libraries weed old and worn material from the collection, newer material can take center stage. As Jeannette Larson writes in *CREW: A Weeding Manual for Modern Libraries*, "It is better to have fresh air and empty space on the shelves than to have musty old books that discourage investigation" (2008, 13).
4. *Authority*: Removing inaccurate or out-of-date material bolsters the library's reputation as a trusted source of information. When patrons can trust the authority of the material on the library's shelves, they can also trust the library.

Librarians also benefit from the weeding process:

1. *Knowledge*: Weeding involves the intense, title-by-title perusal and evaluation of the library's collection. This kind of in-the-stacks activity increases a librarian's knowledge of the contents of the collection.

2. *Planning*: As librarians develop an intimate relationship with their collections through weeding, they also begin to identify previously unknown gaps in the collection and areas that require further development and can begin to plan for filling these gaps and developing these areas of need.

In short, libraries, librarians, and library users benefit from weeding, as this activity makes the library's collection easier to negotiate, ensures that materials are up to date, and increases librarians' knowledge of the collections of which they are the stewards.

Criteria for Weeding

Numerous professional guides to weeding have been published that outline general and specific criteria for the evaluation and deselection of material from library collections. The most common guidelines for weeding are described in two acronyms: CREW and MUSTIE. CREW, which stands for continuous review, evaluation, and weeding, was first described in the 1976 title *The CREW Method*, by Joseph Segal and Belinda Book, and is outlined in *CREW: A Weeding Manual for Modern Libraries* (Larson and the Texas State Library and Archives Commission 2008). This manual emphasizes two criteria for weeding: the age of the material and its circulation. Larson outlines general benchmarks against which to check library materials in various subjects for age, then offers suggestions for weeding material based on the date of its last circulation. MUSTIE, an acronym that describes what Larson calls "six negative factors that frequently ruin a book's usefulness and make it a prime candidate for weeding" (2008, 46), is a second set of criteria for assessing individual items:

M = misleading or factually inaccurate
U = ugly and worn or beyond repair
S = superseded by a new edition of the same title or by an updated book on the same topic
T = trivial or of no contemporary use or relevance (e.g., books about ephemeral topics described from a point of view that emphasizes their past currency)
I = irrelevant to the contemporary needs of the library's users
E = may be found elsewhere in the library's collection in a more accessible or updated form or can be easily borrowed from another institution

Larson describes these criteria in terms of a formula: X/X MUSTIE. This formula, when applied to specific subject areas of the collection, indicates the maximum recommended age of an item in that area of the collection (in terms of the item's last publication date) and the maximum recommended period of time the material has not circulated. When guiding the weeding of a topical area of the library's collection, the formula for weeding a specific area might read 10/3/MUSTIE, meaning that items in that area of the collection more than ten years old should be considered for weeding, as should items that have not been circulated in the last three years, as well as items that meet any of the MUSTIE criteria.

Baumbach and Miller's guide to weeding, *Less Is More: A Practical Guide to Weeding School Library Collections* (2006), elaborates further on these criteria. Arguing that, as the CREW manual maintains, age and use are the primary objective criteria to employ when weeding library material, Baumbach and Miller note that exceptions to these criteria exist. The authors emphasize the need to consider each item from a professional and local perspective and suggest that items that, for example, exceed recommended age guidelines but are still required by local curricula, may be retained in spite of their age. As noted previously, circulation figures may not always be the most illustrative statistics to describe use. When considering the circulation history of an item, librarians should also determine whether the item is more often consulted in-house and thus may not be recorded by the ILS as a circulating item. Materials that are, in the words of Baumbach and Miller, "dirty, roach-eaten, or mildewed," should be removed from the library's collection, as should material with broken bindings, yellowed, marked, missing, or mildewed pages (2006, 13). If these signs of wear are indicators of high use, a replacement copy may be purchased.

The criteria of "ugliness" and "triviality" are always difficult to consider. Although Baumbach and Miller argue that ugliness is a product of age, "ugly" may also represent outdated styles of presentation. Although these "ugly" titles may be appealingly retro to some librarians and might be retained by libraries on the basis of this value, it is important to remember that our adult conceptions of "appealingly retro" are more often than not decidedly different from those of the young; "retro" titles may be quirky to us, but they are often just ugly and outdated to our young patrons. The criterion of "triviality" has the potential to pose a similar challenge to librarians. When considering, for example, a biography of Britney Spears, a 2004 title might seem, to the non-Britney fan, to suffice, and to the aging fan, a historical artifact; however, to the Britney aficionado, the title is both outdated and trivial, because it fails to take into account the star's latest three albums and her adult perspective on her career. These caveats should emphasize the importance of professional, rather than personal, thinking and judgment in the evaluation and weeding of library collections. Because young adult library collections are developed by adults on behalf of young people, it is important to remember that these collections should reflect their interests, needs, and aesthetics, not necessarily our own.

When to Weed

As CREW suggests, evaluating and weeding library collections is an ongoing preoccupation. Ideally, to maintain current and attractive collections, librarians should be engaged in weeding projects throughout the year. Many libraries and librarians develop and maintain weeding schedules, devoting particular months of the year to the weeding and evaluation of designated sections of the library; however, evaluation for the purposes of weeding can be interwoven in the library's day-to-day processes. Johnson recommends that librarians "review materials for weeding with the same regularity that they add them" (2009, 154). Thus, librarians may wish to scan the shelves for potentially weedable titles following the cataloging and shelving of new titles or, as Baumbach and Miller (2006) suggest, when reshelving circulated material. The Arizona State Library, Archives and Public Records collection development training guide suggests that weeding be "conducted on a regular schedule over a period of 3 or 4 years" and advises librarians to "estimate the number of shelves and storage units" in the collection and divide this number by 36 months to develop a "reasonable" schedule for weeding (2013b, "Schedules," para. 2). Although this recommendation is apt for larger collections, YA librarians weeding smaller collections may wish to reduce the number of months in the divisor of this formula to ensure that weeding is not undertaken at the glacial pace of one book at a time. However the schedule is set, it is important to remember that developing a continuous evaluation and weeding schedule ensures that the collection is assessed regularly.

Preparing for Weeding

Before actually assessing and weeding material from the library's collections, librarians should engage in some necessary preparation. This will ensure that weeding progresses in accordance with professional standards as well as the library's mission, goals, and objectives. Following are the steps to take when preparing for weeding:

1. *Examine the library's collection development policy*: The library's collection development policy should reiterate the mission that guides its collection of material and should highlight any collection goals that might necessitate the evaluation of specific formats or sections of the collection in local terms. For example, a library that makes it a goal to develop and maintain collections of material written by local authors may wish to retain the work of these authors, even if the material is outdated or has not circulated. Examine the policy closely for any locally developed weeding criteria or for reference to professional weeding criteria. Many library policies reference the *CREW* manual or articulate MUSTIE guidelines.

2. *Identify the section of the collection to evaluate and weed*: If the library
   has developed a schedule for weeding, an appropriate segment of
   the collection may already have been identified. Typically, librarians divide the collection into segments based on Dewey or LC
   classification and examine all the library's material in a subject area
   or topical category at once.
3. *Research the subject area or topical category to be evaluated and weeded*:
   Though time-consuming, this step is important for librarians examining sections of the collection dealing with topics with which
   they are unfamiliar. If the library has database access, a quick
   search of the professional literature may reveal subject- or topic-
   specific collection development and evaluation issues that may
   then be applied to the examination of the local collection.
4. *Develop criteria for weeding*: These criteria are arguably described or
   referenced in the library's collection development policy. It may be
   useful to examine professional resources (such as Larson's *CREW*
   or Baumbach and Miller's *Less Is More*) before weeding to review
   guidelines for weeding collections in specific subject areas.
5. *Gather checklists*: List-checking is a significant component of the
   weeding process. Librarians check items considered for removal
   against lists of core titles, summer reading lists, awards lists, and
   course syllabi to ensure that items the library pledges to collect and
   maintain in its policy are not removed.

Following are lists to consider:

1. *Standard Catalogs*: Standard catalogs like those mentioned previously can be used to ensure that core titles are not removed from
   the collection. Although the presence of a title in a standard catalog
   is not an automatic criterion for retention, these catalogs can aid in
   the retention of classic works in nonfiction subject areas.
2. *Summer Reading Lists*: Libraries that support students' summer
   reading requirements should ensure that items marked for weeding are not recommended on summer reading lists. These books
   may receive periodic high use and become worn, necessitating removal and replacement.
3. *Awards Lists*: Libraries committed to the maintenance of collections
   that include "classic" material or material of "literary value" may
   check potentially weedable fiction and nonfiction against lists of
   award-winning titles. Depending on the library's commitment to
   retaining books of literary value, it may wish to retain award-winning titles from the last five years, maintain comprehensive collections of major award-winning titles, or retain both award winners
   and honor books.
4. Libraries that participate in local book award competitions in
   which library patrons vote for award-winning books (e.g., New

Jersey's Garden State Children's Book Award) should ensure that titles on the current ballot are retained.

5. *Course Syllabi*: If the library plays a large role in the support of student work, librarians should check lists of potentially weedable titles against recommended or required reading lists associated with local schools or classes.

Evaluating and Weeding the Collection

Evaluation and weeding is a lengthy process that involves the examination and reexamination of items in the library's collection. To ensure that appropriate and needed materials are retained, it is useful to examine sections of the library's collection in multiple "passes," comparing items in the selected section against specific criteria:

1. *First Pass: Inventory*. Remove a series of items from the area of the collection to be evaluated (e.g., remove all the books assigned to 973.6) and place these on a book truck. Print out an inventory of all items in that Dewey class and compare this list to the retrieved items. Note any missing or "lost" items that are not listed as checked out and consider replacing them.

2. *Second Pass: Age*. Following the X/X/MUSTIE guidelines, determine the benchmark for age associated with the segment of the collection to be evaluated (see below for guidelines). Physically remove those items that exceed the maximum recommendations for age and set them aside for further consideration.

3. *Third Pass: Circulation*. Again following X/X/MUSTIE guidelines, determine the benchmark deadline for last circulation associated with the segment of the collection to be evaluated. Drawing from the latest circulation report for these items, physically remove those items that exceed this recommendation and set them aside for further consideration.

4. Return to the items set aside that exceed age recommendations and determine when they were last circulated. Items that have been circulated recently should be set aside for even further consideration. Items that exceed the recommended circulation benchmark and maximum recommendations for age are on their way to being weeded, but should be considered a final time during list-checking.

5. *Fourth Pass: MUSTIE*. Examine the remaining items to determine whether any meet MUSTIE criteria, considering the following caveats:

- *M = misleading*: Those items that exceed age standards and that have not circulated recently probably fall into this category

- *U = ugly*: Is the material "ugly" because it is frequently used or describes a "messy" D.I.Y. topic (e.g., science experiments, cookbooks)? If this item meets standards for age and circulation, it may be weeded, but should be replaced with a new copy of the same title.
- *S = superseded*: Any book that is cataloged as a second or third edition should be investigated to determine whether a new edition of the same title exists. If a new version of the item in hand exists, and if the item itself meets the standards for age and circulation, it may be weeded and replaced with a new, updated copy.
- *T = trivial*: If uncertain about the trivial nature of popular culture titles, ask young library patrons to weigh in before weeding an item of importance or keeping an outdated resource.
- *I = irrelevant*: Materials that reflect old curricula may be irrelevant to library users. For example, if the local school system has reorganized its history curriculum so that students study colonial American history in middle school rather than high school and modern American history in high school rather than middle school, more juvenile items describing modern American history may be perceived as irrelevant to high school users.
- *E = elsewhere*: Consider how young adults use the library before weeding an item that may be found elsewhere and note that young people may be reluctant to enlist the librarian's assistance in negotiating an interlibrary loan.

5. *Fifth Pass: List-Checking.* At this point, you probably have a number of piles or mini-collections of books:

1. The first pile is those that remain on the cart—the items that are current, enjoy high use, and pass MUSTIE standards. These items may be retained.
2. The second pile consists of items that exceed recommended standards for currency, but have been circulated recently. Consider the contents of the entire collection: Do these older items circulate because there are few contemporary titles related to this topic in the library's collection? If so, check these items against core collection resources, summer reading lists, awards lists, and course syllabi to ensure that they are not classic works or required reading. Retain those that are classic or locally needed and weed the remainder with an eye to replacing them with copies of newer books dealing with what seems to be a high interest subject.
3. The third pile contains items that fall within recommended age guidelines but have not circulated recently. Consider these against the whole collection: Do other books dealing with the same topic circulate frequently? If so, perhaps the presentation of information in this title does not meet the needs, abilities, or interests of library

patrons, and it should be weeded. Before removing this title, check it against core collection and awards lists valued by the library's collection development policy to ensure that something the library makes it a mission to collect is not inadvertently removed.

At this point, any books that remain in consideration for weeding should be checked against the lists identified as relevant to the library's collection and its mission, to ensure that such items are not weeded.

After five passes through the same segment of the collection, you should have a definitive list of material to retain and material to weed. Material to retain should be returned to the shelf, material to weed should be disposed of, and lists of replacement material (new versions of worn but well-used titles, new editions of highly circulated material) should be compiled and those items ordered.

Continuing the Cycle

Weeding library material is one necessary result of a process of collection measurement, evaluation, and assessment that librarians engage in on a regular basis. Although many librarians are reluctant to part with material from the library's collection, it is important to remember that weeding is the result of a considered and professional process of evaluation and assessment. Sally Livingston has argued that a library's collection is divided into two parts: the "core collection," which answers 95–99% of patron needs, and the "weedable collection" of outdated material that is irrelevant to patrons or contains information that is now invalid (1999, 15). Livingston recommends that as much as 5 percent of a library's collection be weeded for age on an annual basis (1999, 15). Removing even this small amount of material from a library's shelves has benefits beyond maintaining currency; it ensures that patrons enjoy much greater access to existing materials and increases the library's professional cachet. Librarians who remain wary of weeding library material may wish to consider Dickinson's extended metaphor for weeding. Comparing outdated library material to milk in the refrigerator that is "past the sell date, has an odor and is curdled and lumpy," Dickinson argues, "spoiled milk can no longer be considered milk, spoiled information can no longer be counted as books" (2005, 26).

Table 7.7. Guidelines for Weeding Library Material

Dewey Decimal Class	Dewey Decimal Number	Topic	Max. Age	Min. Age	Special Considerations
000		Generalities	X	X	*CREW* notes that the broad diversity of material in this collection requires librarians to consider weeding topical titles in tandem with other Dewey areas. For example, books of topical trivia might be considered when materials of that topic are addressed in the collection.
	001	Curiosities and Wonders	10	5	Books in this area tend to circulate often—just as books in the 133s do—and may include faddish publications. Discard material that includes "curiosities" and "mysteries" that may already be solved, paying special attention to titles related to science and technology.
	004	Computers	3	3	Update material related to hardware or software, being sure to retain at least one version prior, as new versions are released.
	010	Bibliography	10	X	Update so that bibliographies reflect material in the current collection; keep local or in-house bibliographies of special collections.
	020	Library Science	10	X	Discard items that refer to outdated practices and library technology.
	030	General Encyclopedias	5 – 8 (circulating)	X	While general encyclopedias may be dated after five years, yearbooks and almanacs should be replaced with each new edition. *CREW* suggests moving general encyclopedias weeded from the reference collection to the circulating collection, but cautions to weed these circulating items when they are no more than 8

Code	Subject			Guidelines
	(Psychology)			...topics of philosophy and psychology, but also self-help material. ASLAPR suggests withdrawing psychology books after 5 years, unless the book is by an important author (e.g., Freud, Jung). Popular psychology and self-help material, especially those books written by celebrity figures, should be monitored for obsolescence.
133	Paranormal Phenomena	X	10	As noted above, this tends to be a high-use area of the nonfiction collection and high incidence of book theft may require closer monitoring. Because of the popularity of the paranormal as well as the persistence of paranormal "fads," books in this area should be monitored closely for both wear and triviality.
200	Religion	10	5	While sacred texts (the Koran, Bible, Torah, etc.) may be timeless, books discussing religious issues can become dated. *CREW* and Baumbach and Miller suggest maintaining collections of "timely and comprehensive" information on the six major international religions: Buddhism, Christianity, Hinduism, Islam, Judaism, and Taoism. The collection should also reflect prominent community belief systems (e.g., Orthodox Judaism).
290	Mythology	15	10	While mythic legends may be historical, re-tellings can make them more accessible. Maintain classic works (e.g., Edith Hamilton's *Mythology*) but consider newer editions of collections.
300	Social Sciences	10	5	Because this subject area is so varied and includes a number of controversial topics, evaluation and weeding in this area should be frequent.

301	Black History	5	20	Baumbach and Miller note that this section of the library's collection is often taxed during Black History Month. This area of the collection should be kept current and "reflect a wide range of contributions [to Black history], not just popular figures in sports and entertainment" (Baumbach and Miller, 2006, p. 36). Older material reflecting out-dated terminology and images should be weeded from the collection.
306	Culture and Institutions	5	X	*CREW* notes that this section includes books on marriage, family life, and sexuality, topics of interest to young adults. Material in this section should remain current (particularly where changing marriage laws are concerned) and may be considered outdated after 5 years.
310	Almanacs and Yearbooks	2	5	Almanacs and yearbooks in the reference collection should be replaced annually; older copies can be moved to the circulating collection, but should be weeded within 5 years.
320	Political Science	5	20	This sub-section includes material related to democracy (321.8), terrorism (322), civil rights (323), presidential elections (324) and immigration (325). As such, material related to democracy and elections should be kept current; material about candidates and democratic process will be in demand in election years and should reflect current practices and a balanced point of view. *CREW* suggests weeding books about past presidential elections when "they deal with issues that are no longer relevant to current campaigns" (2008, p. 53). Books related to the Constitution and the Bill of Rights may be retained longer than 5 years

				...democracy with ~~political systems in other~~ countries that no longer exist (e.g., USSR)" (2008, p. 53). NOTE: Many publishers produce material in quick response to high-profile international incidents (e.g., 9/11) and elections; if these are purchased to meet immediate demand, check back within one year to weed screeds and responsive titles and replace with more thoughtful tomes.
315	Careers	5	20	Titles describing careers—particularly in the sciences and technology—should reflect current practices. Any material describing career trends or projecting employment needs should be reviewed and weeded for timeliness.
370	Education	1 - 5	10	Books describing trends in education may take a historical perspective (e.g., material describing *Brown vs. Board of Education*) or may reflect current movements and interests. College guides should be retained no more than 5 years. Guides to scholarship and funding opportunities should be weeded as they become outdated (e.g., *2011 Scholarship Handbook*). Guides to AP courses and AP, SAT, and other test prep guides should reflect current practices (e.g., guides that do not include mention SAT subject tests or the writing component of this test should be weeded).
360	Drug and Alcohol Education	5	15	Materials in this section of the library focus on drug dependency and drug trafficking (material related to the health effects of drugs and alcohol may be found in the 600s). This material should be current and accurate and reflect contemporary vernacular.

398	Folklore, Folktales	5	20	While folktales and folklore may not go out of date, *CREW* recommends weeding "based on the quality of the telling, especially if racial or ethnic bias is present" (2008, p. 56). Evaluate collection to ensure that it is representative of global rather than solely Western tradition.
400	Language	5	10	This section includes dictionaries, etymologies, books on slang, and linguistics. Dictionaries should be weeded every 5 years. Foreign language materials should reflect those studied in the local curriculum as well as those spoken by the community.
500	Natural Sciences	3 – 5	10	Because science changes so quickly, any material more than 5 years old should be carefully considered. Classic titles (e.g., *Origin of Species, Silent Spring*) should be retained.
507	Science Experiments	3	15	Books describing science experiments should reflect current standards of safety and presentation (e.g., poster or Power Point presentation vs. overhead projection). The collection should reflect contemporary areas of interest, such as forensic science and global warming. NOTE: Some science project books may be classified within the scientific discipline (e.g., chemistry experiments may be classified among the chemistry books).
510	Mathematics	5	10 – 15	Replace older materials related to algebra, geometry, trigonometry and calculus with revised editions.

Dewey	Subject			Comments
			15	that have been written in. Weed books that reflect older trends (e.g., "new math" and the slide rule) in education and problem solving. SAT and AP study guides should reflect current practices and test contents.
520	Space and Astronomy	5	15	Major discoveries in space science necessitate an examination of the collection describing the planets (e.g., Pluto) and space exploration (especially Mars exploration) to determine whether the collection reflects current discoveries. Books that take an historical stance may be retained longer than 5 years. "Stargazing" material describing the constellations may also be kept longer than 5 years.
550	Earth Sciences, including Weather, Volcanoes, and Earthquakes	5	15	Contemporary collections should reflect current and historical weather and geographical phenomena such as Hurricane Katrina and the Asian tsunami. Information related to global warming as it affects the weather should be kept up-to-date. *CREW* advises weeding books that describe historical natural disasters (e.g., Mt. St. Helen's) from a contemporary standpoint and replacing these with material that focuses on long-term consequences. Books describing meteorology should reflect current practices and technologies. Field guides may be kept for up to 10 years.
560	Paleontology, including Fossils and Dinosaurs	5	10	*CREW* guidelines suggest weeding dinosaur titles after 5 years, but allow that field guides, especially those that detail the local region, may be kept longer.

570	Biology and Life Sciences, including Genetics, Evolution and Ecology	3 - 7	10	CREW urges librarians to retain classics (e.g., *On the Origin of Species*), replacing these with new editions as old volumes wear. Titles describing genetics, genetic engineering, human biology and evolution should be weeded every 5 years to reflect current scientific findings. Baumbach and Miller advise retaining taxonomies, but weeding and updating information related to viruses and bacteria.
580	Botany	5	10	Baumbach and Miller advise librarians to ensure that endangered species information is up-to-date. *CREW* advocates examining field guides describing edible plants to ensure they meet contemporary safety standards.
600	Technology and Applied Sciences	5	10	Because this section of the collection includes material related to health, careful weeding and monitoring of this material is a necessity. The minimum age for books in the 600s in general is the recommended maximum age for material in the 610s (medicine and health).
610	Medicine and Health	3	5	*CREW* recommends weeding material describing current medial practices "ruthlessly" and advises paying special attention to books about AIDS, cancer, and genetics. Baumbach and Miller urge librarians to maintain current collections describing STDs but offer that books about diet and exercise may be kept longer.
636	Pets	5	15	Because this section of the collection describes veterinary practices as well as domestic animals, *CREW* advises keeping material about veterinary medicine current.

weed any material that reflects outdated or inhumane training practices.

640	Home Economics, including cookbooks	3	10	Cooking material should reflect current standards of safety, medical and nutritional knowledge (e.g., the Food Pyramid and the Plate Model). Baumbach and Miller argue that this section of the collection should reflect "current cooking trends" (e.g., low-fat, low-carb, keto). In communities and schools in which students are often required to prepare cuisine reflecting countries of study, a strong collection of world cookbooks may be useful.
700	The Arts	3	10	This section of the library includes both current resources and those that take an historical approach. ASLAPR suggests that general histories of art and music be retained, but warns that survey titles over 25 years old are significantly out-dated. The popular music collection should be monitored so that it remains up-to-date and relevant. Contemporary popularity of crafting and D.I.Y. suggests a need to monitor this area as well.
740	Drawing and Decorative Arts, including crafting	5	10	Popularity of handicraft and D.I.Y. makes this an area to monitor and weed aggressively. Outdated looking material or material that reflects sexist generalizations (e.g., *The Girl's Book of Crafts* [1959]) should be weeded from the collection. Drawing collections should include traditional how-to-draw manuals as well as guides to manga and comic book art.
770	Photography, photographs and computer art	5	10	Material in this section should reflect current photography practices, including digital photography and digital photo editing. Digital

Dewey	Subject			Description
			10	photography material should be weeded aggressively so that the collection demonstrates current practices. Computer and digital art material should reflect current practices. As in the Computers section (010), retain the most current as well as last most recent instruction guides to software and hardware.
780	Music	5		Material describing musical instruments and instructional techniques may endure. Historical overviews of musical periods may also age well. Be sure to include material that discusses a variety of popular music styles (e.g., pop, rock, rap, R&B, country, punk) and update these materials at least every 5 years. Material describing particular popular acts or figures should reflect current interests and current perspectives. To keep these current, this section needs to be weeded aggressively.
790	Games and sports	2 (computer games and sports statistics) - 5	10	Baumbach and Miller warn weeders to pay attention to sports teams that have moved or changed names (e.g., Utah Jazz) and make sure the team is represented in its current incarnation. Books of statistics should be kept current and reflect recent wins and losses. Material describing computer games and offering cheats and helps should be updated with regularity. Multiple computer gaming systems should be represented in the collection.
800	Literature	5	15	*CREW* advises discarding critical works discussing lesser-known authors no longer studied in local curricula. Collection should reflect demands of the literature (including Advanced Placement) curricula

year here] titles after five years.

900	History and Geography	5	15	Material in this section of the library should reflect contemporary alliances and borders. While some material may age well, material describing countries in Africa, the Middle East, and Russia and the former Soviet Union should be examined for currency.
910	Geography and Travel	2	5	Baumbach and Miller write, "outdated travel guides are useless" and advise weeding these every three years. Material reflecting the local region should be kept especially current.
920	Biographies	5	10	Biography collections should include historical and notable as well as popular culture figures. Biographies of popular culture figures (e.g., actors, musicians, celebrities) should be weeded regularly—at least every 5 years—so that they remain current. Material describing elected figures should be at least as current as their last election. Pay close attention to biographies of figures required by local curricula.
930–999	History including Native Americans, Presidents, and conflicts	5	15	Material in this section should reflect contemporary understandings of historical events and should include nontraditional perspectives. Maintain primary source material as demanded by local curricula. Pay close attention to material describing Native Americans and Native tribes; these items should be aggressively weeded to remove stereotypical depictions.

Ensure that collections describing the presidents represent the current administration.
Baumbach and Miller advise weeding historical overviews of the presidency every 5 years.
Baumbach and Miller recommend including material on the Spanish American War, Korean War, Vietnam and the Gulf conflicts, as well as the more often read material describing the Civil War and World War II.
Material describing current conflicts and incidents (e.g., 9/11) should be weeded to reflect contemporary perspectives.

EIGHT

Maintaining Library Collections for Young Adults

Collection development is a continual process; it is truly a job that is never done. Although libraries and librarians may develop schedules that dictate when the majority of a library's new book selection is accomplished or suggest a time frame for formal needs assessment and collection evaluation, most young adult librarians who not only select material but also work with library patrons—recommending titles, connecting students with informational resources, and instructing young people in the use of technological tools—engage in "continuous review" of the collection, thinking about how it reflects library users' needs and interests and considering how it could be improved to better achieve the library's goals for serving young adults. While the *CREW Handbook*, the often-cited Texas State Library and Archives weeding manual, associates the term "continuous review" primarily with the evaluation and weeding process, its definition can be expanded to encompass the less formal needs assessment, direct analysis, circulation analysis, and retrospective collection development tasks that YA librarians engage in on an ongoing basis. These maintenance activities contribute to the continual development of a library collection that meets the changing needs and reflects the diverse interests of the population it serves.

The primary task of continuous review is collection maintenance, the ongoing inspection and evaluation of materials in the collection with an eye toward replacing, repairing, or removing these items. Similar to targeted weeding, regular maintenance can and should be done at any time: when straightening the library before closing, selecting topical titles for display or promotion, or shelving new materials. Continuous review also describes a type of "on the fly" data collection and analysis that librarians engage in on a regular basis to inform collection development and goal setting: examining monthly or weekly circulation reports; recording reference statistics; negotiating ILLs; and handling requests for material from schools, teachers, or community groups all contribute to a librarian's understanding of the service community and its needs and interests and inform the development of the tacit knowledge he or she applies to collection development, assessment, and maintenance decisions.

The previous chapters described formal methods for needs assessment, collection assessment, and evaluation on which librarians rely during times of strategic planning, institutional evaluation, and administrative reorganization and that can be drawn on to defend creating collections of new material in new formats. Continuous review and collection maintenance comprise lighter versions of these activities that ultimately become part of the YA librarian's daily practice. These activities overlap with and contribute to a librarian's professional development as well and involve keeping up with publishing and popular cultural trends, learning about changes to the local curriculum, working and consulting with other professionals, and speaking and interacting with young library patrons and the community.

NEEDS ASSESSMENT "LITE": KEEPING UP WITH PUBLISHING, POPULAR CULTURE, AND COMMUNITY NEEDS

Needs assessment is the process of determining the informational, educational, and recreational needs and interests of the library's service population; as described in chapter 4, it can be accomplished through the application of a number of data collection methods, many of which are associated with social science research. This process, advises the Arizona State Library, Archives and Public Records "is an integral component of the collection development function of the library and provides focused and necessary direction for the development of information resources at all levels of the organization" (2012d, "Collection Development," para. 2). To ensure that their collections meet the needs of the community they serve, libraries undertake formal needs assessment projects to inform strategic planning and set goals for the development of new collections and services. Because this process is time consuming and labor intensive, libraries engage in formal needs assessment and strategic planning in five- to ten-year intervals, when required by library governing bodies, or when major administrative shifts have occurred. The work of collection development librarians, however, is continual. To ensure that the library's selections continue to reflect the interests and needs of its patrons, librarians identify and understand emerging needs and interests associated with the populations they serve and respond to these by adding material that reflects contemporary popular culture interests, dominant publishing and literary trends, and the curricular demands of the local education system. To this end, librarians subscribe to and read professional and trade publications and newsletters, access "trend-spotting" websites, and maintain communication with local schools and educational institutions. In addition, librarians serving young adults may visit schools and develop partnerships with school library media specialists and teachers and solicit feedback and suggestions from young library patrons. These activities, though considered components of professional development and service, contribute to a librarian's increasing understanding of the service community and its changing needs and interests and can be considered a form of informal needs assessment.

Things to Read

Librarians count reading professional and trade journals among their professional development activities. This practice—which includes reading reviews published in periodicals like *VOYA*, *School Library Journal*, *Kirkus Reviews*, and *Horn Book*; articles describing new library initiatives and best practices in journals like *Young Adult Library Services* and *Children and Libraries*; and features that detail publishing trends and sales in publications like *Booklist* and *Publishers Weekly*—ensures that YA librarians remain at the forefront of teen publishing trends and popular literary culture. While the cost of subscribing to all of the periodicals mentioned is prohibitive for many libraries, some of them publish content online that librarians may access for free, and some even offer free subscriptions to electronic newsletters and alerts that librarians may request be delivered to their inboxes on a weekly or monthly basis. Following are free resources of particular relevance to YA librarians:

1. *Publishers Weekly: Children's Bookshelf*: Any reader may sign up for a free subscription to the trade journal's *Children's Bookshelf* newsletter, which is distributed via e-mail on Tuesdays and Thursdays and highlights new children's books; it includes author interviews, some review content, and publishing news.
2. *Publishers Weekly: Tip Sheet*: Any reader may sign up for a free subscription to the trade journal's *Tip Sheet* newsletter, which is distributed weekly (Fridays) via e-mail and notes upcoming book releases. It includes Publishers Weekly editors' lists of the best new titles as well as author interviews and essays. The *Tip Sheet* addresses publishing across the spectrum and includes mention of adult as well as young people's literature.
3. *Publishers Weekly: PW Comics World*: Any reader may sign up for a free subscription to the trade journal's *PW Comics World* newsletter, which is distributed monthly via e-mail. This newsletter includes features describing comics publishers, authors, and artists and includes a release schedule for upcoming titles.

4. *School Library Journal: SLJ Teen*: The professional journal offers free subscriptions to *SLJ Teen*, a twice-monthly newsletter distributed via e-mail. *SLJ Teen* features monthly interviews with new authors; reviews of young adult books written by teen readers; and publishing news about print, technology, and media for young adults.

5. *School Library Journal: Curriculum Connections*: The professional journal offers free subscriptions to *Curriculum Connections*, a monthly newsletter distributed via e-mail that recommends and reviews titles linked to common curricular topics.

6. *Horn Book: Notes from the Horn Book*: This review journal's free monthly electronic newsletter features interviews with authors and illustrators, reviews of new material, and news from the children's and young adult publishing world.

The free electronic newsletters described here are useful supplements to the journals that publish them and are particularly valuable sources of timely information and popularity predictions. For example, the *Publishers Weekly* newsletters, which highlight new titles and note promotional efforts associated with these titles, suggest which books, series, and authors may be prominent in large chain bookstores and retail outlets and may be requested by library patrons. The *School Library Journal* and *Horn Book* newsletters often include lists of recommended titles that adhere to a common theme or that may serve as read-alikes for popular titles; these topical resources can help librarians answer patron interest or need when a requested title is not available.

While professional and trade journals attempt to identify publishing trends and predict the popularity of new titles, publishers and librarians recognize popular culture as an important informant of literary popularity, which makes keeping up with popular cultural trends a key collection development task. As teen popular culture includes not only popular literature, but also the popular music, movies, and games that the library collects for young adults, it is important for YA librarians to remain abreast of current trends. Trend-spotting and market research firms trade in information related to teen popular culture and attempt to predict the "next big thing." Retailers and product developers pay these firms for their extensive market research reports, often to the tune of thousands of dollars. However, some of these companies make limited content available online for free. The following resources include market and demographic research and observations related to young adults and their popular culture and media interests:

1. Pew Internet: Teens (http://www.pewinternet.org/topics/Teens.aspx): The Pew Internet and the American Life project conducts research about computer, technology, and Internet use and includes teenagers and young adults among its research population.

2. Pew Internet: Libraries (http://www.libraries.pewinternet.org) and Pew Internet: Libraries in the Digital Age blog (http://libraries.pewinternet.org/category/libraries-in-the-digital-age/): The Pew Internet and the American Life project has recently focused on the role of public libraries as technology and Internet providers as well as on the rise of e-books in libraries. The organization's reports (found on the Pew Internet: Libraries site) and its blog describe technology and service trends in public libraries as well as library use by various demographics, including teens.

3. *Youth Pulse*: YPulse (http://www.ypulse.com/): This market research service briefs readers on teen trends, including those related to books and media. The "Millennial Voices" section of the site features reviews of television shows, books, and musings written by teen members of the organization's "Teen Advisory Board."

4. *VOYA*'s Teen Pop Culture Quiz (http://www.voya.com): Posted online in April, August, and December, the Teen Pop Culture Quiz, written by Erin Helmrich, highlights recent developments in the teen media and celebrity world.

The research and popular cultural observations described in the resources listed here are national in scope and detail dominant teen popular and subcultural trends. Although this information is useful, as it describes the mass media developed for and marketed to young people across the country, local teen library users may not adopt all the trends, brands, and media these resources identify, making further investigation into local young people's particular popular culture interests a necessity.

Because public libraries serve the educational and informational needs of their patrons as well as their recreational and entertainment interests, YA librarians should familiarize themselves with the demands of local curricula to ensure that the library's collection includes material that answers them. Although the Common Core State Standards Initiative has standardized local curricula to some degree, suggesting common learning outcomes for each grade that students in participating school districts will be required to achieve, the implementation of these standards varies among states, districts, and schools. School district and individual school websites are good places to begin looking for information about the local curriculum. District sites may include news and public relations documents describing any initiatives that affect the content or emphases of the local curriculum; individual school websites may include reading lists, course or departmental syllabi, and information about special educational programs or opportunities for students. Any significant changes in a school or school district's curriculum have the potential to affect young people's information demands and thus the public library's collection. For example, students in a school or school district that is developing an expanded AP curriculum may require specific literary or nonfictional texts and may look to the public library to provide AP exam study guides that reflect the subjects of the newly offered college-level courses.

Things to Do

While reading about popular cultural and publishing trends and familiarizing oneself with the local curriculum increase a librarian's understanding of the literary, media, and informational needs of the service population, the trends and fads described in national publications may be differently embraced—or not be embraced at all—by the local population, making consultation with the library's young patrons a necessity. Librarians should also develop collaborative relationships with teachers and librarians to determine whether and how the public library supports the work of students inside and outside of the classroom. By incorporating the following activities into the library's existing programs and services, YA librarians can make patron opinion and feedback a factor in collection development:

1. **Surveys:** Surveys of patrons, notes Lesley Farmer, "act as educational/public relations tools as well as information gathering tools" (2002, 69). Soliciting feedback from patrons via survey need not be an onerous project. Librarians may insert one-question surveys on the library's teenweb site or ask library visitors to cast a vote in response to a question posted in the library.
2. **Suggestion box or binder:** A freely available suggestion box or an open binder in which library patrons can offer comments or make requests can serve as a vehicle for passive programming and soliciting library visitors' input.
3. **School library visits:** Visiting the school library and speaking with its librarian about commonly used resources and student information needs is a must and leads to collaborative relationships that inform collection development in both institutions.
4. **Summer reading list development:** Because the public library often serves as students' primary source of required summer reading material, it is important for public librarians to participate in the development of school- and grade-level required summer reading lists. This activity allows public librarians to publicize the library's collection and ensures that 'it includes the titles young people are required to read during the summer.

Because, as Farmer reminds us, "what students enjoy and what adults enjoy can be two different choices," librarians who encourage their young patrons to express their information and reading interests and needs can develop collections that reflect student interest rather than adult intent (2002, 72). Librarians who do solicit young adult input need to demonstrate that they will respond to patron suggestions, a move that reveals the library's commitment to youth services and user-centered collection development and that encourages young people's further investment in the library and its collections. Public and school library partnerships and collaborative activities further this goal, allowing both libraries to provide their young patrons with what Rebecca Miller refers to as the resources "kids need as they try to finish their homework or find fun ways to explore their worlds" (2012, 11).

DIRECT ANALYSIS "LITE": NIPPING BAD BOOKS IN THE BUD

As librarians strive to develop collections that respond to teen needs and interests, they are also engaged in a continual process of collection renewal, which involves not just purchasing new titles, but also examining existing items, considering shelf space, and making decisions about weeding and replacement. These decisions are often made following direct analysis of the collection, a process in which an outside expert examines the physical collection, consults library patrons and staff, and then offers recommendations for weeding and collection development. Less formal direct analysis happens during weeding, when local librarians examine and assess the collection and apply professional standards to the evaluation of individual items, with the goal of weeding outdated, inaccurate, and irrelevant items from the collection. Weeding projects in libraries are ongoing and are often guided by weeding schedules that identify segments of the collection to evaluate throughout the year and thus ensure regular collection maintenance. Adherence to a weeding calendar does not mean that direct analysis of the library's collection can only occur on schedule. Any time a librarian is working in the collection—selecting material to display or examining and shelving new items—can be considered an opportunity for shelf-scanning and direct analysis.

Things to Do

Every interaction with the library's collection increases a librarian's knowledge of its contents and organization. These interactions also provide opportunities for informal direct analysis in service of collection maintenance and continuous review. Continuous review and direct analysis can be incorporated into a number of activities:

1. **Shelving new material:** Many librarians ask that new material be brought to the librarian for review before being put on the shelves. Following the review of new material, librarians should consider shelving the material themselves to determine what, if any, existing items the new titles have superseded. Donna J. Baumbach and Linda L. Miller (2006) suggest that librarians discard older editions

of titles that have been superseded by newly acquired material immediately upon acquisition of the new edition. Shelving new editions thus becomes a process of addition and subtraction as a librarian replaces an old version of a title with its updated edition.

2. **Developing displays and bibliographies:** Baumbach and Miller suggest evaluating each title for potential deselection when pulling material to include in a thematic display or to examine for inclusion in a topical bibliography. During this process, "obvious weeds"—material with "missing pages or a faded, ragged cover" or "that can't be repaired"—should be discarded immediately (Baumbach and Miller 2006, 19).

3. **Shifting the collection:** When moving books or media from shelf to shelf to make room for new items and facilitate browsing and selection, librarians should take time to scan the items on the shelves in question, noting and removing those in obvious disrepair and examining and evaluating items that appear outdated.

Some of the worn and ragged material discovered during direct analysis may still meet the library's criteria for relevance and retention, particularly if its wear is evidence not of age but of intense usage. Cookbooks, craft books, science fair project instructions, and drawing guides that readers crack open to consult while engaging in activities are examples of material that can wear quickly. Consulting the circulation records for such titles can help a librarian determine whether a replacement copy of the item in question should be purchased. Evidence of recent and avid use, including consistent check-outs and holds on the title, suggest the need for a replacement copy, whereas less recent use suggests that the title has served its purpose.

RETROSPECTIVE SELECTION

Weeding worn or outdated material is not the only outcome of direct analysis. When librarians examine segments of the collection with a purpose—for example, looking for material to include in a bibliography or to promote in the classroom—gaps in the collection may become evident. When these gaps are discovered, librarians should make note of what is needed to facilitate retrospective selection, the process of selecting older material that is still in print, relevant, and needed or requested by library patrons. Classic works of fiction and nonfiction and collections of primary source material are common choices for retrospective collection development; however, titles that have emerged as "local classics," previously published work that has been newly added to summer reading and required reading lists, and new copies of heavily used volumes are often selected retrospectively. As Richard Heinzkill has argued about retrospective collection development, deciding which older titles to add to a library's collection "is based on the judgment that there are works that the library ought to have . . . these judgments are based upon standards of literary worth and academic interest" (1987, 56). A library's collection development policy should elaborate upon and describe which works "the library ought to have"; policy language describing the library's intent to develop collections that include material with historical significance or that represent historical trends in publishing and literature suggests a need for some retrospective selection activity. "Academic interest," a phrase that in the case of the library's collection for young adults denotes required or supplemental reading assigned in school, is an additional consideration for the retrospective selector.

To determine what previously published material should be selected for addition to the young adult collection, librarians must consider the library's collection goals, as outlined in its collection development policy, as well as patron need and demand. Some retrospective selection consists of acquiring new copies or editions of existing material that has become worn with use, but the development of collections in new formats—like a graphic novel collection or a DVD collection—may require librarians to acquire older, classic, and new titles. As with traditional collection development, librarians may consult standard bibliographies, readers' advisory resources, and core collection guides to suggest existing titles to retain or others to add to the collection retrospectively. In addition, librarians should consult library users—particularly when developing new subcollections of material by genre or format—to determine which existing titles or items may be considered locally classic or significant. Required reading and summer reading lists often inspire retrospective selection as well, because these lists typically include a mix of older, classic, and newer titles. Ultimately, retrospective collection development and selection responds to the unique needs and interests of the local population and is undertaken to fulfill the library's mission and goals for its collections. Because retrospective collection decisions are locally motivated, this process is linked to needs assessment and may be affected by outcomes of both formal and informal needs assessment practices.

CIRCULATION AND USE ANALYSIS "LITE": WATCHING OVER THE COLLECTION AND ITS USE

Many libraries make circulation, holds, and usage reports available to librarians in charge of collection development on a regular basis, issuing these reports at weekly or monthly intervals. Regular examination of these reports contributes not just to a librarian's understanding of consistent information needs motivated by the academic calendar, but also to identification of local trends and interests. Although circulation is certainly not the only measure of library use, it is a good idea to examine circulation statistics regularly as part of the continuous review process. Print circulation statistics may confirm a librarian's observations about popular materials; networked resource statistics and statistics describing e-book use may be some of the only indicators of use of these resources that a librarian can access. Statistics describing use of these less visible library resources—the library's networked resources and e-book collections—are important to keep an eye on, as patron use of these materials may not occur in the physical library.

Things to Do

In an article describing the impact of "next-generation catalogs," Andrew Nagy asserts, "By constantly analyzing reports on usage, librarians can better judge how to improve services to meet the demands of their patrons" (2011, 18). Though Nagy is writing about the measuring effects of NGCs—library catalog systems that provide patrons with search results from the library's bibliographic catalog as well as the library's digital collections and some federated database search results—the author's recommendations are applicable to any library service that may be measured in terms of circulation and use. Nancy McGriff, Carl A. Hardy, and Leslie B. Preddy (2004, 29) suggest looking to the library's circulation reports to collect data to answer the following questions, which may inform the continuous review of the collection:

1. How many items are checked out of the library each month?
2. Who is checking out these items (e.g., "youth" or "adult")?
3. Which areas of the library's collection are most heavily used?
4. Which areas of the library's collection are seldom used?

By examining these figures on a monthly basis, YA librarians can note any library use ebb and flow and link circulation spikes or decreases to targeted programming, promotional displays, and the academic and social calendar. In addition, these figures can be used to support needs assessment and direct analysis observations and inform weeding decisions or retrospective materials selection; librarians may also wish to target heavily used sections of the collection for retrospective and new materials selection and scan the shelves of seldom used areas of the collection to determine whether judicious weeding may be in order. Following are data trends that can be derived from a library's regular circulation reports and may be used to inform collection maintenance:

1. **Popular authors or creators and items:** Regular circulation reports will indicate which items in the library's collection circulate with the greatest frequency, as well as which items have been frequently or consistently requested and "held" for library patrons. Authors or creators (e.g., video game studios, recording artists) of materials

with high circulation and that are frequently requested should be noted and may be considered reflective of patron needs or publishing and popular cultural trends identified in needs assessment.

2. **Popular formats:** Regular circulation reports can also be used to determine popular material formats, an important factor to consider when assessing a library's e-book and video game collection. Do certain e-book formats circulate with greater frequency and thus suggest the dominant mode of e-book reading among the population? Do certain video game formats circulate with greater frequency and thus suggest the prevalence of specific consoles among gamers in the community?

3. **Topical areas of interest or need:** Circulation reports may be divided to note which topical areas of the library's collection (identified by Dewey Decimal Number or Library of Congress designation) have been circulated heavily. Consistent and comparatively high circulation in a discrete area (like books about drawing in the 740s) can indicate an area of interest among the population, while circulation spikes in specific topical areas (like books about North American history in the 1940s) may indicate an assignment-inspired need.

4. **Effects of promotion, programming, and display:** Material that has been promoted—during school visits or in library programs—as well as material that has been displayed tends to circulate with greater frequency; circulation statistics can demonstrate the effects of these forms of promotion.

5. **User class:** Some libraries may issue reports that distinguish circulation by user class (e.g., "youth" or "adult"); as young adult material grows in popularity among adult readers, an examination of the library's young adult circulation in terms of user class can reveal the broad demographic characteristics of the collection's users.

In addition to the data that may be mined from circulation reports, many ILSs allow librarians access to the circulation records of individual titles, in which the total number of times the item has circulated, the date of last circulation, and the number of times the item has circulated within the last year may be found. This information is often used to support decisions about weeding or replacing individual items or to defend the purchase of additional copies of a single item.

NEXT-GENERATION COLLECTION MAINTENANCE

Maintaining library collections involves making tough decisions about weeding, retrospective selection, and ultimately, resource allocation. Librarians serving young adults face unique challenges as they work to develop and maintain collections that meet young library users' needs and reflect their interests. Because young people's reading interests and information needs may be motivated by both their everyday life experiences, curiosities, and interests and the mandates of the educational system of which they are a part, YA librarians must consider not only young people's expressed reading preferences, but also the demands of the local curriculum to identify titles and resources to add to or weed from the collection. As library collections for young adults are primarily created and maintained for a population defined in part by its transitional status between childhood and adulthood, these collections must respond to the evolving needs of a maturing user group as well as to the needs and expectations of the collection's newest users. The growth of young adult literary publishing and the increasing popularity of the literary form have led adult readers to these library collections for young adults as well, and these users' expectations for the collection may both overlap with and be distinct from those of the adolescent population these collections were originally created to serve. Thus, maintaining library collections for young adults involves a level of diligence and degree of attention—to the collection and its contents as well as its users and their needs and interests—that distinguishes the development of these collections from others in the library.

Today, young adult collection maintenance involves considering the library's physical collection of material—which is itself diversifying to include technological tools and devices as well as print, video, and audio materials—as well as its virtual collection of networked resources and electronic books. Librarians may rely on techniques associated with the development and assessment of physical collections to develop and maintain these virtual collections, but Linda Braun (2011b) points out a number of additional challenges collection developers should consider when developing, assessing, and maintaining electronic collections:

1. Electronic collections are not as "visible" as the library's print and media collections—"A librarian doesn't see materials as they are circulated or are returned or when walking through the stacks" (Braun 2011b, 28)—thus, it can be more difficult to assess the collection in terms of its age and completeness.
2. Young adult librarians may not be aware of the scope of the library's electronic collection, especially if decisions about this collection and its content are made at the consortial rather than the local level.
3. Patron use of the library's ILS or digital materials catalog to request, download, and place holds on digital content makes determining which titles are popular more difficult.
4. Lack of face-to-face interaction with patrons browsing and downloading materials from home may restrict patron use of the library

to that (somewhat limited) electronic content that is accessible remotely.

Overcoming these barriers to electronic collection assessment and maintenance involves developing strategies for, as Braun notes, "walk[ing] through" the library's virtual collection. To do so, YA librarians should request and examine circulation statistics associated with electronic books and browse and search the library's electronic book collection on a regular basis to determine what may or may not be available to answer young people's informational and recreational reading needs. Weeding outdated material from e-book collections remains an important task of electronic collection maintenance and a potential outcome of this virtual direct analysis. Because, Alene Moroni reminds us, "searches within e-book platforms do not provide the precision of library catalog searches . . . it's important to make sure materials available to your patrons are timely and collection clutter is reduced" (2012, 27). As libraries and e-book providers work together and with publishers to develop more user-friendly and precise solutions for ILS integration, "walking through" the library's collection of print and electronic content via the library's ILS should become easier and allow for the development of circulation reports, virtual "shelf lists," and inventories of print and electronic content.

As the library's collection of electronic books grows in size and content, YA librarians must consider how this growth will impact the size and content of the library's print materials collection. Although current debates over digital rights management and the rights of libraries to lend electronic content to patrons continue to restrict libraries' e-book collections to what select publishers make available for library purchase, as best practices agreeable to libraries, vendors, and publishers develop, libraries and librarians will have to develop policies to guide collection development across formats. These policies will likely specify where and when libraries collect duplicate material in multiple formats and establish priorities for new and retrospective materials selection in print and electronic forms.

LOOKING TO THE FUTURE

The advent of electronic publishing and the widespread and growing adoption of personal devices that allow readers to select, download, and read digital resources have had—and will continue to have—a decided impact on the services and collections the public library provides to its patrons. As these technological advances have changed the way librarians and library users select and access information, they have affected—and will continue to affect—library collection development. Advances in ILS have allowed libraries and librarians to access and organize library use data and have provided collection development librarians with a more realistic image of patrons' material use and information behaviors, information that librarians have used to make data-supported decisions about materials selection and retention. As libraries experiment with patron-driven acquisition (PDA) in the digital realm, allowing library users to select electronic book titles from a catalog of available works that the library will then lease and add to the circulating collection, library users become partners in collection development, selecting material from the library as they would from a bookstore. Critics and commentators have argued that, combined with decreasing library budgets and increasing demands for accountability, this professional shift toward patron-driven acquisition has effected a move from "just in case" acquisition—the selection of a wide variety of materials to meet anticipated ("just in case") patron needs—to "just in time" purchasing—the acquisition of materials in response to patron demand. These shifts in selection and acquisition procedures have led both scholars and professionals to wonder about the future of collection development and the changing role of libraries and librarians in the lives of readers and researchers.

Young adult librarians will face unique challenges in this shifting library environment. Increasingly digital collections require patron access to technological tools that young people, in particular, may find difficult to obtain. Librarians charged with developing collections for youth must ensure that the young people they serve have the means to access these collections and advocate on their behalf for libraries to make the tools required to access digital content freely available to users. Youth advocacy is required at the electronic materials selection level as well. Today, consortia facilitate the majority of public library networked resource and e-book purchasing and leasing agreements and, as Braun has observed, in many libraries this collection building "is occurring outside of a specific department or specific customer focus" (2011b, 28). Young adult librarians must become part of this collection development process and familiarize themselves with the electronic resources the library offers to its patrons, so that they will be better equipped to offer suggestions for further development and promote this collection to patrons. As both school and public libraries face budget cuts, collaborative collection development and resource-sharing agreements will likely increase. While these mutually beneficial relationships can be difficult to initiate, engaging in collaborative collection development allows school and public libraries to build on individual strengths, reduce unnecessary duplication of material, and work toward common goals related to literacy and information provision.

Librarians developing collections for today's young adults are active participants in a field in transition; new materials, new formats, and new processes for selection and acquisition are changing the way selectors do business. One requirement of the job has not changed, however: expert knowledge of young adult literature and information resources remains a professional necessity. Whether the library of the future is completely digital or exists in both a physical and a virtual space, the job of the YA librarian will continue to involve readers' advisory and user instruction. These services may be provided online—via e-mail, chat, or text—in a cooperating classroom, or in a dedicated space or corner in the library; however, they all require professional familiarity with a diversity of materials and an expert awareness of how these materials may be used, read, or connected with one another.

References

Agosto, D., & Hughes-Hassell, S. (2006a). Toward a model of the everyday life information seeking needs of urban teenagers, part 1: Theoretical model. *JASIST*, *57* (1), 1394–1403.

Agosto, D., & Hughes-Hassell, S. (2006b). Toward a model of the everyday life information seeking needs of urban teenagers, part 2: Empirical model. *JASIST*, *57* (11), 1418–1426.

Agosto, D. E., & Hughes-Hassell, S. (2006c). Planning library services for inner-city teens: Implications from Research. *Public Libraries*, *45* (6), 57–63.

Agosto, D. E., Paone, K. L., & Ipock, G. S. (2007). Gender issues in information needs and services. *Library Trends*, *56* (2), 387–401.

Alachua County Library District. (2011). Collection development: Alachua County Library District policy statement. Retrieved from http://www.aclib.us/collection-development-policy.

Alexander, L. B., & Miselis, S. D. (2007). Barriers to GLBTQ collection development and strategies for overcoming them. *Young Adult Library Services*, *5* (3), 43–49.

Allen, C. M. (2007). Are we selecting? Or are we censoring? *Young Adult Library Services*, *5* (3), 5.

American Library Association (ALA). (1981). Evaluating library collections: An interpretation of the library bill of rights. Retrieved from http://www.ala.org/Template.cfm?Section=interpretations&Template=/ContentManagement/ContentDisplay.cfm&ContentID=76533.

American Library Association (ALA). (1990). Challenged materials: An interpretation of the library bill of rights. Retrieved from http://www.ala.org/Template.cfm?Section=interpretations&Template=/ContentManagement/ContentDisplay.cfm&ContentID=31881.

American Library Association (ALA). (1996). Library bill of rights. Retrieved from http://www.ala.org/advocacy/intfreedom/librarybill.

American Library Association (ALA). (1997–2012). Equity of access. Retrieved from http://www.ala.org/advocacy/access/equityofaccess.

American Library Association (ALA). (2004). Access for children and young adults to nonprint material: An interpretation of the library bill of rights. Retrieved from http://www.ala.org/advocacy/intfreedom/librarybill/interpretations/accesschildren.

American Library Association (ALA). (2008a). Expurgation of library materials: An interpretation of the library bill of rights. Retrieved from http://www.ala.org/advocacy/intfreedom/librarybill/interpretations/expurgationlibrary.

American Library Association (ALA). (2008b). Diversity in collection development: An interpretation of the library bill of rights. Retrieved from http://www.ala.org/advocacy/intfreedom/librarybill/interpretations/diversitycollection.

American Library Association (ALA). (2008c). Free access to libraries for minors: An interpretation of the library bill of rights. Retrieved from http://www.ala.org/advocacy/intfreedom/librarybill/interpretations/freeaccesslibraries.

American Library Association (ALA). (2009). Labeling and rating systems: An interpretation of the library bill of rights. Retrieved from http://www.ala.org/advocacy/intfreedom/librarybill/interpretations/labelingrating.

American Library Association (ALA). (2010). Questions and answers on labeling and rating systems. Retrieved from http://www.ala.org/advocacy/intfreedom/librarybill/interpretations/qa-labeling.

American Library Association (ALA). (n.d.). The librarian's guide to gaming: Legal issues surrounding gaming in libraries. Retrieved from http://librarygamingtool-kit.org/legal.html.

American Library Association (ALA) Office for Information Technology Policy. (n.d.). The library in the networked world: The ALA self-Assessment tool. Retrieved from http://www.ala.org/offices/sites/ala.org.offices/files/content/oitp/publications/networkforweb.pdf.

Arizona State Libraries, Archives and Public Records. (2012a). About collection development policies. Retrieved from http://www.azlibrary.gov/cdt/colldev.aspx.

Arizona State Libraries, Archives and Public Records. (2012b). Collection development policy: Component I. Retrieved from http://www.azlibrary.gov/cdt/colldev.aspx.

Arizona State Libraries, Archives and Public Records. (2012c). Collection development policy: Components III, IV, and V. Retrieved from http://www.azlibrary.gov/cdt/colldev.aspx.

Arizona State Library, Archives, and Public Records. (2012d). Community needs assessment. Retrieved from http://www.azlibrary.gov/cdt/commneeds.aspx.

Arizona State Library, Archives, and Public Records. (2013a). Selection: Electronic and Internet resources. Retrieved from http://www.azlibrary.gov/cdt/slrer.aspx.

Arizona State Library, Archives, and Public Records. (2013b). Weeding. Retrieved from http://www.azlibrary.gov/cdt/slrer.aspx.

Aronson, M. (2006). Originality in nonfiction. *School Library Journal, 52* (1), 42–43.

Aronson, M. (2011). New knowledge. *Horn Book, 87* (2), 57–62.

Asheim, L. (1953). Not censorship but selection. Retrieved from http://www.ala.org/offices/oif/basics/notcensorship (April 17, 2013).

Asheim, L. (1983). Selection and censorship: A reappraisal. *Wilson Library Bulletin, 58,* 180–184.

Asher, C., & Case, E. (2008). A generation in transition: A study of the usage and attitudes toward public libraries by Generation 1.5 composition students. *Reference and User Services Quarterly, 47* (3), 274–279. Retrieved from Library Literature and Information Science database (December 1, 2012).

Association for Library Service to Children (ALSC). (1997–2013). Newbery Medal terms and criteria. Retrieved from http://www.ala.org/alsc/awardsgrants/bookmedia/newberymedal/newberyterms/newberyterms.

Association of Magazine Media (AMM). (2011). 2011 average total paid and verified circulation for top 100 ABC magazines. Retrieved from http://www.magazine.org/insights-resources/research-publications/trends-data/magazine-industry-facts-data/2011-average-total.

Association of Research Libraries. (2001). Recommended statistics and measures for library networked services [PowerPoint slides]. ARL E-Metrics phase II report. Retrieved from http://www.arl.org/stats/initiatives/emetrics/index.shtml.

Baker, K. (2012). Meeting the needs of diverse communities. *Public Libraries, 51* (5), 34–35.

Baumbach, D. J., & Miller, L. L. (2006). *Less is more: A practical guide to weeding school library collections.* Chicago: ALA.

Becker, S., Crandall, M. D., Fisher, K. E., Kinney, B., Landry, C. and Rocha, A. (2010) *Opportunity for All: How the American Public Benefits from Internet Access at U.S. Libraries.* (IMLS-2010-RES-01). Washington, DC: Institute of Museum and Library Services. Retrieved from: http://impact.ischool.washington.edu/documents/OPP4ALL_FinalReport.pdf

Behler, A. (2011). Collection development for e-books. E-book Task Force tip sheets. Retrieved from http://connect.ala.org/node/184037.

Bertot, J. C., McDermott, A., Lincoln, L., Real, B., & Peterson, K. (2012). *2011–2012 Public Library Funding and Technology Access Survey: Survey findings & report.* College Park, MD: Information Policy & Access Center, University of Maryland College Park. Available at http://www.plinternetsurvey.org.

Bertot, J. C., McClure, C. M., Davis, D. M., & Ryan, J. (2004). Capture usage with e-metrics. *American Libraries, 35* (5), 30–32.

Bishop, K. (2007). *The collection program in schools: Concepts, practices, and information sources* (4th ed.). Westport, CT: Libraries Unlimited.

Bonn, G. S. (1974). Evaluation of the collection. *Library Trends, 22* (3), 265–304.

Boston Athenaeum (2012a). Acquisitions policy. Retrieved from http://www.bostonathenaeum.org/node/156.

Boston Athenaeum (2012b). At a glance. Retrieved from http://www.bostonathenaeum.org/node/263.

Brannen, J. (2011a, December). All about mysteries for teens. Retrieved from Novelist Plus database (February 20, 2013).

Brannen, J. (2011b, December). All about romance fiction for teens. Retrieved from Novelist Plus database (February 19, 2013).

Brannen, J. (2012a, January). All about fantasy for teens. Retrieved from Novelist Plus database (February 19, 2013).

Brannen, J. (2012b, March). All about science fiction for teens. Retrieved from Novelist Plus database (February 19, 2013).

Braun, L. (2011a). The importance of a whole library approach to public library young adult services: A YALSA issue paper. Retrieved from http://www.ala.org/yalsa/guidelines/whitepapers/wholelibrary.

Braun, L. (2011b). Now is the time: E-books, teens and libraries. *Young Adult Library Services, 9* (4), 27–30.

Braun, L.W., Martin, H. J., & Urquhart, C. (2010). *Risky business: Making and managing risks in library services for teens.* Chicago: American Library Association.

Brenner, R. (2006). Graphic novels 101: FAQ. *Horn Book, 82* (2), 123–125.

Brookline [MA] Public Library. (2007, April 11). Collection development policy. Retrieved from http://www.brooklinelibrary.org/what/.

Brooks, S. (2006). Evaluating evaluations. *Library Journal, Net Connect,* 28.

Brown, G. T. L. (2003, September/October). Searching informational texts: Text and task characteristics that affect performance. *Reading Online, 7*(2). Retrieved from http://www.readingonline.org/articles/art_index.asp?HREF=brown/index.html.

Buchanan, K., & Vanzen Elden, A. M. (2012). Beyond a fad: Why video games should be part of 21st century libraries. *Education Libraries, 35* (1–2), 15–33.

Button, L., Lewellen, R., Norton, K., and Skinner, P. (2011). Reducing unintentional duplication: Adventures and opportunities in cooperative collection development. *Proceedings of the Charleston Library Conference.* Retrieved from: http://dx.doi.org/10.5703/1288284314882.

Buzzeo, T. (2010). Struggling readers: Our greatest challenge. *Library Sparks, 8* (3), 40–44.

Campbell County [WY] Public Library System. (2012, August). Section IV: Collection evaluation and assessment. Retrieved from http://ccpls.org/coldev/html/iv.html#41.

Campbell, P. (1994). YA horror paperbacks. *Horn Book, 70* (2), 234–238.

Campbell, P. (2000). Middle muddle. *Horn Book, 76* (4), 483–487.

Cart, M. (2012). Carte blanche: The latest . . . or is it? *Booklist, 109* (8), 40.

Cassell, K. A., & Futas, E. (1991). *Developing public library collections, policies, and procedures.* New York: Neal-Schuman.

Centris Market Intelligence (2010). Centris white paper: Blu-ray adoption and ownership among U.S. households. Retrieved from http://www.yumpu.com/en/document/view/2459342/blu-ray-adoption-and-ownership-centris (March 1, 2013).

Chaet, H. (2012, June 25). The tween machine. *Adweek Online.* Retrieved from http://www.adweek.com/news/advertising-branding/tween-machine-141357.

Chelton, M. K. (2006). Perspectives on practice: Young adult collections are more than just young adult literature. *Young Adult Library Services, 4* (2), 10–11.

Cleto, C. (2008). ATG special report: 10 steps to implementing an e-book collection: A guide for libraries. *Against the Grain, 20* (1), 47–48.

Coleman, D., & Pimentel, S. (2012, April 12). Revised publishers' criteria for the Common Core State Standards in English Language Arts and Literacy, grades 3–12. Retrieved from http://www.corestandards.org/resources.

Common Core State Standards. (2012). In the states. Retrieved from http://www.corestandards.org/in-the-states.

Connecticut State Library's Advisory Council for Library Planning and Development (2012). *ACLPD e-book task force white paper*. Retrieved from: http://www.ala.org/transforminglibraries/sites/ala.org.transforminglibraries/files/content/CTstatelib-ebookswhtpaper10-2012.pdf.

Cooperative Children's Book Center. (2007). What if . . . library? Retrieved from http://www.education.wisc.edu/ccbc/freedom/whatif/archiveDe-tails.asp?idIFQuestions=67.

Corbett, S. (2005). Why YA and why not? *Publishers Weekly, 252* (35), 30–31.

Corbett, S. (2012). What's new in YA? Mashups. *Publishers Weekly, 259* (40), 24–31.

Cornog, M., & Raiteri, S. (2012). Graphic novels. *Library Journal, 137* (15), 53.

Council on Library and Information Resources (CLIR). (2012). Usage studies of electronic resources. Retrieved from http://www.clir.org/pubs/reports/pub105/section3.html.

COUNTER. (2012). Counter code of practice for e-resources, release 4: Appendix A. Retrieved from http://www.projectcounter.org/code_practice.html.

Crawford, W. (2000). Here's the content—where's the context? *American Libraries, 31* (3), 50–52.

Crowe, C. (2002). De facto YA literature and false expectations. *English Journal, 91* (4), 100–102.

Curry, A. (2005). If I ask, will they answer? Evaluating public library reference service to gay and lesbian youth. *Reference and User Services Quarterly, 45* (2), 65–75.

Danforth, L. (2010). The great (M-rated) debate. *Library Journal, 135* (17), 56.

Deahl, R., with Rosen, J. (2012). New adult: Needless marketing speak or valued subgenre? *Publishers Weekly, 259* (51), 4–6.

D'Elia, G., Abbas, J., & Bishop, K. (2007). The impact of youth's use of the Internet on their use of the public library. *Journal of the American Society for Information Science and Technology, 54* (14), 2180–2196.

Dickinson, G. (2005). Crying over spilled milk. *Library Media Connection, 23* (7), 24–26.

Digital Content and Libraries Working Group [DCWG] (2012). *Digital rights management tip sheet*. Retrieved from: http://www.ala.org/transforminglibraries/drm-tip-sheet.

E-Metrics Instructional System. (n.d.). Selecting e-metrics for use decisions, slide 5. Retrieved from http://emis.ii.fsu.edu/module_slide.cfm?moduleid=4388C008-ED6E-4FAE-9806232D93EEDE09&fk_presentationid=47BB471B-7AB5-4081-9021CDE90F23E808&slideid=D235893D-65BF-85C2-13B45D67B787C18B&slide-number=5&hideNotes=yes&hideToc=no.

Enis, M. (2012 August 2). Patron preferences shift toward streaming. *The Digital Shift*. Retrieved from: http://www.thedigitalshift.com/2012/08/media/patron-preferences-shift-toward-streaming/.

Entertainment Software Rating Board (ESRP). (n.d.). ESRB rating and content descriptor guide. Retrieved from http://www.esrb.org/ratings/ratings_guide.jsp.

Evans, G. E., & Saponaro, M. Z. (2005). *Developing library and information center collections* (5th ed.). Westport, CT: Libraries Unlimited.

Fantasy. (2005). In *Continuum encyclopedia of children's literature*. Retrieved from http://0-www.credoreference.com.library.simmons.edu/entry/kidlit/fantasy.

Farmer, L. S. J. (2002). Collection development in partnership with youth: Uncovering best practices. *Collection Management, 26* (2), 67–78.

Fisher, H. (2003). The teenage view of the public library: What are the students saying? *APLIS, 16* (1), 4–17.

Fitzgerald, C. (2009). What do teens want? *Publishers Weekly, 256* (43), 22–26.

Fitzgibbons, S. A. (2000). School and public library relationships: Essential ingredients in implementing educational reforms and improving student learning. AASL. Retrieved from http://www.ala.org/aasl/aaslpubsandjournals/slmrb/slmrcontents/volume32000/relationships.

Florida Library Association. (2012, June). Standards for Florida public libraries. Retrieved from http://www.flalib.org (March 12, 2013).

Flowers, M. (2010). Libraries catch up with the twentieth century. *Young Adult Library Services, 9* (1), 35–37.

Flowers, S. (2008). Guidelines for library services to teens. *Young Adult Library Services, 6* (3), 4–7.

Forbes Library. (2012). Collection development policy. Retrieved from http://www.forbeslibrary.org/policies/collection.shtml.

Franklin, P., & Stephens, C. G. (2009). Use standards to draw curriculum maps. *School Library Activities Monthly, 25* (9), 44–45.

Gaming @ the library. (n.d.). Advocacy. Retrieved from http://gaming.ala.org/resources/index.php?title=Advocacy.

Giroux, H. (1996). *Fugitive cultures: Race, violence and youth.* New York: Routledge.

Giroux, H. (2003). *The abandoned generation: Democracy beyond the culture of fear.* New York: Palgrave.

Glander, M., & Dam, T. (2007). *Households' use of public and other types of libraries: 2002.* U.S. Department of Education. Washington, DC: National Center for Education Statistics. Retrieved from http://ies.ed.gov/pubsearch/pubsinfo.asp?pubid=2007327.

Gleason (Carlisle, MA) Public Library. (2011, April 20). Collection development policy. Retrieved from http://www.gleasonlibrary.org/collectiondevelopment.htm.

Gray, D., & Copeland, A. (2012). E-book versus print: A per-title cost and use comparison of a public library's popular titles. *Reference and User Services Quarterly, 51* (4), 334–339.

Gregory, V. L. (2011). *Collection development and management for 21st century library collections: An introduction.* New York: Neal Schuman.

Grogg, J., & Fleming-May, R. (2010). The concept of electronic resource use and libraries. *Library Technology Reports, 4* (6), 5–35.

Gross, M. (2006). *Studying children's questions: Imposed and self-generated information seeking at school.* Lanham, MD: Scarecrow Press.

Hadro, J. (2010, October 14). Patron-driven e-book model simmers as Ebrary joins its ranks. *Library Journal.* Retrieved from http://www.libraryjournal.com/lj/communityacademiclibraries/887246-419/patron-driven_ebook_model_simmers_as.html.csp.

Haras, C., Lopez, E. M., & Ferry, K. (2008). (Generation 1.5) Latino students in the library: A case study. *Journal of Academic Librarianship, 34* (5), 425–433.

Harris, C. (2012a). The end of nonfiction. *School Library Journal, 58* (3), 16.

Harris, C. (2012b). How to get started. *School Library Journal, 58* (4), 28.

Harris Interactive. (2007). *American Library Association youth and library use study.* Chicago: American Library Association. Available from http://www.ala.org/ala/mgrps/divs/yalsa/HarrisYouthPoll.pdf.

Haverhill [MA] Public Library, (2012, January 19). Teen services collection development policy. Retrieved from http://www.haverhillpl.org/about/policies/teen-services-selection-policy/.

Heinzkill, R. (1987). Retrospective collection development in English literature. *Collection Management, 9* (1), 55–65.

Hill, R. (2012). All aboard! *School Library Journal, 58* (4), 26–30.

Hiremath, U. (2001). Electronic consortia: Resource sharing in a digital age. *Collection Building, 20* (2), 80-87.

Historical fiction for children. (2007). In Tom Burns (Ed.), *Children's literature review* (vol. 124, pp. 121–192). Detroit: Thompson Gale. Retrieved from Literature Criticism Online database.

Hobbs, F., & Stoops, N. (2002). *Demographic trends in the 20th century.* U.S. Census Bureau: Census 2000 special reports, series CENSR-4. Washington, DC: U.S. Government Printing Office.

Hochadel, C. (2010). Who's hot and who's not in teen magazines. *VOYA, 33* (5), 404–409.

Hodges, D., Preston, C., & Hamilton, M. J. (2010). Patron-initiated collection development: Progress of a paradigm shift. *Collection Management, 35,* 208–221.

Hoffmann, F. W., & Wood, R. J. (2005). *Library collection development policies: Academic, public, and special libraries.* Lanham, MD: Scarecrow Press.

Holley, B. (2012). In defense of traditional collection development. *Against the Grain, 24* (1), 2–4.

Horn Book. (2013). Submissions. Retrieved from http://www.hbook.com/about-us-2/submissions/.

Howard, V. (2011). What do young teens think about the public library? *Library Quarterly, 81* (3), 321–344.

Hughes-Hassell, S., & Mancall, J. C. (2005). *Collection management for youth: Responding to the needs of learners.* Chicago: American Library Association.

Hughes-Hassell, S., & Rodge, P. (2007). The leisure reading habits of urban adolescents. *Journal of Adolescent and Adult Literacy, 51* (1), 21–33.

Indiana State Library. (2011). New director's one stop guide. Retrieved from http://www.in.gov/library/3290.htm.

International Coalition of Library Consortia. (2006, October 4). Revised guidelines for statistical measures of usage of web-based information resources. Retrieved from http://icolc.net/statement/revised-guidelines-statistical-measures-usage-web-based-information-resources.

International Federation of Library Associations and Institutions (IFLA). (2012, August 6). *Key issues for e-resource collection development: A guide for libraries.* Retrieved from http://www.ifla.org/news/ifla-electronic-resource-guide-now-available.

Japson, A. C., & Gong, H. (2005). A neighborhood analysis of public library use in New York City. *Library Quarterly, 75* (4), 446–463.

Jenkins, C. (2000). The history of youth services librarianship: A review of the research literature. *Libraries and Culture, 35* (1), 103. Retrieved from Academic OneFile Database.

Jervis [Rome, NY] Public Library. (2000). Collection development policy. Retrieved from http://www.jervislibrary.org/policies/Collection_Development.html.

Johnson, P. (2009). *Fundamentals of collection development and management* (2nd ed.). Chicago: American Library Association.

Johnson City [TN] Public Library. (2012, September 11). Collection development policy. Retrieved from http://jcpl.net/index.asp?speed=high&screen=wide&css=yes&section=info&page=policies.

Jones, P. (2001a). Nothing to fear: R. L. Stine and YA paperback thrillers. *Collection Management, 25* (4), 3–23.

Jones, P. (2001b). The real stuff. *School Library Journal, 47* (4), 44–45.

Jones, P. (2003). To the teen core. *School Library Journal, 49* (3), 48–49.

Jones, P. (2007). Connecting young adults and libraries in the 21st century. *APLIS, 20* (2), 48–54.

Jones, P., Gorman, M., & Suellentrop, T. (2004). *Connecting young adults and libraries* (3rd ed.). New York: Neal-Schuman.

Jones, P., & the Young Adult Library Services Association. (2002). *New directions for library service to young adults.* Chicago: American Library Association.

Jones, T. (2007). Annual policy statement 2007. Retrieved from http://www.schoollibraryjournal.com/article/CA493806.html.

Kaufman, L. (2012, December 21). Beyond wizards and vampires, to sex. *New York Times.* Retrieved from http://www.nytimes.com/2012/12/22/books/young-adult-authors-add-steaminess-to-their-tales.html?_r=0.

Kelley, M. (2013, January 3). Top e-book distributors, ILS vendors, to have sitdown with Readers First library coalition. *The Digital Shift*. Retrieved from http://www.thedigitalshift.com/2013/01/ebooks/top-ebook-distributors-ils-vendors-to-have-sitdown-with-readersfirst-library-coalition/.

Krueger, K. S. (2012). The status of statewide subscription databases. *School Library Research*, 15. Retrieved from: http://www.ala.org/aasl/sites/ala.org.aasl/files/content/aaslpubsandjournals/slr/vol15/SLR_StatusofStatewide_V15.pdf.

Kuzyk, R. (2011). Now hear this. *Library Journal, 136* (9), 34–35.

Lancaster, F. W. (1982). Evaluating collections by their use. *Collection Management, 4* (1–2), 15–44.

Larson, J., & the Texas State Library and Archives Commission. (2008). *CREW: A weeding manual for modern libraries*. Retrieved from https://www.tsl.state.tx.us/ld/pubs/crew/index.html.

Le Guin, U. (2005). Genre: A word only a Frenchman could love. *Public Libraries, 44* (1), 21–23.

Lenhart, A. (2012a, March 19). Teens, smart phones, and texting. Retrieved from http://www.pewinternet.org/Reports/2012/Teens-and-smartphones.aspx.

Lenhart, A. (2012b, April 13). Digital divides and bridges: Technology use among youth. Retrieved from http://www.slideshare.net/PewInternet/digital-divides-and-bridges-technology-use-among-youth#btnNext.

Lenhart, A., Purcell, K., Smith, A., and Zickuhr, K. (2010, February 3). Social media and young adults. Retrieved from: http://pewinternet.org/Reports/2010/Social-Media-and-Young-Adults.aspx.

Library Journal. (2011). America's star libraries: LJ's index of public library service FAQs. Retrieved from http://www.libraryjournal.com/article/CA6705616.html.

Library Journal. (2012a). Budget and circulation survey: U.S. public libraries. Retrieved from http://c0003264.cdn2.cloudfiles.rackspacecloud.com/2012%20LJ%20Budget%20and%20Circ%20Report.pdf.

Library Journal (2012b). *E-book usage in public libraries, 3rd annual survey*. Retrieved from: http://c0003264.cdn2.cloudfiles.rackspacecloud.com/Ebook-Usage-Report-Public.pdf.

Library of Congress. (2006). Introduction: MARC 21 holdings. Retrieved from http://www.loc.gov/marc/holdings/hdintro.html.

Littman, J., & Connaway, L. S. (2004). A circulation analysis of print books and e-books in an academic research library. *Library Resources and Technical Services, 48* (4), 256–262.

Livingston, S. (1999). Weeding school library media center collections. *Kentucky Libraries, 63* (3), 15–19.

Ludwig, S. (2011). *Starting from scratch: Building a teen library program*. Santa Barbara, CA: Libraries Unlimited.

Maine State Library. (n.d.). Complete library template. Retrieved from http://www.maine.gov/msl/mrls/policies/index.shtml.

Malczewski, B. (2011, November 15). Still loading: AV spotlight on streaming video. *Library Journal*. Retrieved from http://www.libraryjournal.com/lj/home/892497-264/still_loading__av_spotlight.html.csp.

Malczewski, B. (2013, February 15). DVDs? Blu-ray? Streaming? Media access and the sense of "a la carte." *Public Libraries Online*. Retrieved from http://publiclibrariesonline.org/2013/02/dvds-blu-ray-streaming-the-present-of-media-access-and-the-sense-of-a-la-carte/.

Maroni, A. E. (2012). Weeding in a digital age. *Library Journal, 137* (15), 26–28.

Maughan, S. (2002). Betwixt and between. *Publishers Weekly, 249* (45), 32–36.

Matthews, J. (2007). *The Evaluation and Measurement of Library Services*. Westport, CT: Libraries Unlimited.

McCann, S. (2009). Systems showdown. *Library Journal, 134* (7), 73.

McGriff, N., Hardy, C. A., & Preddy, L. B. (2004). Collecting the data: Collection development. *School Library Media Activities Monthly, 20* (9), 27–29.

Mentor [OH] Public Library. (2012). Collection development policy. Retrieved from http://www.mentorpl.org/collection-development-policy/.

Meyers, E. M., Fisher, K. E., & Marcoux, E. (2009). Making sense of an information world: The everyday life information behavior of preteens. *Library Quarterly, 79* (3), 301–341.

Miller, R. T. (2012). We need tag-team librarianship. *School Library Journal, 58* (5), 11.

Miller, Rebecca T., & Girmscheid, L. (2012). It takes two. *School Library Journal, 58* (5), 26–29.

Monroe County [IN] Public Library. (2012, March 28). Collection development policy. Retrieved from http://mcpl.info/geninfo/collection-development-policy.

Moran, B., & Steinfirst, S. (1985). Why Johnny (and Jane) read whodunits in series. *School Library Journal, 85* (31), 113–117.

Moroni, A. E. (2012). Weeding in a digital age. *Library Journal, 137* (15), 26–28.

Moyer, M., & Coulon, A. (2012). Live at your library! *American Libraries, 43* (11/12), 46–48.

Muller, K. (2011, May 11). Ask the ALA librarian: Sample policies. *American Libraries.* Retrieved from http://americanlibrariesmagazine.org/ask-ala-librarian/sample-policies.

Mustafoff, M., & Teffeau, L. (2008). Young adult services and technology in public libraries. *Public Libraries, 47* (1), 10–15.

NA Alley. (n.d.). What is "new adult"? [blog]. Retrieved from http://naalley.blogspot.com/p/about.html.

Nagy, A. (2011). The impact of the next-generation catalog. *Library Technology Reports, 47* (7), 18–20.

Nelson, S. S. (2008). *Strategic planning for results.* Chicago: American Library Association.

Nicholson, S. (2009, June 12). Gaming in libraries session 10: Five gaming experience archetypes. Retrieved from http://www.gamesinlibraries.org/course/?p=79.

Nixon, J. M., Freeman, R. S., & Ward, S. M. (2010). Patron-driven acquisitions: An introduction and literature review. *Collection Management, 35*, 119–124.

November, S. (2004). "What some escape to, some escape": Why teenagers read genre fiction. *Young Adult Library Services, 2* (3), 32–33.

OCLC. (2011). *Perceptions of libraries, 2010: Context and community.* Dublin, OH: OCLC. Retrieved from http://www.oclc.org/reports/2010perceptions.htm.

Overall, P. M. (2010). The effect of service learning on LIS students' understanding of diversity issues related to equity of access. *Journal of Education for Library and Information Science, 51* (4), 251–266.

Oxford County Library. (1992). Introduction. In *Focus on the future: Needs assessment and strategic planning for county and regional libraries: A how-to manual.* Retrieved from http://www.ocl.net/needs/one.html.

Park, S. J. (2012). Measuring public library accessibility: A case study using GIS. *Library and Information Science Research, 34* (1), 13–21.

Partridge, E. (2011). Narrative nonfiction: Kicking ass at last. *Horn Book, 87* (2), 69–73.

Pasadena [CA] Public Library. (2012). Collection development policy. Retrieved from http://cityofpasadena.net/library/about_the_library/collection_development_policy/.

Pearlmutter, J., & Nelson, P. (7 December 2010). When small is all. *American Libraries.* Retrieved from http://americanlibrariesmagazine.org/features/12072010/when-small-all.

Peters, T. A. (2002). What's the use? The value of e-resource usage statistics. *New Library World, 103* (1/2), 39–47. Retrieved from Emerald database.

Pew Internet. (2012). Libraries, patrons and ebooks: Where people discover and get their books. Retrieved from http://libraries.pewinternet.org/2012/06/22/part-2-where-people-discover-and-get-their-books/.

Philadelphia Free Library. (2012). Children's literature research collection. Retrieved from http://libwww.freelibrary.org/collections/collectionDetail.cfm?id=3.

Pierce, J. B. (2003). Picking the flowers in the "fair garden": The circulation, non-circulation, and disappearance of young adult materials. *School Libraries Worldwide, 9* (2), 62–72.

Polanka, S. (2011). Purchasing e-books in libraries: A maze of opportunities and challenges. *Library Technology Reports, 47* (8), 4–7.

Pomona [CA] Public Library. (2004). Collection development policy. Retrieved from http://www1.youseemore.com/pomona/about.asp (October 26, 2012).

Pritchard, K. (2010). Let's get this party started. *School Library Journal, 56* (3), 34–37.

Purcell, K., Rainie, L., Heaps, A., Buchanan, J., Friedrich, L., Jacklin, A., Chen, C. and Zickuhr, K. (2012). *How teens do research in the digital world.* Retrieved from: http://www.pewinternet.org/Reports/2012/Student-Research.aspx.

Pyles, C. (2012). It's no joke: Comics and collection development. *Public Libraries, 51* (6), 32–35.

Queens Borough [NY] Public Library. (2012). Collection development. Retrieved from http://www.queenslibrary.org/about-us/collection-development.

Rabey, M. (2010). Historical fiction mash-ups: Broadening appeal by mixing genres. *Young Adult Library Services, 9* (1), 38–41.

Rauch, E. W. (2010). GLBTQ collections are for every library serving teens. *VOYA, 33* (3), 216–218.

Recording Industry Association of America (RIAA). (2013). Parental advisory. Retrieved from http://www.riaa.com/toolsforparents.php?content_selector=parental_advisory#background.

Reynolds, T. (2011, July). Into the mix: Cross-genre fiction and its appeal for teens. Retrieved from Novelist Plus database.

Roach, M. (2010). Video games: A primer for libraries. *VOYA, 33* (1), 44–45.

Romance Writers of America. (n.d.). The romance genre. Retrieved from http://www.rwa.org/p/cm/ld/fid=578.

San Francisco [CA] Public Library. (2002–2012b). Teen collections. Retrieved from http://sfpl.org/index.php?pg=2000011101.

Schmidt, K. (2012). ERM ideas and innovations. *Journal of Electronic Resources Librarianship, 24* (4), 300–307.

Shanklin, W. (2012, November 8). 2012 game console comparison guide. *Gizmag.* Retrieved from http://www.gizmag.com/2012-game-console-comparison-guide/24938/.

Sharon [MA] Public Library. (2004, January 24). Sharon Public Library collection development policy. Retrieved from http://www.sharonpubliclibrary.org/about_policycollectiondev.htm.

Shenton, A., & Dixon, P. (2003). Models of young people's information seeking. *Journal of Librarianship and Information Science, 35* (1), 5–22.

Shenton, A., & Dixon, P. (2005). Information needs: Learning more about what kids want, need, and expect from research. *Children and Libraries, 3* (2), 20–28.

Sin, J. S. (2012). Modeling the impact of individuals' characteristics and library service levels on high school students' public library usage: A national analysis. *Library and Information Science Research, 34*, 228–237.

South Carolina State Library. (2005, June). Technology standards for South Carolina public libraries. Retrieved fromhttp://www.statelibrary.sc.gov/docs/techstand2005.pdf

Springen, K. (2012). Are teens embracing e-books? *Publishers Weekly, 259* (8), 20–23.

Stephens, W. (2012). Serving teens with e-readers. *Young Adult Library Services, 10* (4), 28–30.

Sullivan, E. (2000). More is not always better. *School Library Journal, 46* (4), 42–43.

Sullivan, E. (2001). Some teens prefer the real thing: The case for young adult nonfiction. *English Journal, 90* (3), 43–47.

Swan, D. W., Owens, T., Miller, K., Beamer, D., Bechtle, S., Dorinski, S., Freeman, M., & Sheckells, C. (2011). *State library agencies survey: Fiscal year 2010.* IMLS-2012-StLA-01. Washington, DC: Institute of Museum and Library Services.

Tatomir, J., & Durrance, J. C. (2010). Overcoming the information gap: Measuring the accessibility of library databases to adaptive technology users. *Library Hi-Tech, 28* (4), 577–594.

Tatomir, J. N., & Tatomir, J. C. (2012). Collection accessibility: A best practices guide for libraries and librarians. *Library Technology Reports,* October 2012, 36–42.

Todd, R. (2003). Adolescents of the information age: Patterns of information seeking and use, and implications for information professionals. *School Libraries Worldwide, 9* (2), 27–46.

Top shelf fiction for middle school readers 2011. (2012). *Voice of Youth Advocates, 34* (6), 540–544.

Trott, B., & Novak, V. (2006). A house divided? Two views on genre separation. *Reference and User Services Quarterly, 46* (2), 33–38.

Uhlmann, D. (2011). Pick me! Pick me! *School Library Journal, 57* (4), 80–84.

Vavrek, B. (2004). Teens: Bullish on public libraries. *Library Quarterly, 23* (1), 3–12.

Wales, B. (2002). Charter schools in libraries: A content analysis. *Teacher Librarian, 30* (2), 21–26. Retrieved from ERIC database.

Weisman, K. (2006). An inside look at series nonfiction. *Booklist, 103* (4), 58–59.

Welch, R. (2008). From platforms to books? I'm game. *Young Adult Library Services, 6* (2), 30–31.

Whalen, S. P., & Costello, J. (2002). *Public libraries and youth development: A guide to practice and policy.* Chicago: Chapin Hall Center for Children at the University of Chicago. Retrieved from http://www.chapinhall.org/research/report/public-librar-ies-and-youth-development.

Whelan, D. L. (2009). Dirty little secret. *School Library Journal, 55* (2), 27–30.

Williams, P., & Edwards, J. (2011). Nowhere to go and nothing to do: How public libraries mitigate the impacts of parental work and urban planning on young peo-ple. *APLIS, 24* (4), 142–152.

Wolfson, G. (2008). Using audiobooks to meet the needs of adolescent readers. *American Secondary Education, 36* (2), 105–114.

Woolls, B. (2009). School and public libraries: Partners in student learning. *International Association of School Librarianship, selected papers from the 2009 annual conference* (pp. 1–9). Retrieved from ProQuest Education Database.

Young Adult Library Services Association. (1997–2012). Popular paperbacks for young adults: Policies and procedures. Retrieved from http://www.ala.org/yalsa/booklist-sawards/booklists/popularpaperback/popularpaperbacksyoung.

Young Adult Library Services Association. (1997–2013a). Alex awards. Retrieved from http://www.ala.org/awardsgrants/alex-awards.

Young Adult Library Services Association. (1997–2013b). Fabulous films for young adults policies and procedures. Retrieved from http://www.ala.org/yalsa/booklist-sawards/booklists/fabfilms/policies.

Young Adult Library Services Association. (2008, January). Amazing audiobooks poli-cies and procedures. Retrieved from http://www.ala.org/yalsa/booklistsawards/booklists/amazingaudiobooks/policies.

Young Adult Library Services Association (2008). Creating online surveys. Retrieved from: http://www.ala.org/yalsa/sites/ala.org.yalsa/files/content/teentechweek/ttw11/images/techguide_onlinesurv.pdf.

Young Adult Library Services Association. (2009, August). Quick picks policies and procedures. Retrieved from http://www.ala.org/yalsa/booklistsawards/booklists/quickpicks/quickpicksreluctantyoungadult.

Young Adult Library Services Association. (2010a). *YALSA's Competencies for Librarians Serving Youth: Young Adults Deserve the Best.* Retrieved from http://www.ala.org/yalsa/guidelines/yacompetencies/evaltool.

Young Adult Library Services Association. (2010b, February). Best fiction for young adults committee policies and procedures. Retrieved from http://www.ala.org/yal-sa/bfya/policies.

Young Adult Library Services Association (2012a). Advocacy. Retrieved from: http://www.ala.org/yalsa/advocacy

Young Adult Library Services Association. (2012b). Teen space guidelines. Retrieved from http://www.ala.org/yalsa/guidelines/teenspaces.

Zickuhr, K., & Smith, A. (2012, April 13). Digital differences. Retrieved from http://www.pewinternet.org/Reports/2012/Digital-differences.aspx.

Zickuhr, K., Rainie, L., Purcell, K., Madden, M., & Brenner, J. (2012, October 23). Younger American's reading and literary habits. Retrieved from http://libraries.pewinternet.org/2012/10/23/younger-americans-reading-and-library-habits/.

Index